T0326568

Arab Development Denied

Arab Development Denied

Dynamics of Accumulation by Wars of Encroachment

Ali Kadri

ANTHEM PRESS
LONDON · NEW YORK · DELHI

Anthem Press
An imprint of Wimbledon Publishing Company
www.anthempress.com

This edition first published in UK and USA 2014
by ANTHEM PRESS
75–76 Blackfriars Road, London SE1 8HA, UK
or PO Box 9779, London SW19 7ZG, UK
and
244 Madison Ave #116, New York, NY 10016, USA

British Library Cataloguing-in-Publication Data
A catalogue record for this book is available from the British Library.

Library of Congress Cataloging-in-Publication Data
A catalog record for this book has been requested.

ISBN-13: 978 1 78308 267 4 (Hbk)
ISBN-10: 1 78308 267 4 (Hbk)

Cover image © Joshua Rickard

This title is also available as an ebook.

To Maged

CONTENTS

ACKNOWLEDGEMENTS

I am indebted to too many people to name for the completion of this work. However, I would like to particularly thank Professors Martha Mundy and Adam Francis Cornford for their helpful comments. I also would like to thank Professors Timothy Dyson and Stuart Corbridge from the Department of International Development at the London School of Economics. I would especially like to thank the National University of Singapore for providing me with research facilities.

INTRODUCTION

Over the last three decades, the Arab world (hereafter referred to as the AW, as per the definition of the Arab League) has undergone a process of reverse development. *It has de-developed.* The quality of its capital stock has depreciated, median incomes have plummeted, unemployment has soared, and restrictions on already constrained civil liberties have tightened. When wars and civil wars in Sudan, Yemen, Iraq, Libya, Somalia, Lebanon, Palestine and Syria are considered, the scale of humanitarian disasters could possibly compete with those of the Congo. In short, the AW has failed the test of development, broadly defined as a process of economic growth, with expanding output and employment, technological progress and institutional transformation that steadily improve the well-being of working classes (ESCCHR 2004).[1] That the Arab ruling classes would bring about development was the lie that their bought intellectuals peddled. Instead of development, or 'the realisation of the right to development and the fulfilment of a set of claims by people, principally on their state but also on the society at large, including the international community, in a process that enables them to realise the rights set forth in the International Bill of Human Rights', working classes in the AW have experienced the reverse (ESCCHR 2004).

Most astounding is not the obliviousness of the 'international community' to violations of human rights and gutting of working-class living standards by Arab regimes; it is the degree of US-led intervention and overt support for the these regimes. Until several people across the AW burned themselves to death in the street, the mainstream's assessment of Arab development was as rosy

---

1 I have replaced the 'people' with 'working classes' in the definition given to development by the Economic and Social Council Commission on Human Rights (2004). Also my employment of the concept of freedom differs from its meaning as a set of choices aligned with given probabilities from which the individual chooses. This is a formalised definition of freedom. Human rights are inseparable from communal or working-class rights and freedom is the appreciation of the necessity in the mediation of the individual in the particular or, simply, the complementarity between the part and the whole.

as could be. In reality, few other regions in the world can match the rate of developmental descent experienced in the AW and the success with which the ideological instruments of capital have depicted bane as boon.

There is plenty of evidence to support the hypothesis of de-development. Ironically, there is even evidence in the lack of evidence. Whereas states on the road to development produce evidentiary statistics to assess their own course of development, most Arab states have ceased to produce adequate statistics. This is so not because of national security concerns—these states have little national security left. It is because de-development has become so pervasive that producing knowledge in the form of statistics exceeds their productive capabilities. These nations have hollowed out the production of knowledge, which is additional evidence that they have undergone a process of de-development. In the 1960s and 1970s, Iraq, Egypt, Algeria and Syria produced sophisticated input–output models meant to guide planning in the economy. Now, the paucity of data in almost all areas of economic and social activity tells of retrogression. The data gleaned from the available macro records tell the story:

- poor long-term growth (three decades for the amalgamated weighted average, UN data);
- oil revenue-dependent growth (World Development Indicators, WDI);
- some of the highest levels of unemployment globally (Key Indicators of the Labour Market [KILM] various years);
- increasingly unequal income distribution, which is also some of the most extreme in the world (University of Texas, Inequality Project);
- outflows of real and financial resources (the Gulf states oscillate between the third and fourth largest buyers of American debt); and
- infringements on human rights rarely seen elsewhere (Amnesty International, 2009).

What is more unusual is that when positive growth did take hold, as happened over the last decade, absolute poverty *grew*. After a decade of around six per cent real growth in Egypt, the Integrated Regional Information Networks (IRIN) reported in 2009 that nearly a third of Egyptian children suffered from malnutrition. In Yemen, more than half of all children are malnourished (UNICEF, 2012). When one assesses the degree to which Arab ruling classes are subordinately tied to international financial capital, one is apt to ask why the more sophisticated organised dimension of US-led capital has not intervened to halt regression when it takes so little in money capital to do so.

De-development should not be confused with relative underdevelopment vis-à-vis Western formations or with a delinking of developing formations from the global accumulation process. De-development is the *purposeful* deconstruction of developing entities. Primarily, it involves stripping by force the working classes in those entities of the right to own and control their resources and use them for their own benefit. The fact of de-development is an argument for capitalist decadence, made manifest by the acute degrees of misery in security-exposed peripheral countries. Decadence—the lethargic stage in development akin to forms of primitive accumulation or dispossession without the re-engagement of resources in national production, like enclosures of common land without the rehiring of peasants in wage-labour activity—hits new lows when wars socialise whole countries, leaving their resources up for grabs.[2] This is not the developmental *locus classicus* of evicting thousands of peasants from the land and thereby transforming them into social labour in search of wage work; wars dislodge and evict massive national resources to be more likely decommissioned than engaged in the international market because of the rise of financialisation. Capacity deficiency and lack of technological progress underline much of underdevelopment, but when war and abjection combine in a given territory, the (relative) sovereignty of states and geopolitical considerations provide a sounder understanding of the disaster. This book is an attempt at such understanding.

Although it is possible to observe narrow strips of accumulation via commodity realisation or market expansion by the sale of goods in the AW, violent social dislocation, value grab structured around oil, and commercial as opposed to industrial activity are unequivocally the overarching characteristics of the prevailing mode of accumulation. Because development, security and sovereignty are an intercausal whole determined by the well-being of working classes, the imperialist forces must always ratchet up their power and exercise, often with the support of their local class alliances, the worst forms of atrocity against the Arab working classes.

In short, the Arab nation-state power deficit is a working-class power deficit. Whether real or perceived, the disempowerment of the working classes imperils national, communal and individual security. Of all the deficits in knowledge, democracy or capital formation—underdevelopment is a deficit in almost all the social variables—it is the working-class power deficit that deprives peoples of the right to shape their future. Without a rearticulation of the regional security arrangement to redress the sovereignty deficits of national states whereby working-class power becomes preeminent, the AW will not be

---

2   I make extensive use of the concept socialise and socialisation throughout this text. Socialisation, that is, the process by which the private is converted into social, occurs in the following forms: a) to socialise a human being is to deprive him or her of the means of subsistence and to make them social labourers; b) to socialise countries by war is deprive the working classes in those countries of their rightful ownership of their resources, and; c) socialisation implies the nationalisation of private assets.

able to own the means and tools of development. Without the restoration of power and sovereignty to the working classes—the right of working people to determine the conditions of their livelihood—development, seen more generally as the betterment of human spiritual and material life, will remain elusive.

Since the second half of twentieth century, the AW and its surrounding region have experienced the highest frequency of conflicts on earth. War and the spectre of war obliterate the prospects for sound development. Occupations in Palestine, dormant or flaring wars, civil wars in several countries, and countries living with the threat of abrupt and violent conflict incarnate the condition of accumulation by encroachment wars and violent conflict. The drive to accumulation by belligerent encroachment and dislocation originates in the global crisis of capital accumulation, which necessitates the subsumption of Third World labour and resources to US-led capital. Organised violence against working classes in the AW, by the imperialist forces or by the local ruling class—which are in any case inseparable—engenders redistributive antidevelopmental outcomes and holds determining primacy over the course of historical events. By primacy I mean a determining moment in the set of social relationships that necessarily but not exclusively govern historical development. Modern Arab history as of the mid-twentieth century is a story of struggle leading to defeat in the face of better-armed US-led imperialist forces, including Israel.

Encroachment wars and military routs, structurally or directly, have reconstituted national class formations to imperialist will. The Arab state has been robbed of the autonomy by which it could practice development. Botched development, manifest analytically in the poor interface between development policy and outcomes on the one hand, and in weak national security that takes away autonomy over policy on the other, cannot be fully explored by building separate arguments for each of its constituents. A dichotomised approach can be informative, but it is also misleading. Because of fundamental social differences, the standard conceptual tools of macroeconomic policy become irrelevant in an Arab context. Arab de-development is a holistic process commandeered by a historical subject that is alien to Arab working classes. In this context, development and working-class security, mediated through the sovereignty of the nation-state, are indivisible. In a process of appropriation where the subject of history—US-led capital in alliance with Arab ruling classes—forcibly dislocates Arab resources and labour, to pose the problematic in a classically analytical fashion is not only complacent but specious. The causes of de-development are overdetermined. At its most fundamental, development is working-class security wrought in the course of the class struggle. It is both means and end of the sovereignty of the working class.

Political security is a determining moment for Arab development. Insecure Arab social formations have lacked the autonomy required to devise developmental policies of their own. In the AW, *realpolitik* and violation of international law mark the course of events. Successive defeats, socialist ideological retreat and neoliberal policies that enable the siphoning of resources have eroded Arab working-class and national security. The labouring classes have not constructed through the medium of the state an effective anti-imperialist front, nor have they compelled national redistributive policies that would build their capacity to produce. De-development has mirrored Arab security exposure and the retreat of anti-imperialist fronts.

Acute intraclass fragmentation and polarisation fed by petrodollar-propped imaginary (sectarian) identities, together with repressive regimentation of the labour process, has severely compromised Arab sovereignty and the rights of working classes to partake in economic and political life. For rival imperialists vying militaristically for position in a strategic area, it has been imperative to strip working classes of any control they might exercise over their means of development. The imperialist beholden Arab state, which is in its state of debilitation capital's ideal form of social organisation, has estranged itself from the working classes. The private person of civil society has been denied effective citizenship. Social institutions of civil society and NGOs, selectively designated by the nominal Arab state according to the whims of imperialism, have assisted in supplanting the transformation of private person into public person or ideal citizen. In Egypt, for instance, the Muslim Brotherhood have declared that they have been engaged with US-sponsored NGOs since prior to the uprising (MB spokesperson, 2012).[3] Where the secular state was absent, the citizen was absent, but the private religious person was present. The synergy between particular aspirations that coalesce in organised general institutional forms to improve social conditions perished in this induced social disarticulation. Implosive divisiveness reigned instead. The imperialist power vortex, or all the substructures intermediating capital by the strengths of its ideology, swallowed the national bourgeoisie, integrating it into the global financial (dollar) space, until there was little 'national' left in Arab nationalism.[1]

---

3   Spokesperson of the Muslim Brotherhood speaking at a public lecture at National University of Singapore, 22 February 2012.

4   The vortex or the eye of capital's ideological storm grows exponentially after the collapse of the Soviet Union. This state of affairs cannot be comprehended fully from noting the separate working-class struggles around the world. There is not an international labour front to dent the progress of capital, but there certainly is an organised capital, ideological and political machinery. Where the constraints on US-led capital from its would-be competitors mount, as in the case of Iran, the ideological vortex emerges as the Saudi Royal family and Israel rally for an Iran attack. This aggressive stance ties in

Arab states, which did not embody much of the working class even during the era of 'socialist' pan-Arabism, under US-led imperialist assault have extricated themselves almost completely from their citizenry. Their class structures have metamorphosed correspondingly to absorb the terms of successive defeats. The corrosion in development has been less the result of poor policies than a subordinate outcome of imperialist wars of encroachment.

Imperialist positioning for control of oil has occurred alongside wars. Not only does oil control boost imperial standing, but because militarism itself is a province of capital accumulation in imperialist nations, wars and conflicts in the AW become ends in themselves for imperialism. The resonance of terror bolsters military technology and spending as well as financial capital. Wars also weaken Arab states and their corresponding working classes and institute the US-led imperialist hegemon as the sovereign over a strategic region. Imperial rents attendant upon control of the Arab region and the standing of US-led financial capital vis-à-vis other ascendant powers grow in proportion to the control US-led capital exercises over the flow of resources from the region. Just like the flow of oil, the flow of war in the Arab region is a tributary of capital accumulation. For capital, the social relationships of control and domination supersede the generation of the money form per se. Much in the way that capital regiments the labour process in the Western hemisphere—such as via the recent austerity imposed in the US, the UK and Southern Europe— US-led imperialism conducts wars of aggression and control to subordinate whole working populations in the AW.

Irreversible Damage

At any point in this degenerative development, it was plain to see that driving Arab working classes further into poverty was unsustainable, unless of course the repressive apparatus reaches newer heights, which, short of genocide, was no longer possible. This deepening poverty was not an unintended consequence; it was deliberate at every stage. History as the 'immanent development of dialectical historical forces and interacting oppositions', mediated progressively in real time by forms of social organisations defined in terms of class power, cannot be reduced to self-indulgent notions of intended and unintended acts (Davis 1960). It cannot be more obvious that it is not the individualised

---

with US-led strategy to push forward its agenda as an ideological bonus resulting from its victory and the amassing of momentum by the growth of its ideological vortex. The segmented struggles of labour lacking a clear structure that mediates them in their transition, formation and transformation prove to be the essence of Left ideological defeat.

worker, politician or professor who runs the UN Security Council, the IMF, the World Bank or similar structures; it is their mediation in complex forms of social organisation of which the ruling social class encapsulates the agency. Counter-reforms against Arab labour have dispossessed the working class not only of its material necessities, but also its potential for political ascendancy. More important: when US-led capital provides Arab ruling classes with their security coverage, it can also influence how much they weaken and how much pressure can be exerted on them by their working classes. Under this pervasive and determinative influence, any social platform from which the working class might potentially challenge the hold of US-led imperialism had to be and was dismantled.

In retrospect, slightly more civil liberties and a little more in direct payments to the lower strata might have briefly redressed the inequitable political and distributional arrangements and delayed the onset of uprisings. But such measures were not even entertained, let alone implemented. In this, capital's institutions, which have so far ensured its resilience, were not being short-sighted. Global capital accumulation in the modern age still proceeds by commodity realisation, reinforced by neoliberal ideology and, more determinedly, by encroachment wars and violent dispossession. War and repression comprise the ultimate instrument of dislocation. In the AW, wars, including repressive regime violence, have served the deliberate purpose of dispossessing working people of their political and social rights and of their resources. Working-class security has waned and so have national security and the sovereignty attendant thereupon.

Though undertaken under the rubric of international law and humanitarianism, these military assaults are in fact encroachment wars whose real function is to 'socialise' massive resources. Wars dislocate workers and farmers and remove national resources from even potential political control by national working classes. Much of the private and national wealth, including workers themselves, will sit idle, waiting to be called into production very cheaply when international capital deems it necessary. People as well as things become the inexpensive material of capital.

The power of capitalist ideology also makes the costs of imperialist war appear to exceed the gains. Interlocutors of capital in Western policy think tanks or news media can claim democratisation and a civilising mission rather than control over oil or other raw materials as the principal purpose of the war. However, when demystified, prices and the sums of financial resources they amount to can be shown to be brokered by a structure of power from which Arab working classes have been excluded. After the usurpation of the greater share of value by US-led capital and its subsidiaries, the Arab ruling classes, the resources remaining for the Arab labouring classes have been insufficient to maintain a historically determined decent standard of living. A dispossessed and disempowered working class cannot negotiate the conditions of its survival and social reproduction. Development in the AW, in fact, *has* to be continually denied so that the security of working classes, and consequently national security, remains compromised. The power of US-led capital is leveraged by the disempowerment of Arab working classes. Hence, the terms of power that underlie exchange and the reproduction of global accumulation and its attendant financial structure will also favour US-led capital.

The deepening crisis of capital implies further escalations in encroachment wars or dispossession processes. Alongside enforced public-to-private transfers under neoliberalism, wars act as the instrument by which Arab moneyed and non-moneyed resources are coercively engaged in the formation of value under capitalist accumulation. Wars on a continually defeated and redefeated AW accomplish multiple goals. They maintain US-led capital's control of oil supplies through direct military presence; they stabilise a financial order in which the dollar remains the world reserve currency and wealth-holding medium; they reinforce militarism and its associated financing and technological superiority; they foment religious and ultranationalist ideologies; they assist in the compression of the global wage; and, ultimately, they allow US-led capital to hold at bay ascendant and competing imperialist powers. Wars also tax the working classes everywhere to various degrees. In the US, workers are taxed to fund the war effort; and in the AW, many workers die.

In the AW, war as a feeder of accumulation by militarism became an end in itself. War is either constant or easy to instigate. From the wars of decolonisation, by way of the regional hot wars of the so-called Cold War, the war on Iraq and selective US and NATO bombings, to the recent and ongoing civil wars, violence has engendered more violence. When central-nation wages do not rise enough to buy the overproduced products on moneyed central markets and when pressure builds on profits to fall, militarism saves capital by restructuring value relations and value shares. So far, there is little evidence that any of the heavyweight players in the AW have tried to defuse regional tensions. Judging by the rate at which the Israeli settlements grew during the 'Peace Process', in fact, there is every reason to believe that war – or the deconstruction of societies by liberalising treaties – is the purpose for which everyone negotiates. The fact that US-led imperialism heightens the intensity of the Arab–Israeli conflict, which was absurdly meant to resolve the Jewish question by relocating European Jews to land inhabited by Palestinians, is proof of the inherent imperialist drive for war. If a proposal as phantasmagorical as the resettlement of millions by the promise of 'Yahweh' becomes a fact by imperialist fiat, then, anecdotally, reconciling different ethnicities over the same territory in a secular democratic state would be an easy task in comparison. Anecdotes aside, the historical momentum of wars waged on the AW mediate interimperialist rivalries, which have mutated in the financialisation phase of imperialism into differentiated structures in which capital's class interests have risen above national affinities. The financial interests of capital did not supplant nationalism; they just further subordinated it. I have considered nationalism to be a means of capital accumulation. The contradiction between US-led capital's oversized share of international financial rents upsets other rising powers with national productive bases whose wealth is held in dollars. These powers vying for a bigger share of the rents require an orderly US debt workout not only so as not to endanger the dollar as the world's medium of wealth holding, but also to ensure a smooth transition in the power standing of the US such that its declining imperial stature will not cause precipitous dollar devaluation. That is the catch-22 situation these rising powers (like China) face.

There is always a social process antecedent to economic money facades. Demand and supply are real-life processes that involve union busting and Third World–country bombing. Capital accumulation moulds the social conditions for production. Profit-driven relationships invest in sections of the working class and divest from others. The long internalised dislocation of Arab working classes necessarily but not exclusively contributes to regulating capital's rate of profit. In an integrated and closely interlocked global circuit of capital, in which Arab oil and development form principal moments of the totality, denial of Arab development and regional insecurity become themselves instruments of accumulation. Both the usurpation of resources and rising capital's ideological hold imparted through war—specifically of ideologies that fragment and differentiate working classes into subnationalist, tribal, ethnic and religious sectarian identities—form self-reinforcing constituents of capital.

Arab de-development, then, significantly contributes to the reproduction of global capital in social, physical and ideological terms. Apart from militarisation, the immiseration of Arab working classes facilitates the engagement of non-priced or underpriced value-forming constituents in production. The values *cum* profits extracted from the pauperisation of the Arab working classes, however, are not solely to be gauged on the basis of the absolute value produced from longer working hours or poorer working and living conditions. Relative to the global product, Arab social product is puny in money terms. Arabs constitute around 5 per cent of the world population, while their total income is around 2.5 per cent of global income. When we remember that most of that income is enjoyed by a very small population in the Gulf (around 5 per cent of the total population), the real Arab share of global income falls to around 1 per cent, of which the share of the working class weighed by labour share would be roughly 0.3 per cent.

In comparison, sub-Saharan Africa comprises around 13 per cent of global population and receives a little less than 2 per cent of income. Hence, the surplus (in money form and not value) obtained from the repression of the Arab labour force measured in Arab-derived profits is small. But where does one draw the line between the share of value in a single commodity derived from the Third World and the share derived from the First World? Is it not the case that the value of unskilled human lives should be at par across national boundaries? Why is it then that the lives of fallen people in bombardments of oil-control wars do not represent as much value when measured in money form? In a commodity, value (socially necessary labour), the natural form of value (use value) and the social form (exchange value) are inseparable and contradictory. These forms of value are moments of the *same expression of value*, which belong to one another and are reciprocally conditioning and inseparable from the fetishism attendant upon the production of commodities: 'fetishism which clings to the products of labour as soon as they are produced as commodities and which is therefore inseparable from commodity-production' (Marx 1867). Once fetishism enters the picture, the materialisation of value in exchange becomes determined by a social rapport in which the ideological power of ruling classes and their labour aristocracy sets the exchange rate of the human input/life in production. At times, human beings serve as inputs by their very demise under bombardments, at differentiated levels determined by reified national boundaries. Before we arrive at production, resources excluded from contributing to production have been forcibly dislocated and cheaply priced by the dominant powers. They are thus necessary constituents of capital accumulation.

The social product derived from imperial control of Third World and Arab assets, which is the outcome of the practice of depriving working classes of the right to own and deploy their resources for their own benefit, is hugely significant. From the deformation of Arab industrial and infrastructural development under colonialism to successive recent assaults on Arab working classes, a historical surplus value has been amassed by US-led capital, the illegitimate heir of past colonialists (Abdel Malek 1985).

From a purely quantitative angle, little also would it matter for capital had Arab development proceeded by productivity gains and higher wages. The monetary gains from selling and buying in the AW are insignificant when compared to the power that US-led capital draws from its hegemony over this region. Power is central to capital, which is a relationship of appropriation by means of control. US-led capital's oil control backing the dollar, its pricing oil in the dollar and its higher share of imperial rents are determined by its degree of hegemony over the AW. In a global metabolic rate of capital reproduction, the depth of social dislocation is equivalent to the heights of social prosperity (Mészáros 1995). The betterment of working-class living conditions and the empowerment of working classes enhancing national security would undermine the power of US-led hegemony. This is not a problem that a reified policy package of exchange, interest or tax rate can solve. A solution can only emerge from understanding the specifics of the history of imperialist assault on Arab working classes.

Conceptual Clarifications

The following addenda refer to five concepts that I employ throughout this text.

1) **Working class:** The notion of a working social class in the AW is made to appear elusive when it should not be so. In the Marxian definition of classes, class *relationships* prevail over class definitions per se.[5] For Marx, social classes cannot exist outside class relationships that tie them together, and the analysis of class in diverse socioeconomic formations must begin there. It is within these relationships that class structures, including their history and evolution, are constituted. What a class is and does depends on how it is situated in relation to other classes—foremost among these in late capitalism is the relationship of that class to imperialism. The structure of classes, or the ensemble of interclass relationships, is decisive in determining the qualities of a social class. In other words, classes are a macro-sociological expression of relations between classes, including their subjective, cultural and symbolic dimensions. These relationships between classes are founded upon social relations of production, which are capitalist and will have to be defined in their specificities and development. Here the specificity is the oil-based formation in the AW, in which the relational matrix of the ruling class is composed principally of an alliance *cum* subservience of the Arab ruling classes to the international financial elites. To the extent that these relationships between classes rest upon relationships of production, they are essentially, but not exclusively, relationships of domination, exploitation and imperialist control. In these social relationships of production, owners organise not only their own relationships to the means of production but also distributional arrangements in relation to the pace of capital accumulation. This is the organised dimension of capital, a political process mediating the growing scope of capital in which state power is the key articulating moment. Working classes in relation to the dominant class maintain their organisation, anti-imperialist struggles and experience, which influence the cohesion of the working population as a whole, including the peasantry. The imperialist

---

5   The outline I provide draws on the work of Poulantzas, *Classes in Contemporary Capitalism* (1975).

assault-and-control element is a determining moment that holds primacy in the restructuring of peripheral social classes.

In a specifically Arab context, Shiite/Sunni, Palestinian/Jordanian, Arab/ Berber and other historically shifting notions of identity are often presented by orthodox commentators as constituting fundamental divisions that criss-cross beneath classes and other fault lines of bonding and organisation. They are taken as evidence that the cultural and tradition-based determinants of 'class' are more pronounced than economic ones, as if economic determinants are in a competitive game with traditions. Recognising the ends this sort of language serves, one can discern that social science is being purposely debased to suit imperialist doctrine. This discourse, in other words, is intended to divide the working population, conceptually and thence practically. However, in these tradition/culture definitions of class, cultural characteristics can easily proxy for genetic differences. Otherness by culture resembles otherness by race. Though cultural demarcation lines are arbitrary and set according to shifting ideological forces, individual acquisition of specific economic and cultural qualities would decide where one is situated in the class system. Perversely, the atomised approach to class asks not how a class devolves to the formation of the individual; it instead asks how the individual through personal endeavour and attainment of certain economic and cultural values can come to belong to one predetermined class or another. Class is thus conceptually turned into a club to which people with similar characteristics belong. In this schema, a class can continually change according to the changing characteristics of its individual members to the point where it ceases to exist, given the endless and ever finer demarcation lines that may exist between one set of people and another. In this way, class as a concept is redefined in relation to the ideological power of capital. In the state of retrogression into which social ideology in the AW and elsewhere has decayed, the collapse of class into sect and ethnicity appears quasi-permanent.

To reiterate: class is *not* the sum of various characteristics common to some group of people. Class exists in relation to other classes and as a relationship to property and/or modes of appropriation, in which political, social and legal arrangements enact the division of labour according to the prevailing power balances within the political structure. At a very abstract level, class is the mediation of a particular state of being that is materialised in the more general political form. These social and cultural characteristics in their commonalities and differences are the outcome of the degree of cohesion in a class and of the balance of forces, including ideological ones, within a political structure. Classes as forms of political expression constitute a historical process. Again, to stay at a general level, class in capitalist society is the genus of the relationship between capital and a subject of history in which the reproduction of social conditions is *materially* determined. Various attributes and qualities are devolved to social classes as outcomes of class struggle. A class therefore is not the sum of common characteristics; it is a process that divulges the manifold social characters that exist in relation to it (the universal, or rather the general, in the dialectical relationship) (Ilyenkov 1974). The repression endured by the working classes in the AW in relation to imperial oil control emerges as disarticulation between social condition and consciousness.

Most Arab formations are oil abundant. The class to which oil is relevant is the class of US-led capital. The relationship of oil revenues to class is extranational and construed by a constellation of global powers to which the disempowerment of Arab working classes is a means to an end. Thus, while working-class fragmentation under the capitalist ideological barrage in terms of religion and other cultural categories is pursued everywhere, oil rents and their imperial control shatter even more forcefully the terrain on which social conditions might lead to working-class political action. That working classes in the AW do not identify themselves politically in terms of a social class is far from exceptional in a comparative sense. And much like others, they do not exist socially outside the class system either. It is the role of science not to succumb to the fetishism or the illusion that identity falls above class.

2) *Social formation*: Broadly, the concrete whole comprising social practice. Particularly, an Arab state/country as a deployable concept, fraught with contradictions and unravelling as it is, would be less than adequate to encapsulate the role of social forces in a political process. The Arab countries were already on a downward path, which is *post facto* proof of the dominance of class over state. For the purposes of this book also, the concept of social formation is not a formal interplay between atomised agency and structure, but an articulation of classes that may be reconstituted in the struggle against imperialist aggression.

3) *Imperialism*: Imperialism refers to the process of capitalist accumulation on a world scale in the era of monopoly capitalism, and the theory of imperialism is the investigation of accumulation in the context of a world market created by that accumulation (Weeks 1983). Anouar Abdel-Malik notes that the study of imperialism seems to be safely geared to the political-economic individual approach, but his contention is that the Leninist view is fundamentally sociological. Lenin's *Imperialism* is a study of the functioning of early twentieth-century capitalist systems in the framework of the international balance of forces and the united world front of working-class and national movements, facing the constellation of conflicting colonial and imperialist forces.

From the underconsumption-crisis side of accumulation, the crisis of the centre was driven by low wages depressing demand. Lenin viewed underconsumption as a by-product of blind competition, which produces both overproduction and underconsumption simultaneously. In reaching this conclusion, he principally relied on production-based social crises that develop a momentum of their own under capitalism. Capital recreates symbolic and real social structures that mediate class positions and regenerate overproduction crises. The social forms, fetishes, reifications and superstructure in general reflect the requisites of accumulation, hence Marx's oft-quoted remark: 'Accumulate, accumulate! that is the Moses and the prophets' (Marx 1867).

The political-economic side of the crisis cannot be dissected into realisation versus overproduction. The track of blind accumulation and the primacy of production makes the crisis one of overproduction with overtones of underconsumption or under-realisation scenarios—there need not be a pragmatic dissection of supply and demand sides under which the real history of accumulation by violent encroachments disappear (Niebyl 2005). The details of how wages decline, how demand falls or how profits hit a steady state ignore the pillage of the Third World. Lenin's schema of imperialism emerging from the rise of finance capital, of monopolies and the concentration, centralisation and export of capital, are analytical breakdowns of the constituents of accumulation on a global scale. The historical and more decisive side has been the functioning of capital in the sphere of politics, manifest in measures of crisis aversion of which war is the most important. For Lenin, imperialism is synonymous with war.

The question is: what means other than war could there be under capitalism to overcome the disparity between the development of productive forces and the accumulation of capital on the one side, and the division of colonies and spheres of influence for finance capital on the other? (Lenin 1916)

After years of financialisation, in which industrial capital assumed the role of finance and industries behaved like banks, the restructuring of society has proceeded unabated since Hilferding noted the transformation:

> The development of finance capital changes fundamentally the economic, and hence the political, structure of society. The individual capitalists of early capitalism confronted each other as opponents in a competitive struggle. This conflict prevented them from undertaking any common action in politics as in other spheres. It should be added that the needs of their class did not as yet call for such common action, since the negative attitude of industrial capital to the state did not allow it to come forward as the representative of general capitalist interests (Hilferding 1910).

Given the retreat of socialist ideology in the present epoch, it is a divided working class that confronts capital as the universal monolith—the dissolution of national capitalist classes into financial dollar-internationalised imperialism. Hence I use the terms US-led capital or US-led imperialism interchangeably. Also, one may note that the issue of the descent of the US adumbrates the fact that capital, which has become more international, is in ascendancy.

4) *Merchant capital*: Capital in the AW, viewed in its social dimension of consuming and allocating resources, has edged close to a mercantile mode of accumulation whose principal characteristic is the near absence of positive intermediation between private and public wealth. The merchant mode revolves around quick private gains and does not require productive reinvestment in society; the usurpation of value by financial means is a subsidiary outcome. The practice of merchant capital mimics that of financial capital, in the sense that money is transmuted into money without direct involvement in production processes. Rentier or rent grab may be too general a categorisation; it is also something of a misnomer, meant to support an *ad hominem* (and faux-nationalist) argument which conceals the fact that value transfers away from the working classes are conducted by national as well as by US-led international financial capital. The resurrected merchant mode of accumulation is a reincarnation of early modern mercantilism in a modern guise and, as was pointed out quite early in the industrial age, 'wherever merchant capital still predominates we find backward conditions', (Marx 1887b, 327). The broader context from which this condemnation stems is as follows:

> Yet its [merchant capital] development, as we shall presently see, is incapable by itself of promoting and explaining the transition from one mode of production to another. Within capitalist production merchant's capital is reduced from its former independent existence to a special phase in the investment of capital, and the levelling of profits reduces its rate of profit to the general average. It functions only as an agent of productive capital. The special social conditions that take shape with the development of merchant's capital, are here no longer paramount. On the contrary, wherever merchant's capital still predominates we find backward conditions. This is true even within one and the same country, in which, for instance, the specifically merchant towns present far more striking analogies with past conditions than industrial towns. The independent and predominant development of capital as merchant's capital is tantamount to the non-subjection of production to capital, and hence to capital developing on the basis of an alien social mode of production which is also independent of it. The independent development of merchant's capital, therefore, stands in inverse proportion to the general economic development of society (Marx, *Capital*, vol. III, 327).

A qualification is in order to allow for the juxtaposition. Save slavery, imperialist aggression and colonial genocide, the evolution from the merchant mode as Venetian traders began to control and own upstream cottage-scale or small manufacturing undertakings represented progress and a turning point in the organisation of social production around wage labour (Engels 1891).

Integrating the merchant mode with an industrial one designated a cultural step forward— culture here meaning the universal store of humanity's knowledge. What has occurred in the AW is the gradual disengagement of national industrial capital from merchant capital, after which the latter became the dominant mode. Value usurpation policies, inherently uneven development, blocking the homogenisation of labour and value grab by imperialist conquest are some of the processes that have underpinned the resurrection of merchant capital in this instance. Here I am relying on Mészáros's notion that capital as a social relationship regulates its metabolic rate of reproduction in relation to value grab and value creation, albeit within a context of class struggle and its associated power structure (Mészáros 1995). The case can be generalised in the sense that the security-exposed states of Africa and the AW fall on the 'grab' side of capital as a historical process, and dividedness becomes the defining feature of the their historical subjects—that is, the classes that shape their history. Another distinction arises between a comprador class and a dominant class that commandeers merchant-capital processes. Whereas a nationalist bourgeoisie differs from a comprador class according to whether the sphere of accumulation and its circuit are nationally or internationally linked respectively, the merchant-capital leading class is more fully fused with international financial capital because its concrete activities are inclined to short-term investment wherein the costs of plant removal are also negligible. It is not just that the rate of imports is nearly at half of income in the AW; merchant capital emulates its international financial counterparts in many areas. Apart from buying abroad and selling at home, its principal endeavours at home are, as noted, in the speculative areas of a FIRE economy (finance, investment and real estate). This class has little to lose from forfeiting its production base in the home economy. Its principal activity is to tap into national resources (national assets and foreign exchange earnings) by speculation, devalorisation of national assets and the sale of imports to the national economy. This merchant class does not contribute in any significant way to the development of working classes. These merchant-capital leading classes are either detached from the process of industry within or exhibit an ephemeral link to it. Like the classic comprador class, they are subordinate partners of (US-led) capital.

The pressures of imperialist hegemony and the instilling of the merchant mode have together reinforced the downward (de-)development spiral. Already in 1980 a prevalence of oil revenues and geopolitical flows obviated the prospect of productive job expansion. The AW thus became an economy that could not for structural reasons produce jobs, and where profits without effort had gripped the ruling-class mindset. In this context, cheapening life and reducing people to commodities became part of the shift to the merchant mode and the value usurpation process. For the Arab working class, this is a process that religious alienation—imaginary projection of the causation of worldly misery onto a supernatural power—can only momentarily redeem. As working people endure harsher conditions, it appears that the Islamisation of political life offers a short-lived reprieve to the merchant-leading class. In the absence of a social alternative toward which popular movements can strive, however, change need not imply progress.

5) *Capital accumulation*: 'Capital can also be understood as a way of organising production and economic activity, so that the accumulation of capital is the extension of this form of organisation into areas in which production, exchange and distribution were governed by other rules' (Eatwell et al. 1998, 14). Capital is typically considered to be a mass of goods or money associated with a special form of organisation. However, this definition is lacking on three interrelated levels. Firstly, goods and forms of organisation have always existed and, hence, simply stopping at the definition of capital as a heap of goods and a form of organisation renders capital transhistorical. Secondly, the very coming into being of goods in other historical epochs was determined by concrete social relationships, which means that forms of organisation are also historically specific. Thus, the nature of accumulation varies drastically and acquires a new content in different historical epochs. Thirdly, under capitalism and with the prevalence of the money form, the production of goods is no longer an end in itself, but a means to acquisition of money capital (Mészáros 1995). This form of capital accumulation is specific to capitalism. Moreover, for Marx, capital is not a thing, but rather a definite *social production relation*, belonging to a definite historical formation of society, which is manifested in a thing and lends this thing a specific social character. 'It is the means of production monopolized by a certain section of society, confronting living labour-power as products and working conditions rendered independent of this very labour-power, which are personified through this antithesis in capital (Marx [1959] 1894). Capital manifests the seminal contradiction between socially produced wealth and the private appropriation of that socially produced wealth (Mészáros 1995). Capital accumulation is the process by which social classes under capitalism relate to each other in the process of production, exchange and distribution. Broadly speaking, a crisis of capital accumulation is not a rupture within this social process (this is not an equilibrium approach), but inherent to capitalism on a global scale as peripheral classes bear the burden of dislocation resulting from accumulation by blind competition.

Summary of Chapters

This book explores the obstacles to development in the AW by delving deeper and deeper over the same principal points with the aim of highlighting the forces that obstruct sound development. It begins with a summary of the economic history of the AW, and then moves into a discussion of the apparent macroeconomic phenomenon and policies. It is a generalised approach and, as in every broad view of things, many details are submerged within it. But I aim to make the level of generalisation adequate enough to deliver a meaning that would not be grossly altered by additional details. The way to do this is not to abstract from the quantifiable outside manifestation of conditions, but to focus on their modus operandi. It is at this point that it becomes necessary to discuss the social dynamics and framework in which development has failed. The topics of class structure, democratisation, war, oil and imperialism are taken up at length in several succeeding chapters. The final chapters assess the ways Arab disintegration leverages the hegemony of US capital and the impact of de-development in commodifying human lives. The following are synopses of the contents of each chapter.

Chapter One: Stocktaking and assessment

The purpose of this chapter is to explore the empirical background of the Arab economy and to lay bare the underpinnings of the business cycle. It exposes the record on the basis of available statistics, and shows that the business cycle is determined by US-led imperialist concerns. It also addresses some of the falsifications that painted a rosy picture of the period preceding the Arab uprisings.

Despite the immediate postindependence aggression of imperialism against leading Arab countries, state-led development had demonstrated a better welfare and developmental model than the neoliberal one. When the state-led development model collapsed, the rates of poverty, hunger and repression rose under neoliberalism. Compared to the latter neoliberal experience, the rates at which literacy, living conditions and other welfare measures rose in the *étatiste* postindependence period (I am not going to use statist instead of *étatiste* here because later I will employ 'statism' as Balibar uses it to mean repressive non-law-abiding states) show that the Arab 'socialist' model, at least with respect to welfare and dynamic economic criteria, performed better (Ayubi 1995). If we view development as the retention and redeployment of resources in the national economy, the anti-imperialist positioning exercised by the then newly independent Arab states represented a necessary step for galvanising real resources in their national economies, one that invariably resulted in favourable developmental outcomes.

Chapter Two: De-development and conventional policies

This chapter reviews and criticises existing macroeconomic policies. Arab countries claim to have weathered the onslaught of the global financial crisis (2007–08) just prior to the ongoing uprisings. Indeed, Arab governments appeared successful in using available monetary and fiscal measures to dodge the downturn. The real issue however, which was intentionally overlooked, is that oil prices remained high enough before and after the great financial crisis. Consequently, in an oil export–dependent growth region, there was no downturn to speak of anyway. The economic growth rates were positive all along and had nothing to do with how the policies in place reacted to a downturn. Macroeconomic and social policies did not budge. In any case, they could not move in any direction because most currencies were pegged to the dollar and fiscal deficits were bound to a minimum. Ever since the rise in oil prices in 2002, all Arab countries, of which the majority are oil producing, have registered steadily positive growth rates of around five per cent. However, this 'growth' was hollow and degenerative, like the swelling in the bellies of malnourished people. In point of fact, the uprisings erupted when Syria, Tunisia, Yemen, Libya and Egypt were enjoying record real-growth rates. The chapter criticises existing policies and concludes that in the AW, the resource curse is the curse of the imperialist assault sustained by the Arab working classes, and that an examination into the re-empowerment of the working class within the political process is required.

Chapter Three: Class politics masquerading as democracy

Politics hold primacy in the AW. There must be *a priori* an introduction to the role of democracy in development. Democracy became the veneer beneath which conflicts ravaged Iraq, Libya and Syria or the obfuscation by which class structure was preserved by political Islam. The mainstream discourse is blatantly racist. After bombing Arab formations, instituting divisions within their constitutions, and letting them slip into endless civil wars, the mainstream would note that these violent transitions are necessary for democracy. But how could democracy of any sort arise in a state redistributing value around religious sects or ethnic entities? The constitutions of the AW are not allowed to become universally democratic, supposedly because Arabs are inherently sectarian and/or primitive. Waiting to see how the bloodbath of civil war transforms the savage into the democratic man reveals the racism that seeps through the mainstream's literature. What is more, the very idea of bringing democracy to Syria, a country whose structural destruction would leverage US–Israeli power over the region, is the most absurd of the Arab democratisation stories. In countries where sectarian strife has not led to outright civil war, ballot-box democracy became the rule of a box over society—'boxocracy'. In Egypt it brought to power a political Islam whose spokesperson wanted to mimic the 'small government' of Thatcher in development. Political democracy, understood as the protection of basic civic and political rights, equality before the law, freedoms of speech, of the press and of political organisation is increasingly a farce even in the Western hemisphere. It is obvious to any informed observer that the Arab countries depart widely from this definition and are at a democratic low ebb of their own, around which they wash back and forth by minute degrees. Arab working classes are insecure and their insecurity weakens national sovereignty. The penetration of a Wahhabi doctrine of rights into political Islam, which absolutely places equality of opportunity before equality of condition, strips the state of reasonability. The function of political institutions has more to do with arresting the evolution of socialisation and devolving their legal and institutional powers into newly reinvented forms of social organisation meant to fragment the labouring classes. In this chapter, the thorny issue of transition to an institutional framework that would allow Arab working classes the right to a degree of power in the state is investigated.

Chapter Four: The stillborn and decomposing Arab state

When colonial powers revamped the Ottoman form of social organisation into the modern Arab states, they projected their models and objectives as to what constitutes a state in the Arab colonies. They refounded institutions that organised social relations in line with their strategies and ideologies. Many Arab countries thus constituted are quickly decomposing as a result of military defeats, the daunting balance of forces or neoliberalism. It is important to note upfront that the neoliberal turn in the AW is not separate from conflicts or military assaults; it is an outcome of political defeat and waning sovereignty. No cohesive social entity represented in a state would tolerate the draining of its resources and wealth under neoliberalism over many years unless it were in a condition of surrender—or, more pertinently, unless its social classes were in a state of acute conflict and on the way to destroying the state. Wars and defeats imposed wealth-draining policies by shifting national class structures to accept the imperialist terms of surrender. More recently, many of these states have fragmented into loosely governed territories, and many others teeter on the brink of failure. Libya, Iraq, Lebanon, Yemen and Syria can now be added to Afghanistan and Somalia. However, these failures are not a one-time occurrence after which their states will be resurrected in better forms. Many Arab states have devolved into a continual condition of depression, violence and collapse. It is not only that their effectiveness in development is declining; as forms of social organisation, they actually engender ruin.

Chapter Five: Wars and oil control

Their hubris notwithstanding, successive American administrations have designated the Arab–Israeli conflict as the foremost source of instability globally. But in reality, wars are an integral part of the global economy. They reshape social conditions that produce value and uphold the power of the social class that relies on the war economy for reproducing itself. Also, wars galvanise the development of 'civilian spin-off' technology by public funding, maintaining an edge for US-led capital in technological advance and intellectual property patents required for supremacy in the global production process.[6] Financially, wars expand the indebtedness of the state. They raise the dollarised money supply that has to be underwritten in turn by further military expansion and hegemony over strategic resources, namely oil.

In the financial age, the growth of moneyed debts spent on wars also requires higher tax levies and a lower share of wages for the central working classes. Wars reproduce the social relations by which real assets are devalued, including human resources. They resituate the balance of forces not only with respect to the occupied or aggressed Arab nations, but more importantly vis-à-vis other advanced capital circles. Wars as a social process recalibrate social conditions with the aim of grabbing the most human wealth for the few via the least costly inputs and the least expensive real or symbolic forms of power directed against the working class. The AW is a war flashpoint and the recruiting ground for the 'war on terror'. It not only consumes war materiel and human lives; it foments the conditions for war elsewhere as well. Combined with the power emanating from oil control, wars in the AW are a principal social condition of global capital accumulation.

---

6 The US federal government still funds about half of investment in research and development (R&D), which is a little less than 3 per cent of GDP. More than half of the government R&D budget is intended for defence spending. Also, military corporations are principal contributors to R&D spending. National Science Foundation, Science and Engineering Indicators, 2012, tables A4-7 A4-8, A4-9 and A4-10.

Chapter Six: Dislocation under imperialist assault

The least developed countries—mostly in Africa—and Islamic states where the extraction of raw material is vital to global capital accumulation and where the *rapport de forces* favours the imperialists are areas where the case for de-development *cum* abjection can be made. The belligerence of US capital in the AW expand in proportion to oil's importance as a strategic commodity and, equally, in proportion to US capital's dependence on oil, not so much for energy use or the technologically enhanced imputed derivatives it provides (oil enters practically all production processes in one form or another), but more so for control and geostrategic positioning. US seigniorage and imperial rent acquisition require that competing colonialist and imperial partners dissatisfied with the present unsteadiness of interimperialist redistribution via the financial order be held at bay.

Chapter Seven: Arab disintegration and the rising power of imperialism

'Rents' from natural resources are said to account for Arab dividedness. The spin-off of this story is the capacity to earn income without effort from the sale of an asset that is found in nature, and that need not be capitalised, expanded or improved upon. But the fact that the Arab working classes endure so much in relation to their own US capital–backed ruling classes that relinquish sovereignty over resources makes their increasingly imperilled survival anything but 'earning without effort'. Rather, it is earning with huge effort that involves weathering the wrath of imperialist wars and policies. National revenues and resource distribution between local labour, comprador and international capital are determined by a process of control and coercion. Stripping the working classes of their resources constitutes the very basis of the regional circuit of capital. The merchant class cannot benefit from redistributing assets. Uncertainty erases the long term and affords primacy to short-term commercial gain. This renders extremely elusive the goal of welfare-associated gains without an integrated regional industrialisation project along with a more equitable income distribution.

Chapter Eight: Commodification of labour

For more than two decades before the uprisings of 2011, economic supply-side policies dominated the development landscape in the AW. When for every five entrants into the labour market there were little more than two jobs being created, the neoliberal policy advice was that the educational system produced people who were unqualified for the existing jobs. When wages and incomes were steadily falling and led by public-sector compression in incomes, the policy advice was that the labour market was too rigid. With national income stifled, declining productivity, rising inequality and an absence of autonomous civil society institutions, wealth was generated by absolute, as distinct from relative, measures: that is, by extending the hours of labour without a corresponding increase in wages or more generally by paying working people less than what was needed to maintain their living conditions. In a world where technology and market forces have disengaged billions of working people from production, the commodification of human life implies the perverse and murderous fusion of working people with the labour power they sell for a wage. By dispensing with some of the working people by means of wars, neoliberalism or some related form of socially produced disaster like the persistent deaths from hunger globally, capital demonstrates the worthlessness of the labour-power commodity. Unlike in a Malthusian model, where welfare measures enacted to help the poor would later cause the mayhem that reduces swelling populations and then drives up wages, by the late twentieth century surplus labour is so huge that by destroying human lives, capital gets rid of unnecessary commodities and cheapens already engaged labour. When there are 1.1 billion officially unemployed persons globally (the official ILO estimate is closer to 200 million but the head of the ILO is probably too ashamed to report it as such so he included some of the unofficially employed at poverty wages and raised the figure five times), reducing the supply of labour power does not raise the wage. When the slack is in the billions, the death of several millions does not reduce labour supply; it traumatises and dislocates more people to cheapen wages and labour. This vast surplus and its reduction by war and starvation demonstrates the irrelevance of labour; it justifies the low returns to labour given its 'not so scarce' position; and it exerts downward pressure on the wage rate everywhere.

Chapter Nine: Coming to conclusion in times of socialist ideological retreat

Poor development derives first of all from the politics of imperialist aggression and secondarily from the interface between 'free-market' policies and their antidevelopmental outcomes. The stranglehold of free-market ideology is such that after three decades of developmental failure, there is neither an indictment of past failed policies nor of the agents who implemented those policies. In countries where the uprising led to ballot-box democracy, the new Islamic governments overlooked past policies and attributed failure to corruption as a moral category. According to the Islamists, the problem was not that the 'free market' inherently channels social wealth into private hands and promotes waste—it was the falling away of those in power from monotheistic ethics that squandered resources. In more concrete terms, AW development exists in the shadow of international ideological and power play. It retrogresses according to the degree of tacit or open interimperialist rivalry. As US capital differentiates itself from other competing capital circles in term of its share of imperial rents, the autonomy of Arab states over the execution of their own policy diminishes. To be sure, the AW tested the limits of interimperialist collusion when US-led imperialism breached the covenants of international security and occupied Iraq. The divergence of imperialist opinion over the occupation of Iraq demonstrates the relevance of the AW to imperialism and the boundaries to which financialisation diluted the national identity of capital.

Arab development does not elude policymakers. It is policymakers who reshape development as an elusive goal. The scope and scale of coordinated economic and social policy, which augment national productive capacity via international linkages, are capped by the meagre sovereignty of the Arab state. The crisis of underdevelopment undermines the security of working classes, which in turn blights sovereignty. Sovereignty in the practice of development is that state of government which affords working classes with control over their resources and improves their living standards. The exposure of national security simultaneously undermines the security of person, community and democratic institutions. Battering these components of security vitiates a genuine sovereignty substantiated by working-class hegemony over society and the state as the principal agent of development. One stands confronted with a self-reinforcing vicious circle. This chapter brings back the necessity of working-class representation in the state. It concludes that there need be a reinstatement of policy concepts such as egalitarianism, distribution, land reform and nationalisation.

A Note on the Data

Data about the AW is scanty and generally of poor quality. The retreat of the state meant that the state capacity to produce data about its own economic development retreated. The only data that could be counted upon with any degree of accuracy deals with the financial records of the balance of payments, and that is because these data form part of the imperialist control arsenal. Today, the AW cannot be accurately assessed by macro data. It is more amenable to assessment using micro anthropological surveys than macro data as was the case before the formation of modern states. It is rather strange that so many publications about the AW cite the data without cautioning the reader about its quality. For instance, official unemployment in Syria would fall from 15 to 2 per cent between 1997 and 2000, then would rise to 12 per cent in 2002 and fall to 8 per cent in 2005. In the case of Syria, the World Bank recommended counting the seasonal workers during olive-picking season as fully employed at around 2007. The problem was that the rate of unemployment hit a plateau of around 8 per cent up until the uprising, which meant that the olive picking season was not a season but a permanent condition. That is highly unrealistic. In the case of Tunisia, the rate of unemployment would fall from around 16 per cent in early 2000 to 12 per cent in mid-2000. In the case of Morocco, it would fall from around 20 per cent in late 1999 to around 10 per cent by 2004. In the case of Algeria, it falls from around 30 per cent in early 2000 to 10 per cent by late 2000. When one peers behind this astounding success, one sees that while unemployment was declining, the number of persons registered as employed in the informal sector was rising on a nearly one-to-one basis. These wild improvements in unemployment illustrate some of the misrepresentations and data problems. Had there been such improvements in unemployment in such short periods of time, the AW could have been an unsurpassable model of sound development. In the case of investment rates, when the World Development Indicators database is accessed before the uprising, the average rate of investment for several years before 2010 dips to below 20 per cent. When the database is accessed in the post-uprising period, the same figure is revised upward and rises above 20 per cent without a commensurate rise in the growth rate; oddly, the growth rate remained nearly the same. Moreover, Iraq withdrew much of its past data from the World Bank database. Its data now is very spotty. Lebanon has practically no statistical office; a private bank actually estimates national data. Whenever I collect data on the AW in the 1960's, I only use about two-thirds of Arab countries for which data that far back exists; I always include Egypt, the largest Arab country.

Chapter One

STOCKTAKING AND ASSESSMENT

The Arab 'development' experience of the last three decades cannot be understood outside a context of *de-development*. The uprisings that erupted because of misery and repression—and, foremost, because of a crisis of rule by the ruling classes (Gramsci 1971)[1]—notwithstanding, wars, civil wars and the continued Israeli occupation of Palestine characterise the recent history of the region. Instead of mobilising resources for development, the surplus petrodollars of the Gulf states fund the formation of divisive sectarian identities, contribute to wasteful consumption and bolster regression. While there are differences as well as commonalities in Arab development, it is somewhat scholastic to define the various discrete shades of developmental malfunction. Rather, the scope of the research here presented addresses the social relations that repeatedly generate disasters over time. In any case, all Arab countries have fallen short of real development by different degrees. Detailing the minute differences between countries would add little to our understanding of the historical dynamics behind the collapse in development common to all Arab countries; the mere accumulation of such detailed distinctions is a form of empiricism leading to theoretical nihilism.[2] Examining the shared social relationships that *shape* poor development is a more useful form of analysis, because it allows us to conceptually address the underlying causes.

Foremost among these social relationships are those linking Arab ruling classes to international financial capital. These variants of capital have much more in

---

1   Absolute and relative inequality is omnipresent under capitalism. The spark for the revolutions does not emerge on account of growing inequality, but on account of a crisis of the ruling class. For Gramsci in particular, so long as the bourgeoisie retains its hegemonic position, the prospect of revolution remains improbable in relation to the emphasis on deteriorating social conditions.

2   Sure there are differences of quality and quantity, but to study the reasons of the pervasively poor developmental showings from a standpoint of social relations—that is, the human agency mediated in social structures that emanates antiworking policy— would contribute much more to knowledge in terms of the capability of knowing as opposed to how many different things we know, or empiricism leading to theoretical nihilism.

common with each other than they do with their own working classes. Among the
many destructive manifestations of this relationship, generating sectarian/ethnic
divisions in the working class within and across Arab states stands out insofar as
the eruption of civil wars serves to destroy the material basis for the reproduction
of working people. States such as Iraq, Syria, Libya, Egypt, Bahrain and Lebanon,
among others, face the prospect of continued implosion or have crumbled already.
The fragmentation of Arab working classes has reached a nadir in places like
Syria and Iraq. There has been little effective effort to arrest the carnage.

Development bolsters security. Hence the Arab working-class population
is being splintered in this way precisely because economic and social policies
supporting a broader development strategy in the AW can principally be
achieved through closer working-class alliances. Hence, to splinter the working
population is to underdevelop it. Working-class alliances superseding rent-
bolstered sectarian identities would provide crucial preconditions for the
self-reliance needed for better growth and distribution, but these alliances
have become difficult to form. The retrogression in socialist ideology has
worsened steadily since the 1980s and implicates the labour process and its
attendant working classes across the globe. Sound working-class alliances
mediated through the state, had they existed in the AW, would have generated
momentum within the region's policy space to promote productive investment
and the environment required for the implementation of a development
project. By itself, a cooperative economic infrastructure arising from
working-class integration across the AW would for instance turn the Nurkse
problematic—small markets or low demand levels resulting from poverty
leading to low investment—on its head. But the reverse of rising investment
has happened. Because of the divisiveness, all macroeconomic components
have been heading in the wrong direction.

Another manifestation of the alliance between Arab merchant classes
and international financial capitals is that the process of accumulation has
increasingly shifted to commercial activity away from manufacturing. Buying
abroad and selling at home has gradually supplanted industrialisation and
the homogenising forces of an industrialised market economy. In addition to
the role of the imperialist–comprador class alliance that erects and subsidises
cultural modes of social segmentation, the move away from industrialisation
all by itself entrenches social differences both within and across countries,
rendering sacrosanct the despotic forms of political rule in each one. Also, the
distinct economic structures of the Arab countries—their respective sizes, their
foreign asset holdings, natural resource endowments and differential depletion
rates of these endowments, and their subordinated mode of integration
into the global economy—together offset the centripetal forces that would
otherwise bring Arab working classes together across borders. The closing of

factories (where they existed) and the creation of a mass of people employed in patronage-like schemes annul the public or collective spaces in which workers would meet to organise. The inherent and perpetual drive of capital to divide working people colludes with emerging facts that are in themselves promoters of disunity. Harmonisation for economic and social integration both within and across countries confronts the formidable forces of a local ruling class whose principal activity is commerce devoid of industry, and for whom the social contract is signed with international financial capital, not its subject population. For this ruling class, the function of the social structure is to accelerate resource and value grab. These are some of the issues that this book will deal with extensively. In this chapter, however, I start by depicting facets of the full reality by highlighting and exploring some relevant empirical facts. What follows, then, is a short economic history substantiated by data, where the availability of evidence allows us to scan the surface of the AW, before I go on to introduce the process of accumulation as it is determined by US-led imperialist policies and aggression.

A Synopsis of Economic History

The recent history of economic growth in the AW can be divided into three distinct periods: a period of high growth driven by comparatively heavy government intervention beginning in the early 1960s and ending in the early 1980s; a period of low growth typified by collapsing oil prices, 'free market' reforms and gradual structural adjustments extending from the early 1980s until early 2000; and a period of high oil prices and highly inequitable growth beginning in early 2000 and continuing to the present. Vulnerability to external shocks in the AW is crucial to capital's growth process there. In an environment fraught with uncertainty, economic shocks were further compounded by the liberalisation of the financial market, a freer trade regime and a public sector that became increasingly privately owned by the ruling classes. The business cycle moved ever further away from a developmental growth free of external shocks and ever closer to an antidevelopmental process. This evolution reached the point that if economic growth kicked in, commercial as opposed to industrial sources accounted for the rise, industrial value added retreated and inequity grew. This state of affairs continues to characterise the post–Arab uprising economies. The new regimes in Egypt and Tunisia, the two countries that escaped post-uprising collapse, remain set in their ways and pursue the same path as that of their predecessors.

Mainstream research on Arab growth performance using the method of growth accounting finds that the knowledge-based sector and internally developed technologies are either absent or yield a net negative impact on economic growth on account of fiscal leakage (Sala-i-Martin 2002). AW growth is said to be driven principally by its extensive components or net additions to capital and labour without the scale-enhancing effect of the knowledge economy, or what is referred to as the intensive component. This is not, however, unusual in deindustrialising economies. According to the UNIDO data base between 1970 and 2010, the shares of industry in Syria, Egypt, Algeria and Iraq went down respectively from 19 to 5, 21 to 15,[3] 10 to 2 and 12 to 4 per cent. So the sector that requires the most knowledge to be infused in production is in decline. It is no anomaly therefore to see Arab economies steering away from knowledge-based economies into low-productivity ones.

In the case of Arab economies, the high rate of leakages in assets, low capital-output-ratio investment and capital flight establish the relationship that underlies the allocation of resources. Not only have investment rates declined from a high 30 per cent in 1974 to around 18 per cent in 2010, but much of the investment has poured into areas that are of little or no relevance to productivity growth.[1] The bigger share of investment goes into short-gestation-period capital and into what are commonly known as FIRE economies (finance, insurance and real estate). High imports generate most of the value added in import-led economies. The financial-capital assets that accrue circulate abroad as dollar assets. A greater part of consumption is composed of imported goods; capital flight in the case of Saudi Arabia can represent about a quarter of GDP (UN 2008b). Without the ploughing back of generated money capital into the social infrastructure, and plant and equipment, the mobilisation of national resources proceeds at rates below what is necessary to upkeep the working class and/or to absorb population growth effectively in productive employment. Under *étatisme*, in the immediate postindependence era and up to the early 1980s, regulating exchange and interest rates to stem the outflow of resources at prices set far below value— as was needed to maintain living conditions for local populations—was the policy choice. Thereafter, in the neoliberal age, macro prices, wages, and interest and exchange rates were deregulated at the behest of international financial capital to restrict/downgrade the expansion of the national capital stock. Variations in growth rates became more dependent on the share of

---

3   The data from Egypt may be corrupt. National sources cite a manufacturing rate of
     9 per cent around 2009.
4   The WDI database was accessed in 2010. When accessed after the uprising the
     investment rate appears to fluctuate wildly (from 20 per cent in 2006 to 26 per cent in
     2009), while growth rates remain steady and low. Upon closer examination of the data,
     Saudi investment data appears to have been reformulated, thus influencing the overall
     erratic movement in the rate.

oil in total product, which grew over time. Mislaid investment, high levels of imports and a considerable leakage in assets have typified the neoliberal era.

Evidently, oil prices and revenues considerably impact the economies of the AW. However, the issue is not merely the 'oil curse' itself insofar as it invites imperialist aggression. Also crucial to this investigation is the changing macroeconomic environment that veered oil revenues away from contributing to equitable growth and development. The region is beset by conflict and allocates at least twice the world's rate to defence spending (SIPRI and World Bank WDI database, various years). Consequently, defining its economic attributes and establishing the threshold at which oil revenues would seep into development is by no means easy. *A priori*, what matters for regional development is not so much the level of oil prices or revenues *per se*; rather, it is principally value preserving policy and, secondarily, the oil price level that offset the costs of uncertainty and begins to trickle into productive investment activity. All other things considered, a higher level of political instability underscored by working-class insecurity and imperialist belligerence necessarily imply that for regional development to take root, oil revenues must offset defence spending, smooth out government consumption and act as a propeller of public investment while defraying an insurance premium for private investment. With persistently high levels of political tension in the Middle East, that may be too much to ask from oil—one of the most volatile export commodities in world trade (Mayer 2002).

For the time being, it appears structurally prohibitive to abandon oil dependency—to 'kick the oil habit'. Persistent dependence on oil is not haphazard; it is defined and reproduced by a consortium of Arab ruling classes and US-headed imperial powers. Assuming that development were to occur, the effects of Arab development on the sway of forces that thrive on accumulation by encroachment and militarism would be significant. This is a war region, in which the state of conflict itself is an input into global accumulation and that the world has come to internalise as a necessity. To say that the AW faces 'difficulty' in escaping the oil gridlock is a serious understatement. The share of oil relative to national output has risen over time and is now at more than half of national income.[5] The forces that tie down development supersede Arab national boundaries. An industrialisation process in the AW resulting in a higher consumption of petroleum at home would reduce the quantity remaining for a world dependent on oil. The obliviousness with which the misery of the AW has been handled is an outcome of that global dependency, which may have led to a tacit accord on encumbering the process of Arab development.

---

5   Oil share from GDP is computed after deducting the share of oil from GDP using OPEC data.

The Impact of Conflicts

Conflicts and the persistent threats thereof exact a heavy toll on the AW. In 1991 there was a 14 per cent loss in AW output (mainly from Iraq's losses in GDP) in the immediate aftermath of the First Gulf War. This was equivalent to about US$50 billion in 1990 prices (around a tenth of total Arab output). Had the war not occurred and where the growth rate in the region would continue to rise at a modest 3 per cent after 1990, the cumulative losses in constant 1990 prices from 1990 to 2002 are estimated at around US$600 billion. (These are the hypothetical values-added losses, not the real losses, which are almost certainly astronomical especially the loss of Iraq as a cohesive entity.) The recovery from the war was lethargic and inadequate. It took about five years for output to regain its pre-1990 levels. Although this number is difficult to assess, the foregone employment possibilities were potentially between six and seven million jobs in the 1990s alone. Directly or through destabilising threats, the calamity of war imposes a heavy and unrelenting burden on the regional economy. The spectre of war also circularly justifies the rise of the class in power and the security apparatus that sustains Arab regimes and, by implication, shifts resources from productive investment to stabilisation efforts.

In the past fifty years, the Middle East has witnessed more wars than any other region in the world (SIPRI database 2009). Despite the heavily negative impact of wars on human development, there are surprisingly few studies that try to assess the effects of militarised conflicts on growth in the AW. Mainstream literature on that subject is limited to the link between militarised conflicts and trade, and assesses the direction of causality between trade and war. However, a broader perspective needs to underscore the negative effects of wars in withering a considerable part of the human and physical infrastructure. Lebanon and Iraq never fully replaced their past losses. Wars affect long-term growth, particularly by destruction of productive capacity and, in an Arab context, by the tailoring of policy to the implicit or explicit terms of surrender. Devastation wrought upon the AW ensures that the balance of forces is further tilted in favour of imperialist powers that have a direct interest in cheapening and grabbing Arab as well as other Third World resources. Notwithstanding the sale and exchange of commodities on the market, imperialism is a relationship in which undervaluing and grabbing resources by more advanced countries contributes to their profit rates.

War is costly in the sense that it increases public debts and tax burdens and distorts industrial production through the disproportionate expansion of militarised manufacture and imports. However, this is not why the impact of war in the Arab region appears to be not merely lingering but permanent. In the AW, there are very low tax rates, the public domain is privately controlled and most weapons are imported; hence, the tax consequences of war are less relevant to economic performance. The artificial exaggeration of world addiction to oil time and again reinforces the scramble for the region's resources to the detriment of the working population—not only in the AW but around the globe, as a result of the costs of war and to the environment. Pauperising the Arab working class and subjecting it to the misery of war serves by the demonstration effect to prop up an ideology of ultranationalism in the centre. By the lifeboat ethic, the hordes of barbarians are said to be at the gate of the great Western civilisation.

Nation-states, at the behest of capital, subjugate the working classes within them and pursue their vital interests, whether by wars or other nonviolent means of aggression. However, placing their own class above the fetish of the nation-state, the merchant Arab classes in charge of development disempower working classes in particular by stripping them of their sovereignty over national resources. Of all the instruments of dispossession, war is the most powerful tool for socialising Third World assets, that is for depriving the national working class of owning its resources. Far worse than foreclosures that evict peasants from their property so that they join the non-owning (waged) labour force, wars prevent whole populations from owning their natural resources. War is useful in resource grab, or the process by which developed formations garner the resources of the Third World under highly inequitable terms imposed, more often than not, by military superiority. As will be explained in Chapter Four, in a strategic region targeted for imperialist control, the Arab ruling-class alliance with US-led capital promotes the reproduction of war.

Past Performance of the Arab World

Over 30 years, the AW has been characterised by one of the lowest real average per capita growth rates in the world (the average yearly real per capita GDP growth is 0.5 per cent, according to the World Bank Indicators [WDI] database). The average includes the high rates of the early 1970s during the first oil boom. That the AW is rich in capital is a false dictum that nonetheless dominates the development discourse. Real development is about the mobilisation of real resources, not the mass of money capital. Arab regimes, by virtue of their shared security and sovereignty with the US, are mere custodians of an oil resource that is effectively not theirs. Most of Arab private financial resources abroad are of a personal and/or private nature. These assets remain unrequited transfers or uncashed cheques and are practically unavailable for regional development.

Thus, insofar as the mainstream media projects an image of rich Arabs, the broader picture, in which around 50 per cent of the population survive on less than two US dollars a day and spend more than half their income on basic foods, is purposefully concealed and/or overlooked.[6] In any case, the one or two dollars thresholds are arbitrary benchmarks that mean little in an Arab context. The Arab countries are the most food-dependent countries globally. These one- or two-dollar poverty criteria in countries highly dependent on food imports tell us little about poverty conditions. In India, where food is mostly home produced, a dollar goes a long way. In Iraq, Lebanon and Libya the dollar is spent on imported foods whose prices are determined internationally, so the locals pay international prices from meagre salaries. Yet rising poverty rates have often been concealed. A cursory look at the figures before the uprisings would imply that absolute poverty rates—those below one dollar per day—were around 5 per cent (WDI, various years). These are low by global standards. Following the uprising, these figures were revised upward considerably (to around 20 per cent). In any case, the purpose of these falsifications was to embellish the picture of development conditions and to strengthen the allies of US capital.

However, in spite of higher growth as of early 2000, Arab poverty worsened. A 'growth' in which maldistribution prevailed was occurring in states that were mainly at the disposal of foreign powers. These were US satellites directly or indirectly by virtue of conceding to the World Bank's and the International Monetary Fund's (WB/IMF) policy. It may be relevant at this juncture to dispel the image of 'rich Arabs' and to state things as they are: within the strict terms of economic wealth there are rich individuals in the AW, but the majority of working Arabs are pauperised. According to the University of Texas Inequality Project, the AW exhibits one of the highest income inequality rates of all regions (EHII, various years). The figures one gets from the WDI on poverty, where they exist, are misleading. Egypt in the WDI, for instance, appears as egalitarian as Austria and to be holding steady to that trend; whereas in the Texas Income Inequality Database, the data shows Egypt to be one of the most inequitable countries in the world.[7] Despite the formal change in ruling faces in some 'Arab Spring' countries, the flow of resources remained the same and the divide between the private

---

6   All the computations are based on the UN database or the World Bank WDI database. Also see the national accounts database for the League of Arab States, Ataqrir al Arabi Almouwahad, various years; and the World Bank, online: http://www-wds.worldbank. org/external/default/WDSContentServer/WDSP/IB/2011/05/27/000001843_20 110601143246/Rendered/PDF/P126506000AWIFS000PID000Concept0Stage.pdf (viewed 4 June 2013).

7   'Estimated Household Income Inequality Data Set' (EHII). Online: http://utip.gov. utexas.edu/data.html (viewed 8 October 2012).

internationally integrated capital and the social spheres continues to grow, only aggravating past conditions.

Upon a closer examination of the per capita income performance, the broader picture tends to conceal some varying patterns, the most visible of which is that since about the early 1980s, the more diversified economies (less dependent on oil) have consistently outperformed the big oil-exporting economies. These more diverse economies have proven to have a more stable growth path and, consequently, were less exposed to disturbances caused by external shocks—notably, falling oil prices. More diversified countries internalise value in complex production chains, whereas the Gulf countries only superficially absorb new value in their shallow production structure. Although the received view holds that low oil prices were the culprits behind this poor growth performance, a broader analysis finds that this is a very partial assessment. Driven by higher output levels, export revenues, principally composed of oil revenues, have risen at an average yearly rate of 2 per cent between 1985 and 2002 (this is the low oil price period, which means that low growth occurred more because of policy shift than falling oil revenues). Since 2002, oil revenues skyrocketed as a result of oil prices rising from a plateau of 20 dollars per barrel to a current plateau of 100 dollars per barrel. The chief issue remains, however, that this revenue did not bolster the investment rate or the principal component in the growth mechanism. With the onset of neoliberalism in the early 1980s, the accent in policy shifted to private sector–led investment. The investment rate, dependent on risk considerations and uncertainties—chiefly nonquantifiable risks—decreased on average by about two percentage points over the 1990s. By contrast, in the 1970s, export earnings had increased at a much higher rate (8 per cent) with proportionately more resources spilling over into economic investment activity and, hence, a much higher investment and growth rate.

Higher oil prices in the 1970s, conditioned by *étatisme*, meant that more resources were available for productive investment in spite of the perennial tension plaguing the region. National security and development concerns ran parallel to each other in the immediate postindependence period (roughly 1960 to 1980). Although spending on defence and other security considerations bit off a comparatively large chunk of available resources, the remaining funds propped up productive capital intended for civilian use. The correlation between economic growth and investment was such that for every 1 percentage point of growth there needed to be 3 percentage points of investment (WDI, various years). When the macro context was first liberalised in the early 1980s, this relationship changed considerably. It would then require around 5 per cent of growth in investment to register 1 per cent of economic growth. Under *étatisme* and regulated markets, by contrast, the growth rate responded favourably to the channelling of public savings into an investment–growth nexus.

A continued state of instability along with a laissez-faire framework (introduced gradually since the early 1980s) meant that the investment rate remained low and indeed fell. Investment was to be placed on ephemeral and low capital-output-ratio activity. It is difficult to determine either the threshold level of risk at which regional oil rents would flow into productive investment or the impact of growth on development, which is determined by the *rapport de force* of social classes; but had the region only spent the average world rate on defence, it would be safe to say that because of instability alone, the AW has lost on average roughly two percentage points of growth every year since 1980 (my calculation using the WDI database). This estimate, nevertheless, is hypothetical and only a potential assessment of losses. The real losses from instability-associated conflicts would be commensurate with losses in human and capital assets (capital and human resource destruction and flight), which have indeed been incalculable.

Patterns of Growth

A high variance and an overall poor yearly average growth rate characterise the Arab business cycle. For the periods 1971–80, 1980–90, 1990–2000 and 1970–2000, the average per capita growth rates of the Gulf states respectively were 2.0, –7.5, 0.5 and –2.50. GDP is a value-added calculation that does not include excess savings of Gulf states (that is, it does not include Gulf savings and investment abroad). For the rest of the AW, for the periods 1971–80, 1980–90, 1990–2000 and 1970–2000, the average growth rates were 6.0, 0.0, 0.5 and 0.0. The long-term average per capita growth rate from 1971 to 2000 is at –0.05 (that is nearly zero) and up to 2011, it stood at less than 1.0 per cent (UN data, various years). In the AW, it is possible to grow under stable conditions with low oil prices because the peace dividend could be channelled into infrastructure and productive activity under regulated capital and trade accounts, but the opposite occurred. The rise of merchant capital intertwined with imperialist control motives pre-empts social investment in labour and recirculates capital away from the national formation. Social investment in labour, including the education of women—where it occurs— forms part of the regime stabilisation strategy that does link to development. It follows that under persistent tension and a policy interface facilitating the transfer of resources abroad, the AW exhibited one of the lowest and poorest quality per capita growth rates of all regions over the last three decades. Poor-quality growth performance is even more pronounced in 'adjusting' countries such as Tunisia and Egypt, which were touted as WB/IMF model students.

In both countries income inequality was eroding the income of working people at a faster rate than the high rate of growth in GDP. In sum, three antidevelopmental processes and one outstanding impediment determine the path of growth in the AW:

a) the volatility and dependence of growth on oil price fluctuations in oil-exporting economies, and geopolitical flow disturbances in the case of the more diversified economies;

b) overall poor trade integration in the regional and global economy (principally oil exports)—continued heavy reliance on oil exports and a marked lack of competitiveness;

c) a lower investment rate relative to the 1970s / early 1980s that yielded lower growth rates in the 1980–90s (investment rates fell from 30 per cent in 1980 to around 18 per cent in 2010) including a shift into poorer quality investment marked by the relatively minor contribution of technology and other knowledge-based activities to growth, and;

d) a policy interface allowing for the usurpation of financial and real resource at macro policies and prices set by the agencies of US-led capital.

Although a slower rate of growth in oil revenues can partly explain the decline in investment since the early 1980s, promoting private investment and trade openness, regardless of how far or how fast, resulted in poor investment and trade performances. The investment rate dipped at an average of around –1.5 per cent annually and basic sectors like agriculture and industry declined as shares of output. Manufacturing declined at a rate of about 1.5 per cent after 1990 and agriculture went down to 8 per cent of GDP (measured until 2010 from the UNIDO and FAO databases respectively).[8]

Neoliberal reform policies were implemented piecemeal with the intent to suck resources at prices below value from the AW. These policies are an indirect restoration of colonialism: the control of national resources by an outside power and the below-value resource transfer. Further, despite most Arab countries' adherence to the terms of the WTO, market access problems have persisted for the areas in which the region displayed a comparative advantage, namely textiles and agriculture or, more recently, their remnants. More importantly, on the investment side, where the decline has been substantial, the risks were considerable given the small domestic market, capital-biased institutions, poor regional integration and, ultimately, precarious and uncertain political cycles. Thus, for instance, when 'one-stop shops' intended to reduce red tape and

---

8   These measurements include major Arab countries, the Maghreb and the Mashriq including Egypt, and exclude the Gulf states.

facilitate domestic and foreign investment were set up, very little investment flowed into Arab economies.

Stability concerns beg the question of why an insurance scheme that offsets the non-market-related risks to long-term investment was not considered in the first place—assuming business is afraid of nationalisation or the effects of war . To secure the future in order to draw investment would create regional geopolitical security—it defuses the tensions needed for global capital to boost its militarisation. Developmental investment would have unleashed a forbidden type of economic growth, the rights-based type 'with expanding output and employment, institutional transformation and technological progress that might steadily improve the well-being of working people'. This development would also imply working-class sovereignty or the right of working classes to design and implement policies that conform to their social needs. Because the AW is integrated with global capital via militarism, no effort could be spared by the cross-border class alliance of local merchant capital and imperialism in snuffing any policy that moved toward empowering working classes socially. The extraction of value at fire-sale prices from the AW contributes to lowering the costs of inputs required for global accumulation and to raising the rate of profits for financial capital. War and neoliberalism have worked together to ensure the deterioration of social conditions in the AW. The knock-on effect is not only material but also ideological, spurring warlike attitudes in working people everywhere.

The Mainstream View of Growth

Mainstream investigations of economic growth can be summarised as an effort to find a stable relationship between aggregate output and stocks of physical inputs and technical knowledge. Supposing such a relationship exists, the growth rate of an economy depends on the rate of accumulation of primary production factors such labour and capital and the speed of technological progress. These factors enter as symbols in a growth equation. It is natural to envisage a wide variety of economic and social issues that affect the growth of an economy, but these are said to be the principal factors. The purpose of growth investigations is to provide a framework for examining how these economic and social issues can be counted on in the accumulation of primary production factors and the speed of technological progress, and ultimately their impact on economic growth.

Various manipulations of this growth-research schema have been introduced since its reintroduction in neoclassical growth theory by Robert Solow, but a critical point remained that state intervention boosts growth, otherwise economies decline into a steady state (1956, 65–94).

Specifically, to the discomfort of 'free market' adherents, outside intervention by the state holds sway:

> Once we reject Say's Law and recognize that capitalism is prone to deficiency in aggregate demand, we have to accept that sustained growth in this system requires exogenous stimuli. By exogenous stimuli I mean a set of factors which raise aggregate demand but are not themselves dependent upon the fact that growth has been occurring in the system; that is, they operate irrespective of whether or not growth has been occurring in the system. Moreover, they raise aggregate demand by a magnitude that increases with the size of the economy, for instance with the size of the capital stock. They are in other words different from 'erratic shocks' on the one hand, and 'endogenous stimuli', such as the multiplier-accelerator mechanism, on the other: the latter can perpetuate or accelerate growth only if it has been occurring anyway. 'Erratic shocks' can explain the persistence of business. (Patnik 2012)

For the free-marketers, the notion that government and social policy are necessary for long-term growth ran counter to their belief in self-adjusting markets. That their models always stumble on a steady state—a state wherein all growth falls while its determining variables grow at constant rates—was not a desirable outcome. Further mainstream growth modelling led to a class of endogenous growth models that emphasise behavioural mechanisms and technological conditions through which the accumulation of production factors themselves can be a source of exponential economic growth (Romer 1986, 1002–37). In this class of models, knowledge-related factors enhance predictions of long-term growth. The rate of growth becomes determined endogenously by the economy's dynamic decisions to internalise human or technological capital. The crucial assumption that underlies this class of models is that the dynamic decisions for investment are not wholly subject to diminishing returns. This manoeuvring with algebraic symbols emphasises 'learning effects', research and development activities by firms, and the role of economic institutions as well as social and political ones as direct sources of long-term economic growth.

Endogenous growth theory's predictions of long-term economic growth remained unsustainable in aggregate-scale economies (Reinert 2012). A litany of related research followed and included: a discussion of the role of human capital (Lucas 1988, 3–42); the role of innovation and international trade (Grossman and Helpman 1990, 796–815); the role of politics in economic growth, or how income distribution policy affects economic growth (Alesina and Rodrik 1994, 465–90). These developments grew in an eclectic fashion, overlooking the social dislocation that precedes the making of growth. They furnished symbolic interpretations underlined by reified economic factors, social policy and institutions:

> By their very nature, since they are conditioned by the fact of growth itself, they cease to operate when the system is in a stationary state; they cannot be adduced as an explanation for the system experiencing a positive trend. Such an explanation can only be based on the operation of exogenous stimuli, that is, of stimuli which are not themselves dependent upon the fact of growth taking place. (Patnik 2012)

In these models, capital and labour, the living forms of social organisation in contradiction with each other, fell by the wayside. In all their permutations, real historical conditions were confined to the 'rigour' of mathematical modelling. A multifaceted reality determined by the actions of politically organised social classes inherently at loggerheads with each other was reduced to a manageable system of individual agents enjoying level playing fields and reaching a contract that satisfies an equilibrium condition. Mathematics perverted social conditions. Equilibriums of any sort led to steady states in a rather unsteady world. No matter how much endogenous growth models would tweak the symbols of the growth equation to delay the inevitability of declining marginal returns to factors of production, in the AW there were wars and immense idle labour. The variables that would explain Arab growth are themselves explained by growth—but not the growth of the AW, rather the growth of the central economies. The exogenous stimulus whipping on Arab growth was in fact the disincentive of imperialism.

Mainstream growth theory generated much empirical literature using cross-country data samples that analyse growth and the possibility of poorer countries catching up with the richer ones. For this literature, the problem was economic and not sociological—that is, related to debilitating social conditions in countries saddled by force with colonial institutional structures. The power structure, foremost in which is military power or the threat of military power, is what underdevelops society. More industrially advanced Arab economies succumbed in war and to the inflow of geopolitical petrodollars from the Gulf. They underwent a process of deindustrialisation, while the Gulf states that had no industry appear to have industrialised without acquiring an industrial culture, which is really not industrialisation at all. Moreover, the permanent state of political instability and conflict bolsters the dependence of the region on exports of oil and oil-related products. The process of development differs for historical reasons that cannot be captured by symbols representing governance, institutions or 'corruption' measures. In several empirical trials, statistical proxies for wars explain much of the growth process in the AW (UN 2006).

The mainstream policy message was that economic development depends primarily on the creation of an enabling environment for the private sector, free markets and good governance. When these conditions prevail, the theory says, development prevails. Given that these conditions exist nowhere, advocating good governance to Arab despots is especially absurd. The more astounding parochialism here is that Arab economies would actually grow even if their ruling classes awakened to the rule of law and abided by human-rights principles—as if Arab development would not weaken US-led imperialism's hegemony over oil. In accounting terms, growth can be entirely ascribed to the circulating share of oil in national economies. The recent growth episode beginning in 2002, much like its predecessor of 1973, occurred concomitantly with rising oil prices. In the twenty years between peak oil price periods the growth rate slowed down considerably and per capita average real growth was negative. In light of the variability in oil price and in the presence of mercantile and inherently comprador capital–based institutions and policies—which have an inbuilt tendency to dislocate huge sections of the working classes as opposed to engaging them—the recent growth experience (beginning 2002) was uneven, both within countries and across the region.

Unsurprisingly, empirical assessment of growth performances in the AW shows that capital generates relatively less output per unit than other regions (Sala-i-Martin 2002; El Badawi 2004). There are weak positive effects of capital formation on GDP growth in the AW (Nabli 2004). But the spectre of conflicts, by their corrosive nature, nullifies the contribution of physical capital formation. Moreover, the Arab region lacks the capacity to smoothly absorb technical spillover from foreign investment (Kroegstrup 2005). Trade openness provided no extra inputs to long-term growth (Sala-i-Martin 2002). The arrival of new technology has no statistically significant effects on the growth of labour productivity in the AW region (Kroegstrup and Matar 2005). It is not unusual to witness these results in a region whose average growth rates were nearly on par with its population growth rates—the economy grows on a one to one basis with additional growth in the population. By the natural-growth-rate approach, this implies that labour productivity has experienced no significant growth.

A decomposition of output per capita into GDP over employment, employment over labour force, and labour force over population reveals that the labour-shedding measures have risen. Enforced labour market flexibilisation as of 2000 appears and only appears to have brought up output per worker from 1.5 to –0.7 (WDI various years). Oil prices and revenues distort the output per worker picture. When a simple exercise by which oil revenues is subtracted from output is carried as of 2000, the results show output per capita and output per worker as of 2000 to be negative and significantly exceed the previous period of 1980–2000. Although productivity is very roughly mimicked by output per worker the rates are negative more or less typical of all Arab countries, save the small oil states whose output per worker appears inflated as a result of oil revenues—they brought up the overall average. The rise in the employment to labour force rate as of 2000 underscores the higher rate of participation in informal sector poverty employment and the lower rate of dependency. More persons from the same family would have to engage in employment to maintain the same living income.

Furthermore, the gap between growth and development highlights the poor intermediation between financial capital and real resources. This is not just on account of the Gulf being money-wealthy and in the grip of the US and, hence, why should one even entertain the idea that the Gulf should transfer finance to poorer Arab countries. It is more so on account of cash-strapped Arab countries that are incapable of nationally emitting their own money supply as a result of deregulated capital accounts. Unlike many other developing countries, the AW fails to nationally mobilise real resources with its auto-generated finance. Both real resources, capital and labour, are subject to a misallocational relationship and leakages. Exercising austerity in a capacity-wanting Arab context implies that while labour naturally grows, neoliberal policies cap the expansion of capital (lower investment). Industries shrink even as the population pyramid balloons in the youth tier. This is not a case in which capital and labour are incongruous in terms of skills—the economy needs engineers but we are producing economists, say—but a case in which policy lowered the rate of expansion in productive capital while labour grew. Unless some regulation plugging the leakages and coordination or an expansion of capital is carried out, unemployment grows in absolute terms. High unemployment in the region is structurally rooted in this anaemic accumulation process.

Mainstream Growth Theory: Eloquence and Irrelevance

Mainstream theory is not intended as a mantra of growth, 'its aim is to supply an element in an eventual understanding of certain important elements of growth and to provide a way to organise one's thoughts on these matters'.[9] Yet, invariably, in the literature foisted upon the AW, the policy design for development rests on the basis of complete liberalisation, without due regard

---

9   This description of neoclassical growth theory is taken from *The New Palgrave Dictionary of Economics* (1998).

to the history and particularity of a specific accumulation process under conditions of uncertainty. No matter how complacent one is, one must recognise that liberalisation in a state functionally owned by the class of merchant capital whose interests are vested in extranational territory will mean that national resources will be stifled. There is little chance that the Western-governed WB/ IMF consortium was unaware of this fact. The 'market', even in the fictitious neoclassical sense, is not the unquestionable control of few individuals over allocation; it is a whole set of institutions guaranteeing intermediation and welfare by way of more or less equal power platforms. The usual sermon-like policy of the WB/IMF is to liberalise, increase the effectiveness of labour, and improve technology: 'Restoring growth will require raising private investment [...] and improving the efficiency of investment through greater integration with the global economy' (Page 1998). Given such unrealistic assumptions, these formulaic policy measures are tantamount to obfuscation. Raising growth is not a matter of simple additions to the logical arguments (symbols) of growth—capital, labour and technology in an equation. Growth represents a quantitative benchmark for capital accumulation. Capital accumulation, however, is a sociohistorical process decided by organised power and classes and not something that can be traced to a formal argument- the formal argument can clarify matters but it has to adhere to some realistic assumptions. Thirty years of reforms aimed at expanding and enhancing the efficiency of the private sector have shown no substantive expansion in investment capable of dodging an inequitable growth path. Should this not beg the question as to whether a neoclassical growth framework can *ever* generate reasonable grounds on which a policy for capital accumulation can be formulated? The alternative approach has to be traced in terms of the history of social classes reinitiating change in the region. Foremost among these changes is to enact economic policy that will ensure the recirculation of wealth in the national economies— that is, to shut off the spigots of resource transfer abroad. In one concrete instance, state-generated savings underwritten by future development would be ploughed back into scale-augmenting investment activity.

Apart from investment, which is deterred by uncertainty and small markets, the region experiences a significant leakage of resources and/or affluent consumption, which reduces effective (that is, nationally retained) private or public savings. When so many resources escape and imports represent on average around 50 per cent of GDP (2011 figures), the multiplier theory, according to which one dollar multiplies several-fold in the economy, founders. Capital inflows are channelled into raising consumption, especially on the luxury goods of the merchant class as it emulates its foreign counterpart either directly, or indirectly by shifting resources away from investment. As conspicuous consumption and regional tensions have risen, the private savings retained in the national economy have fallen. Public savings have also fallen with falling tax receipts (under adjustment) or by the change in the composition of government expenditure carried out under structural reforms intended to bolster the savings of the merchant class by tax reduction. In any case, oil revenues in the oil-producing economies, or geopolitical rent injections to stabilise the more diversified economies, have crowded out retained savings as affluent consumption has risen and tax revenues have plummeted (the rich saved abroad). The biggest squeeze on domestic savings, however, remains the combination of insecurity, the compradorial nature of the ruling merchant classes and, just as important, the open capital accounts policy that hijacks the interest rate as a 'savings' instrument.

The Missing Discourse in the Arab Uprisings

Relative to its wealth, then, the AW has been performing far below potential. While the real GDP per capita, for the region as a whole, was growing annually at a rate of 6 per cent during the 1970s, it declined during the 1980s at the average annual rate of 0 per cent and grew at a mere 3 per cent during the 1990s. When it picked up again to an average of 5 per cent in early 2000, it was hollow and inequitable. Inequitable distributional arrangements that dampen demand alongside declining investment rates—especially investment rates in plant and equipment—which are usually associated with long term stability and sizeable markets, are a drag on economic performance. Investment rates in the Arab region were on average around 4 percentage points below the rate in the developing world for the period 2000–2010.

The 2011 uprising coincided with rising regional tensions and a trumpeted larger role for a private sector under Islamic finance. The Arab private sector, now deeply rooted in commerce rather than industry, cannot assume the agency of development. It chiefly buys imports for local consumption and taps into oil revenues. Industrial capital could have had a long-term stake in the region, but the conditions for industrialisation eroded over time. It may be too early to tell, but so far, in states that elected political Islamists, no policy is boosting public investment in the physical and social infrastructure or promoting state-sponsored industrial projects. Development has not been treated as the long-term social project that it is. There has been no redistribution of wealth and land that were earlier confiscated from the working class by the kleptomania of Arab regimes. The 'Islamic' economy is no different from its predecessor.

The region's dependency on oil, its degrading effect on the environment, and the ideologically motivated exaggeration of oil, are causes and outcomes of underdevelopment. Oil itself, the black substance, cannot be given a life of its own that explains underdevelopment. Rather, the explanation lies in a peculiar dependent process whereby the agency of development (the alliance of the merchant class with US-led imperialism) dislocates labour and recirculates the region's wealth outside the region as opposed to within. This *modus operandi* is clearly the explicit policy design of the WB/IMF, which has observed its consequences but pursues it anyway.

But matters were not always as bleak as this. In the 1960s and 1970s, the regulated policy framework offered the chance to improve the AW industrial capacity. Oil revenues, where they existed, enabled the AW economies to command additional resources, boost industrialisation and build an infrastructure, dramatically missing in some cases, like the Gulf states. Additional spending in domestic currency grew as part of the new foreign currency inflows, which were internalised and exchanged for local currency. Currency inflows induce a higher level of activity in the domestic economy and trigger, in some cases, a real appreciation of the currency. This appreciation can become a source of difficulty for the economy if it hinders industrialisation and export diversification, or if it erodes the competitiveness of traditional areas of activity. Later, Gulf financial flows in the form of aid and remittances to the more industrialised Arab countries, like Egypt and Syria, began to be mishandled and contributed to Dutch disease like symptoms (deindustrialisation as a result of an overvalued exchange rate). As will be seen in the next chapter, however, the exchange rate story is only a minimal part of the picture; the principal component behind deindustrialisation is the defeat in wars and the rise of an ideology of defeatism that furnished this merchant class with an alibi by which it could escape its populist egalitarian rhetoric and shift its allegiance to world capital. Thus, instead of boosting the security of the war economies, Gulf funds and remittances gradually increased the structural fragility of the balance of payments and rendered these economies less able to cope with adverse shifts in resource inflows.

In the 1960s and 1970s, the distortion of oil earnings on exchange rates was initially minimal and contained. In this same period, the populist regimes controlled capital accounts and tailored interest and exchange rates to equilibrate saving and investment while protecting the basic consumption bundle, which was part and parcel of national security. These macro prices were construed and monitored so as to arrest leakages and internalise accumulation and knowledge processes. In the 1980s, owing to the shift in the class alliance of Arab regimes already discussed, neither the oil-rich countries with small populations nor the poorer, relatively more populated and less oil-dependent economies internalised the complex chains of economic activity that might have permitted sustained and autonomous development.

Moreover, these private sector–leaning reform policies were built on the implicit belief that the private and public sectors compete for the same resources.

In developing countries performing far below potential they do not, especially when national finances are not exposed to international financial pressures. There is plenty of room in the economy for both private and public sectors to use in complementary fashion. Given the resource demobilisation and the risks that the private sector faces in these countries, public investment serves as a jumping-off point for private undertakings. But instead of a Marshall Plan, with the initial capital injection required for public and private investments to rise simultaneously, the AW got a Morgenthau Plan (the plan offered initially to Germany after the Second World War with the aim of limiting German industrialisation). This was in marked contrast to the immediate postindependence period, when private investment was underwritten by the state's commitment to increasing public investment and the private sector piggybacked on the public sector. Despite the glaring fact that if economies liberalise, the ruling merchant classes will divert resources, the WB/IMF promoted private investment as a panacea at a time when no rational private investor could possibly invest over the long term in the uncertain context of the Arab region.

Slowly, export of primary products came to typify the AW. The earnings from oil, which are the property of working classes as per the second principle of the UN Covenant on Economic, Social and Cultural Rights, became the 'unearned' incomes of merchant and international financial capital. As of 1997, the impact of oil extraction on the environment when factored into the savings rate lowers a positive rate to -10 per cent on average (for the region as whole including Turkey and Iran) (World Bank 1997). Future generations have been left without development and with a degraded environment. Inequitable growth and institutional distortions have paralleled shifts in class relations. These reforms created 'rich countries with poor people'; but here, not as Stiglitz (2004) notes, that is on account of the Dutch disease but on account of rich people abandoning the recirculation of wealth within the national boundary.

Conclusion

Poor performance associated with imperialist assault is not related to Arab oil per se; it is a much broader social phenomenon prevailing wherever imperialism strives for primary-product control by aggressive means. To resolve the debacle, socially, politically and historically specific mediations between capital and labour need to be assessed. WB/IMF policy has (deliberately) overlooked the obvious, which is the ties of Arab merchant classes to US-led imperialism and the war context. Arab ruling classes practicing unsightly forms of human rights abuse do not heed advice to pursue 'good governance'. The fact that the World Bank advises a change in governance strategy where change is impossible merely embellishes the public images of US-friendly dictators. To recommend, as the WB/IMF has in some cases, that a country might be better off ignoring potential sources of oil wealth is also nonsensical. Oil can be a source of funds for continuing economic growth and improvements in social and welfare standards.

Until 1977, to underline this point, real per capita income in the AW grew at about the same rate as that of East Asia. However, after that time, East Asia's per capita income tripled by 1996, while on average per capita income in the AW stagnated from the early 1980s on. The retreat could not be fully attributable to oil prices or revenues, since the latter declined once and started to rise again as of the mid-1980s. Successive Arab defeats, shifts in the mode of appropriation of the ruling classes from industry to commerce, and imperialist oil control/militarisms represent the context of development and the core reason for Arab retrogression. The state was gradually stripped of a sovereignty whose substance is working-class security; hence it lost autonomy over policy. Eroded sovereignty and failure of the state constituted a failure of development. Swings in the regional business cycle could be attributed to pressures arising from external forces, and not to forces generated *causa sui* by the economy's internal mechanisms. The business cycle of the AW exemplifies a case of an 'imperialistically determined cycle' or one mainly driven by outside pressures. Oil prices and revenues are relevant to development only insofar as they exceed the costs of political tensions in a state that mediates the interests of the working class; otherwise, they simply act as stabilisation measures without being transmuted into productive activity. If policy were to implement improvements in social welfare and productive employment via the internal redirection of oil revenues, an empowered Arab working population would loosen the imperial grip on oil, at least to the degree to which they actually hold sovereignty. For Arab development to be denied is key to the hegemony of US-led imperialism over the area. Unless post–Arab uprising policy measures go to empower the working class by locking in the circuit of value, direct redistribution and land reform, development will continue to be a case of de-development. Before I proceed to the political determinants of development, in the next chapter I review and criticise some the macroeconomic policies implemented in the AW since the onset of neoliberalism.

Chapter Two

DE-DEVELOPMENT AND CONVENTIONAL POLICIES

After several military routs, the Arab ruling class, whose interests became progressively more rooted in international financial capital, has relinquished sovereignty and autonomy over policy. The crucial point at which the surrender occurred coincided with the Camp David accords of 1979. These treaties ripped Egypt out of its Arab milieu and slivered the Arab world, further weakening its already flaccid security agreements. In this context, for developmental growth to take hold, oil revenues, or better yet nationally generated finance, ought to more than cover the political instability premium. They should exceed the costs of security as well as the sunk costs of public spending and investment. It is hypothetically possible for an Arab economy to grow under stable conditions with low oil prices because the 'peace' (or defused-tensions) dividend in a state that promotes the rights of labour could be channelled into the social infrastructure and production. In reality, of course, the opposite of this desirable path was followed. The regressive developmental process leading to the Arab uprisings was reinforced at every stage by WB/IMF-proposed procyclical policies. These measures accentuated the many shocks to which the AW was subjected. The downturns were lasting because the vacillation of oil prices intertwined with a precarious political environment to deepen the troughs in the cycle. Rooted in the interests of their own class, the ruling classes' commitment to the WB/IMF neoliberal framework engineered a whole set of macro prices (wages, exchange and interest rates) that ensured antidevelopmental outcomes. Macro prices including wage rates were calibrated to levels insufficient even to maintain, let alone improve, the majority's standard of living.

Prices, to be sure, do not descend from heaven. Prices were reproduced across time by a quasi-colonial power relationship in which Arab resources are undervalued. Money-form explanations cannot suffice for investigative social science; otherwise, accounting could reign as its queen. Prices emerge from a metabolic social process in which workers and nature are consumed by the voracity of production for profit. Owing to the enfeebled power of the Arab working classes, their resources are either snatched for a pittance or, when high prices are paid for oil, the revenues cycled back into the dollar economy. During this process of recirculation, petrodollars wreak havoc on societies and feed the construction of divisive (religious-sectarian, ethnic-tribal) identities splintering the working class. Petrodollars have demobilised real resources.

The neoliberal agenda required theoretical backing. Coinciding with the retreat of socialist ideology, the WB/IMF, employing a neoclassical framework, elevated private sector–led development from a reasoned position with acknowledged drawbacks and failings into a system of belief. This obfuscation reached its zenith in the years just prior to the Arab uprisings, as the WB/IMF spewed out a litany of literature recommending deregulation, requesting that class power–determined prices be freed, and ludicrously as mentioned in Chapter One recommending good governance to Arab rulers. Advising absolute despots of the type of Hosni Mubarak or Ali Abdullah Saleh to govern in 'good' ways was no error of ignorance or idealism; it was measured. Entreating 'good governance' from bad governors was how a phantasm was transmuted into a reality by the power of ideology (World Bank 2007b).

Arab regimes not only codified a whole set of power relations which rendered their functioning possible; they confiscated all power (Foucault 1980). The AW was probably the only place where capital's coercive hold on the economic and political sphere was complete. Hence, implying that good governance and reform were possible under these regimes was a sham used by capital to soothe the working classes and to circumscribe their revolt. By employing the language of reforms in an unreformable situation, the WB/IMF consortium endorsed repression and de-development.

In addition to the uncertainty related to wars of imperial aggression, which acquire the semblance of *force majeure*, the interface between private sector–based macro policy and outcome generated disastrous results. In the double disaster of war and bad policy, the ensemble of privatisation, deregulation, and trade and capital account openness allowed the transfer of value either at no cost or at fire-sale prices. Dislocation of labour and other resources—through privatisation—socialised assets to be grabbed. Typically, the class that earned its keep by private means would lose its means of self-reproduction and join the market in search of employment. In three decades of market reforms, labour's share of total income in the AW dropped to about a third—one of the lowest shares globally (KILM, various years).[1] Class power–brokered prices signalled

---

1   On the basis of available data it is not possible to estimate Arab labour share from total output using the unadjusted labour share which is the ratio of the compensation of employees to the value added (net of indirect taxes and consumption of fixed capital). In a roundabout way, the estimate of the labour share may be derived from the share

for the neoclassical 'equilibrium to be reached' at the point in which capital owns nearly everything and labour nearly nothing. Neoclassical efficiency dogma turned the illusory into the real and crippled developmental growth. Working people had less to buy with and were buying more imported staples, yet that condition was edging toward Pareto efficiency: the poor hit a bottom after which they cannot be made worse off. Hence, the chemistry between Pareto, a long-dead member of the Italian Fascist senate, and US-governed international financial institutions, in a Kafkaesque manner, burned the Arab roadmap to 'development' into the backs of the Arab working class. In this chapter, I review and criticise some of these policies with the aim of motivating the social and political context in which de-development proceeded.

The Boom Years

From 2002 and as a result of rising oil prices, the AW began experiencing another oil boom similar in many respects to a previous boom experienced between 1974 and 1981. Since 2002, excess savings over investment in constant year-2000 dollars (constant prices) for the AW stand at 1.2 trillion dollars (WDI, several years). The capitalised excess savings over domestic investment of the Gulf states since 1970 are estimated at four to five trillion dollars (WDI, several years). Between 2001 and 2011, the uncapitalised excess savings over investment in the Gulf states alone are at around 2.2 trillion dollars (WDI, various years). More so than the previous oil boom, the current boom rides on high oil prices. Between the two booms and as a result of declining oil revenues and faulty policies, the AW exhibited one of the highest unemployment rates, the lowest average real per capita growth rates, and the fastest widening gap in income distribution (WDI, various years; EHII, various years).

---

of consumption of workers from total income weighted by income distribution data, where data are available and given that Arab labour does not save. By these results, the share of labour would be around a quarter of total income, which is close to what the ILO reports intermittently. Guerriero used statistical techniques and arrived at the following shares: Yemen 0.27, Tunisia 0.45, Sudan 0.41, Saudi Arabia 0.36, Qatar 0.29, Oman 0.34, Morocco 0.37, Libya 0.28, Lebanon 0.40, Kuwait 0.32, Jordan 0.49, Iraq 0.11, Egypt 0.29 and Algeria 0.41. Marta Guerriero, 'The Labour Share of Income around the World: Evidence from a Panel Dataset' (Institute for Development Policy and Management [IDPM], Development Economics and Public Policy, Working Paper Series, no. 32, 2012). The 2012/13 ILO Global Wage Report shows that since the 1980s a majority of countries have experienced a downward trend in the 'labour income share', which means that a lower share of national income has gone into labour compensation and a higher share into capital incomes. The same report also shows that real wages fell steadily for countries reporting data on wages between 2000 and 2011.

With openness and lower oil revenues, funding of the social infrastructure shrank. In 2002, for the majority of Arab economies, investment rates were the lowest of all regions at 16 per cent (WDI 2002). Growth in productivity per worker was on average negative, and intraregional trade remained as low as 10 per cent (KILM, various years; UN 2010). Capital flight in the case of Saudi Arabia, the largest economy, accounted for a quarter of GDP (UN 2008b). In spite of high absorption capacity domestically, money capital fled abroad. For twenty years between the first and the second oil boom, the region was in a sort of free fall and was a record holder in key economic variables indicating poorest performance. When oil prices, revenues and incomes picked up again in 2002, apart from high growth driven by a higher imports share, investment and productivity growth remained set on a declining trend (WDI, various years). The money capital pouring in was not going to repair the damage inflicted by the WB/IMF-sponsored policies over the last thirty years.

Unlike the 1974–81 oil boom, when the state handled the allocation of resources, there are distinctive features to the present oil boom, beginning with the heavier involvement of the private sector. While private investment rose, total investment fell as a result of the receding share of public investment. Private investment went into the so-called FIRE economy (finance, insurance and real estate) or into areas of quick gain related to short-gestation capital or speculative activity. Alongside this shift to the private sector, the prospects of expanding regional conflicts implicated the class and institutional structure. The principal agency of development, the alliance of Arab merchant and US-led financial capital, seized the institutions of the state. Whereas in money terms asset bubbles were forming, especially in real estate, as a result of excess liquidity, political insecurity devalued resources in real terms. Assets in war zones are valueless. The cash sunk into real estate and other assets set at speculative prices was hardly being exchanged or was twirling in tight circles of wealthy speculators. Inflated assets and financial exchange generated little value added. However, the separateness of the financialised sector from the rest of the economy was by no means innocuous. Through merchant-skewed central-bank (monetary) policy, the financialised sector drained state coffers and dipped into the public purse, providing finance on asset interactions held by the wealthy at the expense of social assets. One way to visualise this process is to imagine that the central banks created money to expand credit for the wealthier classes, which is not far from the bailing out of Western financial institutions in the 2007–08 financial crisis. Credit-underwritten private-sector assets rose while many governments exercised austerity to service their debts, resulting in primary surpluses in state budgets. While the investment rate was declining, domestic credit to the private sector rose from a range of 15 per cent in the 1960s and 1970s, to a high 46 per cent in 2009 (WDI, various years).

During this process, WB/IMF literature attributed the developmental decline to government intervention in the economy (World Bank 2002). But as the state retrenched, the supposedly 'free market' forces steered resources to a minority that had already captured the state. As low growth, low productivity growth, unemployment and poverty took hold, the retrogressions were assumed by WB/IMF to issue from distortive taxation, subsidies, overvalued currency and rigid labour markets. Despite dipping economic performance, free-market policies, reduction of public expenditures and inflation, open capital and trade accounts, and reliance on the private sector continued to be peddled as the solution. Employment growth, it was said, would ensue from reducing public employment and investment, creating room for the private sector to grow into (Pfeiffer 2000, 113–14). When the public sector retreated yet unemployment rose, morally designated corruption, high population growth and poor governance were labelled the culprits of redundancy. To the ideological panders of the international financial institutions and their stenographers in the business press, the ideal of the free market was irreproachable. Its mathematical symbols—and that's all they were and are, symbols in an equation—were a fiction mimicking reality. They were so far removed from the complexity of real conditions such that they could mean anything at any time.

Fecundity and cultural traditions were implicitly assumed to be short-term policy variables that were supposed to decline with structural adjustment policies. This was 'free market' policy with just two dimensional variables, price and quantity; whenever a real social condition arose, it threw the model off course. The equilibrium model itself was logically (in terms of Neoplatonic logic) valid but inoperable. The WB/IMF policy framework resembled religious catechism to be followed by the unfaithful. The effects of pillage on Arab economies were, in a perfect inversion of reality, blamed on the (non-existent) generic Arab's inadequate embrace of free-market policy. The WB/IMF consortium concealed gaping income inequality and political bias against labour by the token effort taken to improve schooling and labour market participation for women. However, as the working class sank into poverty, real and invented symbols of repression against women intensified. The ever-lower share of income accruing to the working class was redistributed less to the growing ranks of poorly paid men and more to also poorly paid women— though both sexes were actually of course being immiserated.

The WB/IMF consortium abstracted the free market from an actuality that does not exist, imposed modes of conduct on the basis of the abstraction, and employed banalities to place the blame on the patrimonial and cultural traditions of national working classes. That a level playing field, broadly representative institutions, lack of productive capacity and, crucially, a region free of imperialist interventions were necessary developmental preconditions in an Arab context apparently eluded their ideologically blinkered faculties. As the market became freer in the financial age, the wealth and savings of the narrow minority exercising power through the state or under the security cover of US-led imperialism rose. Instead of investing at home, the merchant classes exhibited astute entrepreneurship and invested abroad where the returns were safer. The WB/IMF consortium overlooked the obvious in their cant but in reality always intended to deconstruct Arab social formations. For central capital, union busting at home or social devastation in the periphery are never unintended consequences. They are the social measures necessary to accumulate capital.

From National Policies to Antinational Policies

Prior to freeing the resource transfer channels, many Arab states practiced selective controls on their capital and trade accounts. They devised several interest rates and exchange rates to calibrate savings and investment and to limit capital outflows. Long-term bonds sold on the internal market supported the expansion of the money supply and financed investment. Under neoliberalism, capital accounts were opened up and multiple interest and exchange rates collapsed into single rates. The national currency traded internationally, while states that exported little oil and exhibited balance-of-payments problems (the highly populated states with small oil reserves) resorted to external borrowing to steady their exchange rates. In combination with intensifying imperialist intervention and wars, the risks and uncertainties of the market increased. The growing risk premium within the single national interest rate rose significantly to hedge against capital outflows. The high borrowing costs of financing national projects delayed investment. The short-term stabilisation measures of the fiscal budget implied reduced public investment and, concurrently, shrank the money supply. States could not issue money because their foreign exchange receipts were dwindling or kept in reserves to ensure exchange-rate stability. In low-oil-capacity states, the money space opened up as a result of dwindling national currency was filled by the dollar, and implicit or explicit dollarisation gradually overtook the money markets. Short-term stabilisation introduced welfare-cutting reforms that shortchanged national labour and assets. The negative social impact of short-term austerity built up exponentially over time to the disaster that is the long term. Together, conditions in both short and long terms—which are in reality inseparable—worsened.

In fact, the analytical splitting of the short from the long term was yet another bogus ploy whose effect was to undermine long-term growth and development. The formalised construct of time was taken literally as real historical time. So, after a period of belt tightening and poverty, prosperity would dawn upon the Arabs—another version of pie in the sky to bamboozle the working class into submission. These free-market policy packages were not so much about contracting government spending and money supply, which they achieved anyway. The real purpose was to structurally shift the ownership of these policies away from the national purview to US-led capital and to vitiate the prospects of long-term growth.

In circumstances where production capacity is lacking, state intervention steers development (Saad-Filho 2007). But the WB/IMF sought to shrink the public sector, lower taxation, deregulate, cut public investment and balance the government budget—after which, it claimed, the state would garner sufficient resources to lead development. The Arab state did not. As the biggest agent wielding financial assets, the state provides the credit for large-scale economic activity. State spending ensures a continuous flow of money capital, to which downstream and upstream economic activity correlates. The state's capacity to deliver on financial commitments also acts as the insurer of long-term stability and economic activity. The public sector cushions growth pitfalls and stabilises economic activity, especially in Arab countries where external threats jitter the business cycle. More importantly, state intermediation between capital and labour adjusts the distributive impact of growth (Fine 2006). Such intervention can either boost the savings of the ruling class or the consumption of the working class. When uncertainty and high import rates prevail, the rich save abroad and the working classes consume goods produced abroad. Add to that all the ephemeral economic activity, which treats investment as a short-term speculative procedure, and yet a clearer picture of the merchant mode of accumulation around which lives are organised emerges.

From about 1980, the role of the state in the economy retreated. The fiscal policy stance pivoted from so-called distortive intervention to a supposedly 'unadulterated' price system that was meant to allocate resources in a socially desirable way. Unadulterated, in the sense that, for every imperfection in the market there will be a price that will clear the said market from its own excesses. Arab states, in turn, cut spending, cut taxation, implemented budget austerity and pulled out of the welfare arena, which is underpropped by public investment. These states nonetheless continued to make direct-payment subsidies to the working class, which served the role of pacification—and only pacification. The synergy between demand side and production side tapered off as openness led to the bulk of the consumption bundle being imported from abroad. For instance, all Arab countries are now significant food importers (FAOSTAT 2012). While these measures were being implemented, the erosion of national agriculture combined with coercive dislocation laws and measures caused the biggest exit from the land since the beginning of the twentieth century (UN 2008c).

However, the key aspect that tightened the constrictive grip of neoliberal policies was the investment framework. Another roundabout fallacy of neoliberal policy assumed that fiscal deficits raise interest rates and crowd out the private sector. Crowding out occurs when an economy is near full employment. When there are unutilized resources, there is economic space for an increase in all types of expenditure, both public and private. Even if crowding out occurs in under full employment, it is unlikely to be complete. That is, the elasticity of private investment with respect to government expenditure of any type will be less than minus one (Weeks 2002). The interest rate in an open economy with balance-of-payments constraint, moreover, is administered by central banks to avert capital outflows. It has little to do with financing investment in risky areas with shallow financial markets. Most Arab investment, in any case, is auto-financed to begin with. The projection of measures already performing poorly in the Western hemisphere onto the AW is therefore likely not for lack of imagination, as the WB/IMF policy architects would have been well aware of these facts. The purpose was, then, simply to reduce government spending and with it the value shares of the working class.

The cash-strapped Arab governments could not control deficits as stabilisation spending rose with receding tax receipts. Interest rates also rose, but not because of deficits, rather because of risks and in relation to returns on capital markets abroad. Inflation rates also rose on account of falling national production, monopolies on import patent by patronage, and higher import prices (Ianchovichina 2012). Openness of trade and capital accounts makes the financing of deficits possible mainly through external savings or borrowing, which in turn may cause currency collapse and inflation. Inflation will in turn rise by roughly the rate of imports to GDP. When selective controls are exercised in the trade and capital accounts, by contrast, balance-of-payments constraints are less binding, deficits can be financed from tax revenues, and multiple saving and investment interest rates can be designed to calibrate investment with industrial expansion. This happened in the past in Arab 'socialist' states until lost wars revamped social structures and the class in charge of the state followed its class proclivity and accepted the terms of the neoliberal medicine.

Save the Gulf states, which have enough cash to cushion immediate shortfalls, Arab countries exhibit a shallow tax base and open capital and trade accounts. These governments cannot monetise the debt (because the money they issue flees abroad or buys commodities from abroad) or impose a progressive income tax, despite the fact that the tax rate is at a low of 10 per cent of GDP on average (UN 2006). Instead, these governments implement indirect value-added sales taxes, which criminalise the working folk and are difficult to implement in cash and informal economies. Meanwhile, the exposure of the national currency to international pressure, high import ratios and the hold of the merchant class upon the state apparatuses combined to transform governments into bookkeepers for international financial capital.

Higher interest rates stunted growth, less because investors could not borrow to invest but because they dollarised economies and opened the doors of speculation against real assets and the national currency. Unsurprisingly also, monetary policy withdrew funds from public investment, intensified balance-of-payments problems and inflated the price of basic commodities. For a decade before the uprising, food prices were rising as wages declined, while real-estate prices were supported by a central bank policy ensuring ample liquidity and ease of money convertibility to the dollar at steady exchange rates (Maher 2011). While the assets of the ruling class grew as a result of the exchange-rate policy, the prices of food for the working classes were hiked by the very same policy. Given the high ratio of ruling-class to working-class assets, the pegged exchange rate policy was more of a subsidy to the rich. Their assets had fixed dollar values in the international markets guaranteed by the national wealth produced by the working class.

Interest-rate policy, instead of addressing savings and investment concerns, served the sole purpose of slowing capital outflows. Restrictive monetary policy shrank the credit space into which industry and the wealth of working classes might grow. The AW central banks were organically tied to the structure of merchant capital. They represented a facet of the organised dimension of capital that imposes the rule of money as an alienated form of value above society. The more complex the intermediation of credit—the various layers of claims upon claims, hedge funds and securitisations, all partially resolving value contradictions resulting from the real crisis of accumulation—the more ferocious the deployment of the wrath of the money form upon the working classes, hence the austerity. The gradual shift in the anchor of the national currency from protected national space into the more complex international financial space since 1980 subjected the Arab working classes to austerity unhampered by national opposition. What would soon be imposed in Europe and the US after the 2007–08 crisis had already been tested in the Third World under the rubric of structural adjustment.

Post-uprising monetary policy today is no different than it was prior to the uprisings. Through manipulation of the interest rate, central banks aimed to achieve low inflation and to reduce the balance-of-payment constraint by regulating the pace of economic activity. The high interest rates they imposed reduced the money available to the state and to workers, but did not regulate economic activity. Given the superficial development (meaning its inaccessibility to the working class) of the financial markets, the private banks' demands for high collateral in view of national risks, and their low involvement in financing industrial activity, one deduces that the interest rate was unrelated to the national economy. During the great financial crisis of 2007–08, the Arab states' growth rates remained positive because they had few linkages to the global financial markets. Arab financiers and the Gulf Cooperation Council (GCC)—Saudi Arabia, the UAE, Bahrain, Kuwait, Qatar and Oman—withstood significant losses. The interest rate did not calibrate savings and investment or supply and demand by targeted borrowing from national sources or by boosting investment. All that the interest rates did was to regulate the rate of capital flows with the fixed convertibility of national currency to the dollar. In any case, under open capital accounts, interest rates should remain high, not only to limit the excessive outflow of capital to safer areas abroad, but also to stabilise the currency exchange rate so that money-profits earned nationally can be exchanged at quasi-fixed rates against the dollar. In a sense the whole AW monetary policy apparatus serves to subsidise resource transfers by the ruling class abroad or to maintain the money value of their nationally appropriated wealth fixed against the dollar.

In Arab countries that do not export significant amounts of oil, the interest-rate policy has reduced savings and investment as a result of declining demand, has not significantly affected inflation and has had minimal impact on the balance of payments. The interest rate in an open-capital-account environment and with a pegged exchange rate has redistributed wealth upward. Moreover, because of the long-term risk from holding government bonds, money capital speculates on short-term government instruments and asset markets. Empirically, whenever the interest rate rose or fell it did little to impact economic performance (UN 2006).

In situations with closely observed and regulated capital accounts, the manipulation of interest rates can secure financial and money-market stability and induce savings for the purpose of reinvestment through the issuance of long-term bonds. In the pre-neoliberal policy setting, particularly under 'Arab socialist' policies, the interest rate targeted specific economic sectors: differential interest rates on loans earmarked the relevance of economic undertakings and their linkages to the rest of the economy. Under more developed financial market conditions, the interest rate may influence inflation as a result of varying levels of savings and investment and total income. But when Arab countries import most of their food and manufactured goods and exhibit huge unemployment and squandering of financial national wealth, the interest rate serves mostly to bolster the pegged-exchange-rate policy.

In undercapitalised and underperforming economies, state spending on investment and consumption has a direct bearing on building capacity and improving demand simultaneously (Weeks 2002). In more developed formations, the interest rate may influence industrial expansion and affect inflation as a result of money expansion influencing demand. But Arab private-sector liabilities in the area of industrial development are minimal (AIDMO 2010, 24). Industrial investment migrates into short-term gestating capital (UN 2008a). Moreover, personal loan and credit-card debt are insignificant as a portion of total debt. Most of the state debt, where it exists in non-Gulf countries, supports the expansion of credit to the ruling classes. In the Gulf, the finances of the state are mostly within the purview of the absolute monarchs. In economies of this nature, the interest rate principally raises the servicing of the public debt and augments the deficit. It actually acts as a snatch mechanism for the private bankers who earn a considerable share of debt servicing part of government expenditure and, therefore, serves the opposite purpose to that for which it was ostensibly designed.

Under the neoliberal regime, inflation control policies would allegedly lead to higher private investment and growth. The neoliberal method to curb inflation is to lower the debt, shrink the money supply and reduce fiscal deficits. Privatisation, freer trade, financial and capital account liberalisation were, as it turned out, the necessary precursors to austerity. However, restrictive fiscal and monetary policy in such an environment reduces inflation only superficially. In the presence of high import ratios and contractionary macro policies, the dollarisation of the economy ensues. The expansion of economic activity because of shortage in credit issued nationally occurs via cash dollars. Where the national currency withdraws from the economy, the dollar becomes the de facto national currency. The *de jure* national currency, although it appears steady in terms of the exchange rate along with falling or steady inflation rates, has become only a partial reflection of the national value of wealth; much of national wealth is dollarised. Inflation does not disappear. Growing state debts inflate capital assets owned by the propertied classes in real terms, or in terms of exchange rates fixed against the dollar and supported by national wealth. Add to that, as growth and national money supply decline while the country becomes more dependent on imports, the dollar enters the local market as an alternative currency to cover the rising costs of those imports. Although inflation may have fallen by some insignificant percentage, dollarisation implies that the national currency has at least partially turned into a nominal symbol. National currency is the fake currency while the dollar is the real currency. So, how can one measure the decline in the general price level denominated by a fake currency? Therefore, the lowered inflation rate is illusory. These policies, in the end result, mean that the country forfeits growth along with monetary sovereignty.

High inflation, in an Arab context, is rarely a monetary phenomenon. Food and lodging rental prices did not rise because of higher money supply or debt monetisation. As the central banks pumped liquidity into speculative activity, driving up asset prices, rents on capital rose in tandem. So whereas, for instance, real property owners benefitted from higher real-estate prices, the working class encountered higher housing rents. Food prices rose because of higher agricultural prices globally, and free-trade agreements had eroded a good part of subsistence agriculture. In macroeconomic terms, growth was slowing not because of inflation but because of rapid fiscal and financial leakages. When central banks inflate capital assets owned by the ruling classes by foreign currency reserves at one end, and use inflation as indirect taxation on the working class on the other, the rate and quality of growth plummet.

Inflation of any sort in an Arab context taxes the working class according the degree of the autonomy of labour and labour unions. Unions demand indexed inflation-adjustment ('cost-of-living escalator') contracts that cushion the impact on the working class. However, moderate or immoderate inflation, government spending sprees on stabilisation, and huge deficits are not at the kernel of the problematic of erratic, low-quality growth. The real problem is the deregulation of capital and trade accounts and their associated balance-of-payments framework. As noted in Chapter One, it was the decision to remove controls on these accounts that deindustrialised the Arab states, which until 1977 had been growing as fast as their East Asian counterparts. What the AW experiences is a very particular Arab disease. This disease is the Arab merchant class acting as the suzerain of US-led global empire.

Dutch Diseases and Resource Curses

In the AW, there is neither a resource curse nor a Dutch disease. As mentioned above, the economic sickness is far more severe and is caused by an imperialist curse. Imaginary powers bestowed upon mainstream (neoliberal) economic constructs obscure the shifts in the class structures and class alliances, which have led to the implementation of policies that magnified the negative impact of low productive capacity. Whereas in the Netherlands the appreciation of currency was redressed and the ailment healed, in the AW the illness metastasised into the final stages.

Where working-class political power is strong enough to help shape policy, oil revenues can galvanise dormant potentialities and alleviate poverty. The relative success of the Chavez model in Venezuela is a case in point (UN-ECLAC 2011).[2] But the policy framework that has permeated the AW macro environment over the last three decades has misallocated resources.

---

2   Venezuela cut its poverty rate to 29.5 per cent in 2011 from 48.6 per cent in 2002. United Nations Economic Commission for Latin America and the Caribbean (ECLAC), *Social Panorama of Latin America* (United Nations, 2011).

Although most states pursue stabilisation spending that could invoke positive developmental linkages, the stabilisation pursued by Arab regimes has centred on consumption spending without significant links to production. Spending on healthcare, for instance, was extensive, yet public health awareness and nationally driven research and development were thin. Spending on imported drugs represented a significant leakage; local production accounts only for 45 per cent of consumption (OIC 2012). By historically determined standards, health progress was rudimentary and resulted from the fallout of advancement in science and the import of generic medications produced by scale economies as opposed to internally developed public-health standards. In any case, where life expectancy has risen as an effect of rising historically determined levels of subsistence, it did so as a collateral outcome of the medical product cycle and not as result of internally driven development. (By historically determined, I mean a working class must be reproduced adequately in terms of food, shelter, education, healthcare and so forth for it to achieve a given level of social productivity.) In relation to what it could have been, though, AW life expectancy is still short. That is, although people on average have lived longer lives (in some parts of the AW as in Syria, Yemen, Iraq and Sudan, life expectancy declined), the absence of adequate public health and environmental programs has meant that in comparative terms, their living standards were lacking. The way public health is financed meant that spending on medication was less concerned with better health than with boosting the profits of the drug importers. Suffice it to say that in Egypt, Yemen, and Sudan child malnutrition has grown significantly (UNICEF 2009).

Education expenditure also rose. However, education has emphasised areas of qualification that are by no means attuned to the demands of industry—or of what remains of industry after liberalisation. As industry shrank, workers educated in technical fields either emigrated or remained unemployed, further accentuating the resource-drain and brain-drain syndromes. Rote learning characterised education, and the regimenting aspect of schooling overtook its illuminating function (UN 2006). What is more, AW investment in research and development (R&D) as a share of GDP ranked lowest in the world (UN 2005). In view of the shrinking numbers of jobs, much of the desired investment in education ended up abroad through complex migratory routes. Spending on education that does not connect to the production structure ends up as yet more fiscal leakage.

In the AW, it would have been a boon had the inflow of foreign exchange overvalued the national currency, reduced competitiveness and precipitated deindustrialisation. The areas of the AW, like the Gulf states, that initially exported oil possessed little industry to begin with. The Arab countries that had industrialised in the postindependence era, namely Egypt, Iraq,

Lebanon, Algeria, Tunisia and Syria, underwent deindustrialisation following liberalisation. Oil revenues did not raise the value of the national currency leading to lower competitiveness and deindustrialisation. They did however, as they seeped from the Gulf into the more industrialised countries, create a new Saudi-sponsored class that adhered ideologically to the merchant-consumption model of the Gulf and that bestowed holy powers on commerce and the free market resurrected on the basis of a fabricated history of Islam.

Natural-resource abundance is said to undermine economic performance as dependency on easily earned foreign exchange breeds complacency (Karl 1997; Ross 1999). States can begin to borrow funds in order to sustain levels of consumption during the downturn—funds they might not repay over the long term. Consequently, steadying levels of consumption in this way permanently dents savings rates over time and hence reduces investment—an argument that resembles the one for the uselessness of aid to Third World countries: in teleological order as aid goes in, gets consumed or snatched, lowers savings and yet more aid is needed (Griffin 1970). Oil prices indeed tend to be volatile, keeping long-term spending decisions on edge. But as applied to Arab states, this is a misconception. A state hijacked by a national merchant class whose property is in US-secured oil and dollar savings abroad is really not much of a state at all, in the sense of mediator and protector of the national interest. The vested interest of this class in the GCC countries, in particular, is principally in dollarised wealth held abroad. The GCC countries still produce a narrow range of goods for export, namely oil and some of its shallow value-added derivatives. However, they remain underdeveloped in terms of the definition provided in the introduction. Given that after fifty years of oil profits, jinn can be called upon to testify in their courts, women are forbidden to drive, and every sort of backwardness and superstition continues to shape social legislation, no case for their 'development' in any real sense can be supported.[3]

The channelling of oil revenues in development occurs in a class-determined context. A healthy context is one in which oil revenues mobilise real resources in value creation as opposed to their long history of funding anti-working-class wars and value destruction. In addition to funding imperialist assaults on world liberation movements, including Saudi funding of the Contras in faraway Nicaragua, Gulf petrodollars have supplanted the necessary synergy for development in the intermediation between oil revenues, technological developments and economies of scale. Natural resources have only wrought havoc where imperialist encroachment has reached.

---

3   'Lawyer Wants Jinn to Testify in Court', *Emirates 24/7*, 23 October 2010. Online: http://www.emirates247.com/news/region/lawyer-wants-jinn-to-testify-in-court-2010-10-23-1.307686 (viewed 20 November 2012).

Reducing the real condition to an intrinsic evil residing in the natural resource itself or to the stupidity of a national ruling class existing in a vacuum and unwittingly underdeveloping its own nation conceals the decisive role of imperialism.

Irrational behaviour on the part of political elites, poor resource management, rent seeking by political actors, and states that rely on unearned income and avoid developing their economies are not characteristics of resource-cursed countries only; to one degree or another, they fit all capitalist countries. Development flops in Arab countries resemble the resource curse or the Dutch disease only superficially. Resource curses are context specific in relation to the political structure and institutions in each country, which are in turn determined by the class configuration. When the ruling class is more integrated with international financial capital than the home production base as in the nationalist capitalist state, *that* is when a resource becomes a curse. The Gulf countries did not internalise the complex supply chains implying industrialisation. The other Arab countries that industrialised in the postindependence epoch later deindustrialised as the ruling class underwent a metamorphosis from nationalist to comprador. That wars and civil wars in correlation to natural resources and undemocratic regimes are glaringly in evidence in the AW supports the notion that imperialist war making and weakening of states follows imperialist diktat.

The ostensible goal of WB/IMF policy design is to stabilise the macro economy by reducing public investment, shrinking money, preaching good governance to change the mindset of rulers, making the civil service 'lean', and privatising natural resource and other high-performing sectors (World Bank 1995). Hypothetically, the outcomes of these policies—democratisation, the reduced power of minority groups and consistent backing to private sectors that generate employment—will exorcise the resource curse. However, the closest allies of US-led imperialism have been the undemocratic regimes in the AW. When principally US-governed international institutions advise good governance and privatisation, they do not intend to overthrow the bad governors, but they intend to get the privatisation going and going into the bad governors' pockets. Such basic questions of who did what and why are ignored by a 'pragmatic' policy design that bestows agency on Neoplatonic forms of thought (marginal conditions) or delusional neoclassical efficiency criteria for productivity and their corresponding prices. These concoctions do not comprehend individuals as they are: that is, constituted within a manifold of social relationships and mediated politically into social action by instituted (or popularly generated) forms of social organisation. Instead, they conjure an idealised world of one-on-one relations between 'rational' individual actors. How can any policy generated within this fantastical construct help create the behavioural, institutional or social changes necessary to overcome the curse?

In the WB/IMF framework, the totality of the developmental situation is segmented and distorted and relevant relationships are diluted. Even when the social forces and the contextual and historical patterns that shape the functioning of state institutions are mentioned, they are formalised into symbols with no referent in the realities of the AW. Social classes and relationships, the development process in relation to other processes (principally the ownership of the means of production), the formation of revolutionary consciousness attendant thereon, and the redistribution of wealth become nontransformative objects existing outside real time. The state as the mediation of class conflict vanishes; rather, in the neoliberal schema it exists as if it were a primary school student who could pass or fail an exam. Institutions imagined to be composed of atomised personae are a degenerate version of an ideal type that is too ideal to be real. It is a sort of historicism without the history. The fatal flaw is a mode of abstraction that fails to draw its concepts from historically determined conditions. Neoclassical thought's point of departure is the quintessential transhistorical situation of subject–object: the individual affects his or her environment by a given action. There is nothing to disagree with in neoclassical economics, not because it is right or wrong, but because its symbols could represent anything and its opposite at any time. Where it becomes dangerous is when it 'economises' the truth, as in when it omits wage slavery and imperialist aggression, for instance, as concrete historical conditions.

In the AW, the interface between macroeconomic policies and outcomes is neither misguided nor inadequate; it is a purposeful design and serves specific ruling-class objectives. Oil resources have shored up ownership of financial assets and investments abroad. They have effortlessly assisted expenditure on imports. Petrodollar inflows have financed affluent consumption. The presence of sovereign funds abroad has retracted the extra funds that could have overvalued the currency. So once more, competitiveness did not decline because of overvalued currency. However, industrialisation policy was relinquished and industrial shares shrank as trade accounts were freed. In the less oil-endowed Arab countries that exhibit precarious balances of payments because of import costs, where real currency appreciation occurs, the nontradable sector benefits from demand growth. In the mainstream sense, currency overvaluation occurs when the central bank fixes an exchange rate at a higher point than that defined by market conditions. The state-subsidised exchange rate blunts the impact of import-price hikes on consumers such as the lower price of staples like bread in Egypt and Syria, but much more than that it fixes the wealth of the propertied class in dollars. The high exchange rate may dent the competitiveness of the tradable sector, but industry and the tradable sector are shrinking so there is precious little to actually compete with— supply elasticity is low (UN 2006). Industry was hurt by lifting protection prematurely and across the board, not by higher exchange rates. The macroeconomic debacle is thus twofold. On the one hand, the GCC countries did not industrialise or acquire a culture of industrialisation, and on the other, the petrodollars flow from the Gulf to the more industrialised Arab economies created insidious social models that contributed to their deindustrialisation. They tickled the fancy of state bourgeois classes whose natural course of development is to end up in the lap of imperialism, but they were tied down by their own pan-Arab hubris. What is really harmful are not the macroeconomic effects of petrodollars on competitiveness, but their funnelling into funding the hordes of Salafis supposedly opposed to imperialism but that end up being more pro-imperialist because of their ill-fated strategies and tactics than otherwise.

Why the Private Sector Cannot Lead Development

Neoliberalism, whose defining ideology is laissez-faire economics, recommends 'freeing' (deregulating) all markets, including the trade and capital accounts. Promoting fiscal restraint at the expense of public investment in social and physical infrastructures and relying heavily on indirect taxation in contrast to progressive and capital gains taxes are steps to take before putting the private sector in charge of development. Prices would then determine the efficient transfer mechanisms and resource allocations. But the private sector has failed—spectacularly—at the task of development, and it is this failure that requires explanation.

Private investment growth hinges on prospective returns and the degree of risk. For Kalecki (1935), the investment–growth nexus, defined as the inducement to invest, is determined by the gap between the prospective rate of profit and the rate of interest. Later theoretical advances are permutations of this core idea of demand-led investment. The rate of capital accumulation depends on profitability, which, in a circular manner, depends on economic growth. If interest rates were suddenly to fall, it follows that the risks would be lower, the capital output ratio would be higher, and the growth rate would rise (Targetti 1989). Although analytically sound, this argument is incompatible with the specificities of the AW.

Assuming that returns can be redressed through bolstering balanced growth (meaning proportional growth in all sectors), it is the context or the component of risk that is definitively challenging in the case of the AW. In view of various internal and external security concerns, many Arab states carry within them the potential for collapse. The risks to investment in the AW are serious because the stabilising elements that allow for the calculation of risk do not persist over the long term. Keynes, having lived through a war, differentiated between unquantifiable uncertainty and quantifiable risks. He noted:

> By 'uncertain' knowledge [...] I do not mean merely to distinguish what is known for certain from what is only probable. [...] The sense in which I am using the term is that in which the prospect of a European war is uncertain. [...] About these matters there is no scientific basis on which to form any calculable probability whatever. We simply do not know. (Keynes 1937)

The prospect of war, omnipresent in the AW, alters the background for investment decision making, miring it in historical uncertainty. Thus one cannot assume away the context and a requalification of the concept of risk with regard to the AW is in order.

In analytical terms, the risk function in the AW is only partly associated with typical market and price volatilities. Rather, it is one in which the bulk of capital assets could wither instantaneously as the state fractures. The investment function in the AW is therefore subject to time incoherence and structural shifts, that is real history and not hypothetical time. This, then, is not a case of actuarial risk. Although the ordinary types of market risk will always be present to some degree, the potential for complete collapse is portentous. The uncertainty shifts the ground beneath intertemporal preferences and brings the future closer to the present. There is not much of a future to plan for when the state may abruptly collapse. Investors will be primarily concerned with how returns must redress initial capital costs within a short gestation period. Subsequently, money capital lodges in ephemeral endeavours. Obviously (though not to neoliberal ideologues) raising investment under these tenuous conditions must be preceded by ensuring stability over the long run through enhanced security.

Underdevelopment, in short, cannot be tackled by supply- or demand-side policies that were tailored for developed economies performing at high capacity. It takes both supply side and demand side expansions to boost economies that lack skill, knowledge in production and economies of scale. Taken together, the Arab economies are small, comprising around 2.5 per cent of world income. Nearly two-thirds of Arab income goes to the Gulf, which constitutes around 5 per cent of the Arab population—the GDP measure does not include savings abroad in the case of the GCC. Paradoxically, small markets induce small investment, and the opposite (big markets induce big investment) holds (Nurkse 1952). Nurkse attempted to resolve the enigma by suggesting a state-funded 'big push' approach that would boost demand

and supply simultaneously within regulated capital and trade accounts. The subsequent crowding-in of private investment would raise incomes and break the vicious circle of underdevelopment. The one-sided supply and open-market policies of the neoliberal age, however, did exactly the opposite of that. *Laissez faire* means literally 'let do', roughly translatable as 'let them do as they like'. In the absence of an equal playing field, laissez-faire policies afforded the local merchant class and its international financial capital carte blanche to do as they liked with Arab resources. Development policy became primarily a matter of redressing public-account shortfalls, with much of the spending centred on building political allegiance and or inducing regime stability/instability as per the demands of US-led capital.

The population growth rate has been high since the 1960s, and these policies of contraction meant to restore the fundamentals (mainly stabilise the finances of the state) were supposed to structurally adjust economies for the lift-off into the world of development. But they failed. The failure was, in a classically Malthusian way, blamed on population growth. Yet it was the neoliberal policies themselves, rather than high birth rates, that disengaged real resources and lowered job creation. When trade and capital accounts are open, security-weak industrialising countries will be opened for plunder. Shrinking the productive base in relation to the still-rising population threw millions out of decent work and into poverty wages in the informal sector (more details are provided in Chapter Eight, which deals with unemployment).

The market that neoliberalism claimed it wanted to free did not exist in the AW to be freed. The principal Arab market was state guided and industry protected, financed mainly by internal government borrowing. It became private sector–led, its industry was exposed to superior competition, and its financing depended more and more on borrowing from foreign sources. The economy mutated from an even-distribution, public sector–led economy to a highly uneven economy led by the private sector and a privately owned 'public' sector. The private investment promotion arrangements—one-stop shop, easy profit repatriation, FDI promotions—resulted in overall declining investment rates. FDI in the AW ranked low globally and was centred on resource-seeking activities: the kind with the fewest linkages to the national economies and the kind most environmentally damaging (UNCTAD 2010). Guarantees on repatriation do not offset uncertainties and market-size issues. Moreover, private investment policies were built on the implicit understanding that private and public sectors compete for the same resources. In underdeveloped and financially regulated economies, there is plenty of slack for both types of investment to act in a complementary rather than competitive way.

Development in a class-divided society finally depends on the ruling class's proclivity for capacity building. AW developmental challenges—the contradiction between a restrictive monetary policy and a vigorous fiscal stimulus plan, the disjunction between regional savings and regional investments, and the absence of automatic stabilisers—are issues that cannot be tackled under openness of trade and finance. The retention of resources and their redeployment in national economies through various selective price and protective measures require a degree of seclusion. A broader understanding of the social structure and the institutional framework that might allow for autonomy of policy is a good starting point for assessing policy options. For macro policies to work jointly and interdependently and become developmental tools, the principal structural element underlying the policy framework, which is the linkage of development to security and sovereignty, also has to be tackled. Capital accumulation and long-term investment depend on a rearticulation of Arab security arrangements in a way that guarantees the security of the working classes and national sovereignty.

Closing Remarks

Volatile and unevenly distributed growth has worsened the social condition of the majority of the Arab working classes. Many social areas including education, gender equality and developments in civil society have retreated or stayed below historically determined levels. Social relapse in turn reinforced the downward spiral of poor-quality growth. Instead of raising both public and private investment via establishing stronger regional security arrangements and providing insurance on losses to long-term investment from noneconomic or political causes such as war, the ruling classes did the opposite. Instead of a gradual and selective approach to trade integration preceded by concrete measures to ease into the global economy as a regional bloc, they rushed into the WTO treaty. Instead of strengthening Arab monetary cooperation and imposing capital account regulation, they raised the financial risks attendant on open capital accounts. Add to that their withdrawing from investment in R&D, inculcating a structurally unemployable labour force in religious obscurantism, reducing public investment, foiling the increasing returns from the knowledge-based industry—and one has a still partial but clearer image of the totality that is de-development.

With such deficient national security, it was pointless for governments to erect institutional guarantees on repatriation of profits by foreign capital and investment. The guarantor must be a sovereign state. Principal Arab states were defeated and their sovereignty waned. The cycle of poor growth began in the late 1980s with investment dropping and the transfer mechanisms reallocating resources from the public to the private sector. Trade openness did not sharpen competitiveness or diversify exports, it deindustrialised economies. Selectivity, regulation, and gradualism in trade and capital-account openness, or policies that temper abrupt capital flows and value transfers, were dropped in favour of speculation regimes that were supposed to expedite the resource-allocation mechanism. The WB/IMF idea that the private and the public sectors should compete for the same resources in undercapitalised countries was not innocuous. It was intended to shift the ownership patterns into private hands in areas where there was slack in the economy in order to ensure that the underdeveloped state does not build its own capacity. The asset-for-rent acquisition further hastened the ascent of merchant capital, for which Arab integration was anathema. Disintegration halted many forms of regional and working-class cooperation. In turn, poor quality economic growth bred poor social conditions, and poor social conditions engendered poor long-term growth.

Present and past policies do not, to put it mildly, offer the optimal framework for the achievement of high levels of employment, more equal distribution of income and wealth, poverty reduction, sustainable growth, low inflation and macroeconomic stability in the AW. Macro policies would have to curtail the flow of value in physical, human and money forms away from the national formations. The specific focus of policy should shift into modes of stemming resource flight, recirculating value nationally, revalorising labour and redistributing value through social policies. Long-term investment in the physical and social infrastructure and industrial projects are the very core of effective state policymaking. However, the interaction necessary for these investments between monetary, financial and fiscal policies cannot deliver satisfactory results because of openness and maldistribution. Land reform and the renationalisation of social assets previously stolen via the consortium of merchant and repressive state must occur before anything else can work. The case is very simple: on account of the pittance in wages and assets of the working classes, demand cannot perform its leading function. Demand calls for more egalitarian redistribution. Supply calls for the capacity of the state to finance the future and hence for multiple exchange and interest rates that insulate public investment and the national consumption bundle from the vagaries of the international markets. These are the cornerstones of alternative policies—and they necessitate class restructuring.

In the AW, much of what is consumed at home is produced abroad (most of the food bundle is imported in the AW, FAO 2009b). If wages *were* to rise, they would be of little benefit to the national economy because the goods they would buy originated elsewhere. As evidenced by poor productivity growth and the knowledge/technological nexus regress, openness policies have dragged down the business cycle. Indirect taxation, deindustrialisation, and trade and capital-account openness have severed the positive linkages between various sectors of the economy. The production supply chain became shallow; not many value-added inputs could be manufactured in the home economy. Accompanying that, industrial knowledge also became shallow. It is that cavity in industrial progress that led to the hollowing out of culture as a store of knowledge, which in turn vitiated the ideological impetus necessary for revolutionary consciousness. It mainly withdrew the platform of material independence upon which labour can launch its struggles. The ideological crisis of socialism and the absence of labour organisations holding the promise of resistance further combined to undermine development. In the next chapter, I explore the class politics obstructing resistance and undermining the process of sound development.

Chapter Three

CLASS POLITICS MASQUERADING AS DEMOCRACY

Development, as defined in the introduction, captures the terms by which human potentialities are unleashed and the welfare gains afforded to the working classes are broadened. Development in this sense ensues not as a result of an atomised human agency realised in the state, but rather as a result of political struggle mediated in forms of working-class organisation that improve living standards. Development may be further defined as a balanced outcome that combines civil liberties and 'freedom' from serious want for all (Sen 1999).[1] This notion of development does not preclude freedom from hunger, oppression and anything else that stands in the way of working classes participating fully in shaping their collective future; it is simply a concretisation on Sen's definition; one is free by realising the necessity to be free from want for the whole of the working class. On a less qualitative note, development combines the infusion of knowledge in production, incremental growth in capital and progressive institutional change. Hence, development is both improved living standards wrought in the class struggle and growth in capital stock. It is the realisation of the subject of history as it interacts with the totality of the social condition, the object. Development therefore becomes the articulation of the social forces that shape the outcome of capital accumulation. How does this expanded view of development tally with Arab conditions?

When Arab developmental goals consistently fail to be met despite the presence of idle real and financial resources, the causes have to be explored not in secondary issues like the rate of build-up of industrial and communications infrastructure, but in the way power is shared between social classes.

---

1   The notion of freedom here varies from the probabilistic conditions with which an atomistic individual is faced outside a historical continuum that A. Sen uses in addressing social welfare functions. Social welfare cannot be the sum of various utilities; it is the intermediated gains of the working class in the class struggle. I simply used freedom as the necessity of keeping a distance from wanting basic necessities for survival.

A priori, missing the target of development points to shortcomings in the way various classes and national institutions relate to each other and to the outside world. Where these relationships are manifest is the sphere of politics; hence it is at this seminal level that disparities in development have to be explored. Confronting the political facts of modern Arab history discloses the connections that facilitate or distort the attainment of development objectives. Development—the long-term process—is underwritten by sound forms of social organisation that incorporate the betterment of working class conditions. It cannot be reduced to short-term experimentation with people's lives by way of balancing short-term budgets. Pinning state budgets to the short term in undercapitalised, security-deficient and financially exposed markets inevitably underfunds social development. The mainstream 'social welfare' criterion by which development is gauged cannot be residually derived from better economic performance when the mechanism of transfer from the private to the social sphere is broken. In the presence of immense redundant pools of labour, marginal conditions do not hold and efficiency shrivels. Markets only reach equilibrium—hypothetically because they never do—at levels where wages do not suffice to purchase a handful of calories. *Efficiency in a developing-country context is the progress obtained from letting economic efficiency ensue from social values, not vice versa.* Social values are in turn determined by the values of the class in power and its ideology—hence the significance of the state.

There are commonalities and differences in Arab development. Nearly all the data on development exhibit poor performance. Where they do not, it is because the variable is token-like or materially insignificant. To enumerate these variables at length would be scholastic. It would also add little to understanding of the historical dynamics behind the development failure that all Arab countries share. But to study the reasons for the pervasively poor developmental showings in terms of underlying social class relations would add to knowledge from the point of our *capability* to know as opposed to how much we know—merely adding to a store of often not very useful empirical data. Underdevelopment is a totality in which the degenerate social conditions are both poorly measured and numerous. However, the social relationships that generated the historical dynamics of underdevelopment are those of US-led imperialism. Foremost among these social relationships are those that generate division within and between working classes. Through the state and patronage networks, capital has promoted economic and social policies that breed inter- and intra-working-class conflicts. The key question is to explore the political processes that have fragmented the working classes either by ballot-box elections occurring in devastated societies or by authoritarian repression. As noted in the preceding chapters, Arab ruling classes have moved away from industrial autonomy into a merchant mode of appropriation—from producing goods to just buying and selling goods. This regression from national to extranational development has also vitiated the homogenising forces inherent in a market economy. Capital has differentiated labour and designated unequal labour shares to various sections of the working class from an already declining wage bill. So, in addition to the distinct economic structures, including their capacities, foreign asset holdings and natural resource endowments, the subordinated mode of integration with global capital has further inhibited the centripetal forces of the market. By switching to merchant capital, Arab ruling classes prevented wages arising from an integrated industrial economy from converging. Policy harmonisation and labour homogenisation confronted the formidable forces of an imperialist-partnered merchant class to which a national social contract is anathema. In this chapter, the political preconditions of accumulation by forcible encroachment are analysed with the aim of leading the discussion into the role of the state in the next chapter. The argument will focus on the issue of security as the substance of sovereignty.

Political Aspects of the Problematic of Development

There needs to be an introduction on the role of democracy in development. Fundamentally, most Arab countries are undemocratic. On its own, this common denominator could anchor the argument for the lost-development thesis here elaborated. The politics of the mainstream, the well-known 'art of the possible', is inapplicable to small exposed formations in which imperialist aggression defines the path of history. There are far more 'impossibles' than in the politics of central countries, and where the possible does come into being, it does so by way of internationalist solidarity against imperialism. Some theorists define politics as cooperation, negotiation and/or conflict within and between societies that organise the use, production or distribution of human, natural and other resources (Leftwich 2005, 591). Democracy can thus be seen as the systematic correspondence between the preferences of the majority and the policies selected and implemented by the government. It can also be understood as the accountability of the state, including the protection of civil rights, the subordination of state officials to the rule of law, and their adherence to the standards of behaviour expected by the majority. Once again, these definitions pertain to an ideal world in which class politics is reconciliatory because central capital can offset its losses at home by means of aggression abroad. As seen through Eurocentric spectacles that regard capitalism as a progressive stage in history for all, including the victims of genocide in the colonies, class entente occurs nationally in the centre, but internationally the wars against Third World working classes are not part of class antagonisms (Warren 1973). From this perspective, a Third World working class identified in terms of its nationality is not organically part of the international working class but belongs to some subspecies that is not so technologically advanced. While capital has been for the time being at least victorious in establishing national boundaries as class boundaries in the minds of many, the social classes involved in value relations and value creation are by necessity internationalised. Very few products can be manufactured from solely national sources, and few nations can survive on their own. In this broader optic, the internationalist class struggle, as opposed to chauvinist class reconciliation at the centre, *is* the democratic process. One may note in passing that the wealth of the centre is partly the historical surplus value of the colonies and, for long, the left strategy of tying reform to revolution in central formations has been more of a payoff to central working classes to quell peripheral unrest rather than revolutionary strategy. Of course conceptually it matters whether one uses multitudes, North or South, Third or First World to delineate the scope of reform policy. Where the structure of the thought or concept ends, the political and ideological impact begins. Reform politically centred in the West has rarely delivered an internationalist impact in the East. Unless the calculated risks are high, not a single effort by a central peace movement could avert aggression in the Third World.

In Arab developmental circumstances, the struggle of the working class against a merchant class subordinated by US-led capital defines the politics of democracy. Democracy in a developmental process is manifest in the form of civil liberties and the success of the working class in overpowering the circuit of capital and increasing its (labour's) share. This general definition evades the more thorny issue of the disarticulation between social being and social consciousness. Are the politics of the working classes compatible with the betterment of their living conditions? In intraclass conflict, for instance, one segment of the working class may undercut another by grabbing a higher share of income from a declining wage bill. So, even as labour income goes down, one section of the working class can be better off at the expense of another. Capital's primary political objective is precisely to pit one stratum of the working class against another, including equally a vilification of many of the Third World working classes. Within such strands of thought, class politics is viscerally ideological and conspiratorial.

The ideal notion of democracy comprises the protection of basic civil and political rights, equality before the law, freedoms of speech, of the press and of political organisation, regular elections for the legislature and the executive, civilian government, and civilian control over the armed forces (Dahl 1971). Arab countries (to put it very mildly) depart from this categorisation; they are at a nadir of their own around which they might differ between themselves by minute permutations. Steep economic inequalities further weigh on the democratic process and, by convoluted processes, turn democratic institutions into ancillary structures for the reproduction of wealth by the ruling classes. Arab ruling classes, in fact, control the polity and the economy simultaneously. The collapse of egalitarian (socialist) ideology relieved Arab regimes of the need to justify the fact that much of the social product is being disproportionately appropriated by the ruling minority. Political institutions have become immaterial in organising workers' lives around common goals. The state has contracted in the face of imperialistically funded civil society. Smug with its ideological flow, it has relegated some of its social functions to civil society, and it has also supported the devolutionary splintering of the labouring classes into newly reinvented identities. Although the ideal democratic process is such a metaphysical abstraction that no country can completely conform to it, Arab ruling classes buttress antidemocratisation at two foundational levels: repression and the desocialisation and privatisation of the end products of production. As a consequence, Arab working classes are both impoverished and battered.

Democracy that ascended by the power of the ballot box in fragmented societies was reincarnated as dictatorship by the ballot box, or what has been called, by activists dismayed by the arrival of Islamists to power, *boxocracy*. I will use this coinage to mean the hollowing of the substance of democracy by formal procedure. Idealising the voting process has not bridged the divide between working-class struggles and the combination of civil liberties with higher shares of the surplus. On the contrary, boxocracy puts the same ruling class back in power again and again with different faces, while the persistence of 'free market' policies reproduces and deepens structural inequalities. The biased constitutions, the rules of a political-economic game that promotes short-term grab, and the predominance of imperialistically groomed civil society–identity (religious or ethnic) over citizenship have reduced democracy to the rule of a thing—the fetishised ballot box—over people. A citizen has come to reflect and internalise the social form of appropriation devolved to his or her section of the working class, and as such he or she belongs to sect, clan or ethnicity and rarely to the state. In any case, the open capital and trade accounts side of the market reduces functional Arab citizenship to the size of one's savings pocket book abroad, and only abroad; no amount of cash can buy security at home in the Arab world. The devaluation of citizenship, in fact, is an essential attribute of modern capitalist democracy. The tendency of liberal doctrine to represent the historical developments that produced formal citizenship as nothing other than an enhancement of individual liberty is inexcusably one-sided (Wood 1995, 211). The supposedly representative institutions, situated as they are within a context of unequal power structure, reproduce the power of classes rooted in imperialism. Boxocracy, the rule of the ballot box, is a kind of filter that blocks working-class representation while transferring ever more political power to the ruling classes. It is thus a reified political process behind which lurks the agency of capital. This hollowed-out pseudo-democracy offers a choice between two or three variations of capital's program and its agendas. It is bereft of the bundle of economic and social rights derived from working-class participation in the power structure of the state. As such, bourgeois democracy is, especially in an Arab context, the alienation of the working class (Wood 1995, 216).

Civil liberties vary in inverse proportion to regime insecurity. In advanced formations, civil liberties flourish so long as they do not question or disturb power structures. Paul Goodman's dictum that in America one can say whatever one wants as long as it does not make any difference captures the sham of bourgeois democracy. The greater legitimacy derived from the ballot box, the greater the leverage by which ruling classes undermine the working classes—and by working classes, I mean the global working class. In terms of capital's longevity, efficiency and returns to forms of political practice, unballoted dictatorships fare worse than balloted ones. Western democratic governments have also splintered their working classes. In thirty years of US growth, wages have remained stagnant and inequality has risen dramatically, yet there has been no effective working-class response (Wolf 2006). Illusory freedom derived from national pride, as distinct from freedom from want, appears just as ludicrous as the promise to jihadists of houris in heaven. At least in terms of convincing the working class to vote for a government that would finance televised wars in the Third World by issuing large amounts of debt, US-led capital has ideologically outmanoeuvred Wahhabism in bamboozling the working class (Cui 2005). Set against a background of socially enacted and structural racism, ballot-box democracy breeds divisions to the degree to which workers' organisations pursue sectional interests as opposed to class interests. 'Sectionalism is the product of limited democracy,' but more importantly of socialist ideological retreat (Gindin 2013).

In the dialectic of theory and practice, the internalisation of atomistic modes of existence by workers reduces the possibility of ideological development derived from the conditions of social struggle. Counter-reform counters revolutions, and political failure breeds defeatism and a crisis of alternatives. By reform I mean the measures taken to fuel internationalist class struggle and not the current payoffs to central working classes from colonial loot. Ballot-box democracy operates as part of the arsenal of the dominant ideology, deepening the alienation of an already traumatised worker from the rest of society (the 'traumatised worker' is a term used by Riccardo Bellofiore in his lectures at Turin). It absorbs the pressures from below. No regime, of course, is unresponsive to pressure from below, yet the role of boxocracy appears to be most pivotal in assuring that the 'below' is never cohesive enough to exert any pressure on those above. This is one of the reasons why, after decades of supporting undemocratic regimes, US-led capital is experimenting with the democratisation of Arab formations. In any case, given the retreat of the Left, US-led capital has little to fear. As the 2012 Egyptian parliamentary election showed, the ultrafundamentalists trailed the Muslim Brotherhood. Democracies bereft of working-class rights abort the historical agency of labour. They have proven just as reliable to capital as authoritarianism, perhaps more so. Ballot-box democracy operates within a *pro forma* structural context of social inequality antecedent to nominal political equality. Capital's media and cultural hold, weak working-class organisation, working-class consent generated by ideological and financial means, and the adumbration of social and economic rights are some of the precursors to the ritual of voting in boxocracy. In the AW, on top of all this, reinventing the past as surreal identity politics crowns capital's ideological rule.

The centrality of the state is such that, far more than a private person can achieve in terms of progress through civil society, a citizen in a workers' democracy can improve the quality of his or her existence. Arab capital, or rather the transnational class alliance at the helm of the social relationship reproducing wealth in the AW, by use of repression more so than ideological appeal, moulds the state and the citizen to its desires. With US-led capital embedded in this ruling alliance, it causes the degeneration of the Arab state. The global hunger for oil together with military-industrial capital's need for perpetual war drive it to do so. In central formations, a history of class struggle and imperialist spoils temporarily spliced together the conflicting classes—a joining that is now unravelling as working-class families are almost completely asset stripped by a combination of money-wage stagnation (or decline) and successive financial crises that have destroyed their savings even as the social wage has been cut. But the program of atomisation was so successful in the US that the stably employed (and especially white) working class was successfully rebranded by capital's ideological organs as the 'middle class'—which simply meant one was not 'poor'. Working classes paraded as middle classes, for the term 'middle' substitutes the derogatory-sounding term 'working' to underline status. The working class as such was conceptually suppressed. Unhinged self-perceptions within layers of the working class at both centre and periphery cloud understanding in general. Nonetheless, the state in this reified world appears independent of the class structure, though the contempt in which many working-class citizens now hold their allegedly democratic (boxocratic) institutions is fraying the illusion. In most of the periphery, imperialist central states are loathed because of their contemptuous encroachment and militarism. In the patrimonial Gulf states, however, where there is one domestic servant for every two citizens, nearly the whole of the subject population has ideologically fused with capital. That said, the integration of the Arab national bourgeoisie with international financial capital in non-Gulf Arab states wrenches the state loose from society. The state is weak vis-à-vis civil society and is therefore perceived as weak or biased—hence, the rise of civil society over the state.

As Arab capital abases itself to the mercantilism of empire by deindustrialising, its national allegiance becomes suspect. Imbalances in income, ostentatious displays of wealth and privilege as the merchant class emulates the consumption patterns of its central counterparts, state-licensed merchant activity and resource grab grind down national cohesion, or more loosely, the social contract. An imperialistically determined mode of organising life around importing goods for sale on the national Arab market and exporting the revenues in dollars decapitates national industry. Labour is not only deskilled in this process of shrinking production; it is idled. The price system that shapes the process of exchange is no longer national—the terms of international trade set most of national prices. The citizens—the worker and the working class—do not confront the national bourgeoisie in the democratic process; rather, it is the powers that shape the globe with which national labour has to contend.

Further complicating matters is that the confrontation with global capital happens through the state. The state is a tool for collective action, regardless of the forms of political process and organisation that characterise a social formation. The state, which is in one of its aspects the resultant force of differing political forces both at the national and international level, remains the principal agent of development. A sovereign and capable state, if security strategy is aligned with developmental objectives, can undertake social transformation. Sovereignty does imply at subordinate levels a professional and autonomous bureaucracy, a closed political system and state domination of private actors (Fine 2006). However, more fundamentally, sovereignty's substance is democratic security—that is the security of the working class mediated through national security. In an Arab context, neither national security nor the downstream manifestations of sovereignty appear to kick in. Thus, the state that can develop the AW is missing. The Arab state flies in an imperialist orbit.

Security as the Substance of Sovereignty

Security (or its opposite, insecurity) is often reduced to an analytical construct around certain values or utilitarian ends. In reality, security is an objective condition of existence historically determined within the nexus of the class struggle. Security from want for the working class, quite simply, is development; and this actual security requires a whole set of anti-imperialist defence mechanisms, including national defence, to be exercised. The recent avalanche of recognitions that security is an inherent dimension of development arose from the sense of *ideological* security that imperialism has acquired as a result of socialist ideological withdrawal. Socialist ideology is so weak that capital need not be too underhanded when pursuing its objectives. US-led capital, the principal perpetrator of insecurity, feels secure enough to claim that security is relevant to development. The empire and master of history is capable of exonerating itself of its transgressions. So linking security and development has become a policy fixation for a number of international institutions, government think tanks and academic researchers. For instance, the UN's High-Level Panel on Threats, Challenges and Change recognised that 'in an increasingly interconnected world, progress in the areas of development, security and human rights must go hand in hand. There will be no development without security and no security without development' (UN 2004). Similarly, the Commission on Human Security acknowledged that 'conflict and deprivation are interconnected. Deprivation has many causal links to violence, although these have to be carefully examined. Conversely, wars kill people, destroy trust among them, increase poverty and crime and slow down the economy. Addressing such insecurities effectively demands an integrated approach' (CHS 2003). A similar conclusion was reached by the High-Level Plenary Meeting of the UN General Assembly in 2005, whose draft outcome document stated, 'We recognize that our nations and peoples will not enjoy development without security, nor will they enjoy security without development, and that they will not enjoy either without respect for human rights' (UN 2005a). With the publication of the UNDP HDR (1994) and the World Bank's *Breaking the Conflict Trap* (2003), the security and development debate evolved into a well-established policy and research area.

In this strand of research, poverty, conflict and underdevelopment are dehistoricised. Conflicts and underdevelopment exist independently of colonial history and residue and imperialist aggression. In a new version of the well-established imperialist blame game of White Man's Burden, it is the people of the conflict-stricken and developing territory who cause their underdevelopment and bear the burden of responsibility. Institutional concerns and political preconditions of development have crept up alongside a governance literature whose purpose is to conceptually delink the national ruling classes from their organic ties to the imperialist power centres. Generic Arabs and Africans are alleged to independently govern themselves—badly— and to perpetrate their own insecurity even though security is instrumental to their development. When the topic of security is explored at length, the discourse meanders into putative interventions by 'development' institutions aimed at peace, state formation and nation building. All this high-minded but condescending literature assumes that, whether for genetic or (more usually) cultural reasons, the populations of former colonies are incapable of establishing either security or development, or for that matter doing anything whatever of value for themselves.

Apart from the moderately insecure Arab states such as Algeria, the rest are insecure or in a state of violent conflict. (As noted earlier, *all* Arab states are underdeveloped, including the Gulf, despite its high per capita income— development is a condition of industrialisation, social and economic rights.) Not counting the wars of independence from the direct colonial powers, the Arab states have lost one major war after another: the 1948 Arab–Israeli war, the 1956 war, the 1967 war and the 1973 war. When these states are not losing a war, they are being structurally adjusted to losing the next war. Arab states have been purposely deconstructed by war and/or by the usurpation of resources otherwise destined to the working class. Many working classes in Arab countries, as a consequence of this deconstruction and economic impaction, are at war within and with each other. Insecurity and de-development are two facets of the same process, highlighting the connection between imperialist intervention and peripheral developmental disasters. To isolate security issues and treat them separately outside the continuum of history therefore exonerates imperialism. As for development, imperialism imposes neoliberal rules for Arab countries to follow; but when these countries do not meet the goals of 'good development', it is said to be the fault of their shaky faith in the secular religion of the 'free market'; science impersonates theology.

In the unipolar world that emerged after the fall of the USSR, the growing numbers of wars in the periphery could no longer be attributed to fending off the Red Menace. Wars and civil wars that lead to the destruction of assets swept across the AW. Arab capital does not fully re-engage resources after military conflicts. The principal reason for military aggression is to restructure value relations and values and ratchet up the power of US-led capital. A secondary reason is that Arab economies are nearly fully integrated with the world's advanced economies that are already operating below capacity. US-led capital has also financialised its profit-making procedures, which means it no longer places emphasis on extending its industry or its subsidiaries in the AW. There are far too many industrial assets overproducing goods as it is. Hence, much of Arab industries destroyed in war are not rebuilt.

So far, wars and civil wars have written off years of development. That it became inevitable for scholarly energy to be channelled into the relationships between conflict, security and development is borne out by the course of events. The point of this literature is to limit the reasons for conflicts to intranational problems (Nabli 2004). Countries that are bombed, or countries that are set on a path of self-destruction by WB/IMF 'free market' policies, and whose state apparatuses crumble, are blamed for their own disasters and then dubbed 'failed states'. European colonialists overhauled Ottoman modes of political organisation and erected in their place the 'modern Arab state', which is just another name for a form of political organisation, contra the racist Western discourse about Arabs and Africans as ahistorical and stateless people. The colonialist-drafted constitutions, the identity-biased (religious, ethnic) bureaucracies and legal processes, very poorly matched the requirements of Arab society. Through all this time of the AW struggling to catch up with the European state model, the material shortcomings of society caused by colonial plunder, war defeats and usurpation policies have stood in the way. The overdeveloped state model imposed by Europe was congruous with colonially engendered underdevelopment. In the slack between overdeveloped state and undeveloped capacity, there was always room for comprador sections of the ruling classes to push the state beyond its own sustainability and against itself. Class proclivities outweigh national identity. When nationalism and security were ascendant during the short postindependence period, authoritarianism prevailed over the operational side of the state—its bureaucracy, and development burgeoned. The state did not 'fail'; history is not a pass or fail school test designed by imperialists. The postcolonial Arab state was predestined to malfunction because its initial colonial plan was faulty and it lost the war. Imperialist power-positioning wars at the start of the twentieth century fashioned Arab states as incubators of adversity, and since the late twentieth century, US-led financial capital has collected the tribute.

Security: From the Abstract to the Ludicrous

In addressing security, orthodox commentary moves from metaphysics to empirical ludicrousness (UNDP 1994). Real, concrete security in the context of development is defined in this commentary as *human* security. In part, this means safety from such chronic threats as hunger, disease and repression—but also protection from sudden and damaging disruptions in the patterns of daily life—whether at home, at work or in communities (UNDP 1994). These are the manifold manifestations of security, not security itself. Security as mentioned above is the general principle of the working-class struggle for rights. In the UNDP depoliticised notion of security, from the need for nail polish to the dictum 'the US has to protect its way of life' (a dictum that entered the lexicon of international relations as grounds for just war), security can be said to include everything under the sun. The full gamut of human security includes whatever can be empirically detected in actuality to affect life—that is, tautologically, life itself. Insecurity in this broadest sense is an existential condition, a condition of being alive—but one that nevertheless acquires a particular intensity under capitalism. Fear and want in fact pervade the existence of the great majority in class society and have done so since class society began. In reality, it is specific patterns of social relations, including relations of production, exchange and distribution that generate insecurity. The variations in the social relations reconstituting distribution, rather than the statistical weightings assigned to various manifestations of insecurity, are what require research. In underdeveloped, war-ridden Arab formations, very few of these primary 'human security' needs are met for the majority. Insecurity arises because of structural social transformations (or deformations) instigated by war and neoliberalism. These transformations of the class structure, undermining the resilience of the working class, are the true 'universals' and the creators of insecurity.

Moving on from the ludicrous above, for the Commission on Human Security (CHS), security embraces far more than the absence of violent conflict. It encompasses human rights, good governance, access to education and healthcare, and ensures that each individual has opportunities and choices to fulfil his or her own potential (CHS 2003, 4). On their own, these last words are similar to how Karl Marx defines communism, but is the CHS seeking the annulment of the class system? Human security as a concept 'interconnects' freedom from want, freedom from fear and freedom to take action on one's own behalf. The metaphysical emerges in the way the CHS defines 'interconnects'. For the CHS the class structure is not dysfunctional, and the context in which the individual 'interconnects' is irreproachable. Human security departs from national security, but complements it by being people centred (CHS 2003). Apart from the vacuous term 'people', which buries social classes beneath the text, no aspect of security can depart from national security by definition. Severing any security aspect from national security is blatantly unrealistic, but the breadth of what constitutes human security renders it synonymous with the betterment of social conditions, which is in turn synonymous with state-sponsored development. What the CHS does not mention is that security is a totality in which national security *overrides* (forms the determining moment in a process) the intermediation between the moments of communal and individual security. Widening the concept of security to elucidate the security of people in general and human security as its *numéraire* shifts the intellectual emphasis from what capital is to the social conditions that capital produces. Indeed, insecurities abound, but no individual effort in a lopsided class structure will result in security until the class lopsidedness is levelled. Also, even if everyone wishes as hard as they can for insecurities to vanish, they will not. These definitions dilute the primacy of the class contradictions that shape the allocation of resources. Capital, the private appropriation of social product, is also the process by which resources are engaged to produce for profit. For the latter, capital must dislocate, bust unions or similarly bust entire Third World states by wars of aggression to reduce the actual or ideological costs of its reproduction. This motion from production to dislocation underlies the making of secure or insecure living conditions. It is, to borrow from dialectical logic, the universal law of motion—although in Marxian terminology, the concept *general* is the outward manifestation of the particular, not of the 'universal', or the characteristics that are common to each individual condition (Ilyenkov 1977).

In the structurally defeated AW, national security and sovereignty are the preconditions for all other sorts of security. Very few securities, be they economic, social or political, emerge outside the womb of a nationally secure state. National security necessarily militarises development (CIDSE 2006). However, Arab states emerged as militarily incapacitated states: they were nationalist but because of underdevelopment incapable of self-defence. Israeli victories in blitzkriegs are a case in point. Their underdevelopment in the postindependence period was progressively reinforced by the disempowerment of the working class—reducing the impetus in people's warfare. The lacking military capacity of Arab states and the expulsion of the working class from the formation of national security under neoliberalism lowered the calculated risk to US-led imperialist aggression. Hence, facile imperialist bellicosity rose alongside Arab underdevelopment.

The absence of conflicts together with access to goods and services are an expression of working-class security within the purview of the nation-state. The dissection of security into its innumerable component parts conceals the complex and impersonal social forms that reorganise social action. The individual is not a historical force when particular politics are unmediated through the general forms of social resistance, which require collective action and collective consciousness. Economic or political security is an outcome of social agency, which cannot be a vector sum of individual volitions structured through political institutions. This is not an additive problem it is a qualitatively structured movement. Economic security as the share of value to labour is determined almost entirely within the balance of power between labour and capital. At an abstract level, therefore, an understanding of security begins in the contradiction between these two fundamental processes. The abstract (the general) is the process of transformation in social conditions resulting in security wrought from the success of working-class struggle against capital. In the AW, repression and the decapitalisation of national formations by war and neoliberalism reduced the means available to workers and set further and further back the starting point from which working classes could begin to fight for their security.

Arguing for the primacy of national security does not ignore or underestimate individual security. This is not a race between two independent forms. Nor is it an issue of preference for the whole over the part. The point is to assess their development side by side in the metamorphosis from the particular—concrete working-class organisation, its forms, extent and militancy—to the general, the power of labour within the state, as the historical pattern that actualises labour. Promoting chambers of commerce and banning trade unions, as many Arab states have done, therefore imply that the historical movement is antidevelopmental and antisecurity. More important, can national security in the AW be understood without recourse to a global analysis, especially with respect to the security of global financial capital? Nation-states are not self-enclosed islands, separated from global forces and the interests of other states. Rather, they are embedded in various international relations, chiefly their positions in the international power structure and economy. As such, to explore national security, an exploration of the regional and international contexts must follow. The security of the AW, which has been a victim of destructive international influences, is internationalised. In other words, one cannot make sense of Arab security at the national level without incorporating into one's analysis the politics of oil, the foreign penetration of the area, the after-effects of the Cold War, and the various intraregional struggles for power. These are the international contradictions, which again have to be considered in the process of building security.

Security, understood broadly as an historical process determined within the varying levels of national and international contradictions, underwrites development, in which the absence of conflict is not a necessary condition, but a desirable one. The mechanical sequence from security, to sovereignty, to developmental success did hold for China, the leading growth performer over the last three decades. Chinese and US capital generally see eye to eye. Chinese production is nationally based, and China's differences with the US are about how the US's dollar share endangers the origin of Chinese wealth, which is its national capacity. In the AW, by contrast, US capital wholly subordinates a merchant class that does not earn much from a national production base. The wages of Chinese workers rose nearly three hundred per cent in the decade between 2002 and 2012, whereas labour's share of total product in the AW fell to one of the lowest ranks globally during the same period (KILM, various years). Whether seen as mechanical or as an articulation of historical relations determined simultaneously by coincidence and necessity, the sequence security–sovereignty–development sheds more light on the developmental differences between the AW and other developing regions.

There have been no Marshall Plans for the AW. Losses to war and neoliberalism incurred by national production capacity have lingered. In the power undercurrents of global accumulation, capital requires a certain degree of disengagement of resources both to cheapen inputs—it requires many resources to stay idle under its thumb—and, just as importantly, to strengthen its ideological hold. Because of the frail position of the more exposed classes within the power structure of the global order, their conditions degenerate to the lowest standards of subsistence. Although these 'Third World' conditions boost the living standards of certain sections of the central working class, they return to haunt and depress the conditions of labour everywhere. Social production inherently pulls labour together. The selective fractionation of labour by unequal wage shares invariably fails in times of crisis, when capital has to impose austerity across the board. Labour resurges as an organic whole unadulterated by labour aristocracy every time crisis deepens at the centre— as it has begun tentatively to do in the US since 2011, where the cross-sectoral dialogue of the Occupy encampments brought together skilled professionals, debt-crippled young graduates, unionized workers, low-wage service workers and the destitute.[2] So far, however, labour without labour ideology (class-based, socialist, internationalist thinking) lets the bottom of the Third World sink to one degree or another by way of the sectional improvement of social conditions in the advanced world. Arab states riven by war and internal conflict have borne the brunt of global capital dislocation. Incessant imperialist assault has disfigured their social structures and stripped their working classes of the security necessary for development. In the AW, conflict has become the rule. The weight of an imperialist military that cannot be deterred by conventional military means has sapped sovereignty, unclamped resources and paralysed development.

From Security to Sovereignty

As discussed above, security is a totality of interrelated moments in which national security mediates communal or working-class security. The rights of the working classes in citizenship, the right to economic and social security, the right to social protection and equality of condition as a precondition for equality of opportunity are manifestations of security. In developing formations constantly subjected to imperialist assault, class struggle is primarily anti-imperialist and circularly contingent upon the security of national working classes (Abdel Malek 1981). The universal (the general) is not the social class; social classes are ubiquitous, polymorphous processes, and their commonalities cannot be a rule for their universality. The universal (the general) is the process or forms of struggle by which anti-imperialist

---

2   This analogy was suggested by activist and poet Adam Cornford.

alliances are formed and act politically. Security in this context is gauged by the degree of alliance between labouring classes and nationalist ruling classes that becomes manifest in the independence that developing states maintain from imperial power centres (the case of national capitalism). The realisation of national security through the struggle of the labouring classes and the evolving structure of class alliances and fronts are for developing nations the substance of sovereignty. Working-class agency in the political process, both nationally and internationally, determines the degree of security, which will in turn be transmuted into national sovereignty over national resources and national ownership of development policy. A closer anti-imperialist alliance of national classes, in which the rights of the working classes prevail, denotes sovereignty.

The relationship of sovereignty to security predates modern capitalism. The classical debate on sovereignty emerging from the works of Thomas Hobbes and John Locke is often reduced to an argument over whether the sovereign power would be irrevocable until national security is compromised or else would be revocable even when national security is safeguarded, but when property and personal liberties are compromised (Wood 2012). These positions on sovereignty were aired from different standpoints with respect to the English monarchy. At a slightly higher level of generalisation, security, be it enacted in the sovereign (the power of the state) or extended to personal property and other venues of life, underwrites sovereignty. The fullness of security expands sovereignty. In modern contexts, security of person and security from want are by-products of working-class security.

Sovereignty, substantiated by working-class security, represents the key moment for development. As proven by the case of Iraq, the sham of individualistic civil liberties, or abstract notions of freedom such as the introduction of ballot-box democracy in devastated societies, merely drains away sovereignty. Voting in a disarticulated social milieu, devoid of social and economic rights, results in social implosion. The terms of political organisation under the auspices of imperialism deny labour its rights. The ideological framework upon which the post-2004 Iraq boxocracy was erected redirected the flows of capital away from labour (Iraq exhibits the lowest share of labour from income globally at 11 per cent) (Guerrero 2012).

Sovereignty and development coexist under conditions where the political representations of labour have transcended nationalism. Although anti-imperialist struggle in the periphery requires an alliance between national working and ruling classes, the rise in the power of labour and its share of national income cannot be sectional. It has to be transnational, to the benefit of other working classes. Working-class politics have to supersede national boundaries. Sovereignty in the practice of development transcends narrow nationalist aspirations; otherwise the building of autonomy in smaller countries could end up like the attempt to build socialism in one country—a burden not even Soviet Russia was able to bear. Sectional sovereignty, as in advances of the class struggle without an internationalist support base, produces sectional development. As the degree of autonomy a nation exercises over its own territory grows, favourable developmental outcomes follow. Ideally, when policy establishes labour objectives as central, development assumes a fuller existence.

In the AW, exposed security becomes manifest as frail sovereignty. The labouring classes have succumbed to the overwhelming military powers of imperialism. The ensuing weakness of sovereignty has become the conveyor belt of resource transfers from the AW. This mechanism of dispossession is upheld by an articulation of class powers, both national and international. These set the condition for accumulation by dispossession, which in turn further undermines security, sovereignty and the potential for development. It might have been possible to relate the concept of Arab underdevelopment on the basis of slack in *doux commerce* (Voltaire's notion of merchandise trade without violence or coercion) and/or, by dependency theorists, with respect to the deteriorating terms of trade. But these pale in significance given the violence to which the AW has been subjected. Power relations always underlie contracts and generated prices brokered by unequal power platforms. The terms of power meddle in the terms of trade everywhere. But in the AW, power principally assumes violent forms. Even the semblance of equal power platforms in capitalist trade is ripped away in the AW. Capital, in the AW, grows by encroachment wars or the serious threat thereof. Military power enables US-led imperialism aided by Israel to control Arab moneyed and non-moneyed assets. US-led capital's positioning in the region underwrites its imperial stature and the expansion of its dollar-based financial system.

The real or exaggerated strategic relevance of the AW lines up many countries against Arab working classes for fear of abrupt disruptions to oil flows. Not that the human costs of war and underdevelopment have ever evoked adequate global policy responses; but in the AW, reasserting the imperialist balance of power demands interventions of the most brutal kind. The mere suggestion that the Straits of Hormuz might be closed rallies the whole world behind the US-sponsored hegemony over the region. Even powers that are becoming increasingly concerned with the liability of holding growing American debt tacitly but unwillingly support US regional ambitions. The transition costs to the world from receding US-led supremacy over the region, less in terms of shortages or disruptions to oil supply, but more in terms of a possible setback to US imperial rank and the dollar, unnerve the planetary rulers. The possibility of a disorderly withdrawal from a US-led financial system, which would be accompanied by dollar devaluation and, hence, a decline in the value of the world-saving medium, contributes to an 'ultraimperialism'. One is reminded of Karl Kautsky's (1914) observation about superpowers agreeing on the exploitation of the colonies without recourse to wars, but in actuality the collusion itself is precarious because many are ill at ease with the racketeering of US-led financial capital, an issue which will be discussed at length in the next two chapters. This then defines by negation the formidable task with which the Arab working classes and their allies in the central formations are mandated: to convince the planet that their oil wreaks environmental havoc, that clean and sustainable alternatives exist, and that the dialectic of blood for oil has been more harmful to them than to anyone else.

Development by Encroachment Wars

Oil—in its crude form, in the way it is priced in dollars, and in the infinite technological permutations of its derivatives that add to its value—represents a decisive constituent of global accumulation. Control of oil in all these aspects is central to maintaining the stature of US-led empire, the present global financial order and its associated imperial rents. A cross-border class alliance of global capital and Arab ruling classes reproduces the articulation of the Arab social formation with global capital. Outright military superiority and hegemony over Arab working masses has reproduced the ruling-class alliance and maintained, *pari passu*, Israel's military supremacy over the region. Not only is Arab asset destruction necessary to capital, but the persistence of conflicts, wars (or the threat thereof) in the AW mediates stubborn interimperialist rivalries between the US and other powers in Europe and Asia over its disproportionate arrogation of imperial rents by means of its leading stature and military might. The incongruence between US-led capital rents and its waning imperialist rank manifests itself in growing US military adventurism. US-led capital's recklessness endangers the global financial structure and the dollar as the universal medium of wealth holding. The proclivity of US imperial partners and holders of dollar wealth for future interimperialist collaboration shrinks as the crisis of the republic fails to be redressed by the booty of empire (Petras 2011).

The flip side of the Arab working classes exercising sovereignty over their resources is that the US's position would be downgraded globally. Arab development diametrically opposes the present global wealth-making process and the financial order associated therewith. The immiseration of the Arab working classes is thus revealed to be both an outcome of interimperialist entente and a complex articulation of global powers necessitating the de-development of the AW. Although power can be couched in various symbolic constructs, the concept of power that best befits what is being unleashed against Arab working classes is principally firepower. The manifold and continual aggression has so far resulted in a growing number of fragmented states—Iraq, Sudan, Lebanon, Libya and Syria being the most obvious examples—and the prevalent serious threats of major regional wars. Their boundaries are *de jure* intact but *de facto* nominal and illusory.

US-led imperialist aggression seems more costly than the money-form gains it is set to expropriate from the measly income of the AW. Recalling that part from the Gulf, the rest of the AW resembles the sub-Saharan market in terms of purchasing power. Given the small amounts that US-led capital is likely earning from bombarding the AW, it may very well appear to be conducting a civilising or humanitarian mission, as sardonic as this may sound, as in bringing democracy to Libya, Syria and Iraq. The question is often put in an apologetic way, as in: why should Western powers spend so much on war in countries whose income and resources will not offset war's costs? Imperial wars, seen from this double-entry accounting framework, are explained as part and parcel of a Western civilising (or these days, 'democratising') process, which has already left behind it hundreds of millions of slain 'noble savages' in the last few centuries. Save the racism inherent in all 'nationalisms', one has yet to see the last of the fruits of this 'civilising' endeavour. When stripped of falsehood, the money form—prices and the sums of financial resources they amount to— is brokered by a structure of power from which Arab working classes have been discarded. As already noted, after the usurpation of the bigger share of national wealth by Arab ruling classes and their foreign patrons, the resources remaining to the Arab labouring classes are insufficient to maintain a historically determined decent standard of living. It is not the money derived from the colony proper that explains colonial undertakings; it is the sum total of the monies earned from the status of empire. In money form, the occupation of Iraq does not contribute much to the US. Most Iraqi trade is with Turkey and many oil contracts are signed with non-American companies; in fact, the US may end up footing a bill so high that the combined GDP of Iraq, assuming it all accrues to the US over many years, may never offset the costs of the war. However, the undervalued asset transfers from the rest of the world and the devalorisation of world assets in dollars are in part a reflection of the American fragmentation of Iraq and its show of force there. The exercise of power was never a psychological trip, it is dialectically linked to expanded production or self-expanding value. Growth for the sake of growth, or the ideology of the cancer cell as it is popularly called, requires an indefinite show of power.

Relative to the global product (world GDP), then, the money value seized from the AW will not be significant. But the power structure already distorts exchange rates and price terms. The social product derived from imperialist control of Arab assets is significant in value terms because it partly stabilises global capital's profit rates by underdeveloping the AW. From a purely quantitative angle, it also would matter little to US-led capital had Arab development proceeded by market expansion, productivity gains and higher wages. For such growth by trade expansion would also dim in significance relative to the trade between Western formations assessed in money form. The real reason for colonisation has not changed: simply, it strips working classes of the Third World of sovereignty over their resources. The grand design is to allow the balance of forces behind the scenes to set the price of their primary commodities far below the social value necessary to reproduce the population. In a sense, as the bombings set the stage for the transfer of the raw material as part of constant capital or dead labour from the Third World on terms convenient to the colonialist, there will be in the dead labour not only spent muscle and nerve, but dead Arab and African labourers. In addition to this, wars, by destroying human lives in the presence of 1.1 billion unemployed globally, cheapen labour. The acquisition of Arab labour by means of forced migration, labour that is then engaged in capitalist production in a centre that has not borne the initial costs of reproduction of the immigrant labour force, generates immense value and, hence, profit denominated in the dollar. Imperialism gets something for nothing. There is no departure from a trend set by expansionary colonial capital here; US-led capital must expand by destroying and grabbing peripheral assets. What the pricing in the dollar facade conceals is that short-changed values from the AW boost the profits of central capital.

Closing Comment

Despite vast financial wealth, natural and human resources, the AW remains underdeveloped, including the Gulf states, which are the holders of this massive amount of money capital. Following the 2011 uprisings, social conditions have only worsened. In countries with more peaceful transitions, such as Egypt and Tunisia, boxocracy has re-legitimised the old robber barons. As detailed in Chapter One, income inequality, private-sector hold over resources and low-productivity private investment remain (UN 2012). The regional rates of unemployment have not improved (KILM 2012). More than half the population lives below the two-dollars-a-day threshold in the highest per capita food importing region (Arab Monetary Fund 2009). The daunting terms of power, which determine the terms of trade—even the very making of the price system—are calibrated by belligerent means to favour US-led capital. Alongside enforced public-to-private transfers under neoliberalism, wars against working masses are the definitive instrument by which social and non-monetised resources and labour are coercively engaged in production and the formation of value.

Wars also serve to militarise the global economy. For several decades already, the global economy has internalised the wars or warlike internal conditions of the AW. Markets have developed a cohabitation strategy, albeit an uneasy one, with these conditions. However, the fear cloud spun around Islamic terror, the Arab–Israeli conflict and Iran's nuclear 'ambitions' infuse global production with steady doses of militarism (Petras 2011). Unlike primitive accumulation, however, which gradually socialised the English peasantry, wars socialise whole countries at once for the purpose of plunder (in the sense that they weaken the state as the form that allocates the national assets to the working population). What is more, indebtedness due to war and the militarisation of US industry restructure the partition of value in favour of US-led capital as it imposes austerity measures on the central working classes.

That democratic and developmental processes in the AW seem to fail cannot be attributed to cultural differences. Tradition and folk mores cannot be reduced to culture or account for lack of democratisation. The Shiites and Sunnites of today share but the name with those of the past. Ideas do not transcend history because their contents change in relation to the real material conditions of survival. Syria's elected parliament of 1955 passed some the most progressive land reforms and social protection laws (Chouman 2005). But culture as the store of knowledge of humanity (patented as private property by central capital) can only very partially explain why the AW did not develop. The difference between the AW and more developed Western countries is in the quality of social structures. As explained above, the working class of the AW is at the mercy of a continual joint assault by Arab ruling classes and US-led capital. The development and security of Arab working classes obtained via an insurgent democratic process would block the oppressive two-headed behemoth, but the recent uprisings did not restructure the social classes into an anti-imperialist front. The military coup in Egypt aborted democratisation and victimised a political Islam (the Muslim Brotherhood) that actually pursued worse neoliberal policy than its predecessor—the Mubarak regime. The opposition and the incumbent government play out their struggle on imperialist-laid fields. The post-uprising policies have shunned policies of land reform, controlled capital accounts, selective protection of national industry, progressive income taxation, egalitarian income distribution, needs-based social policies and, more generally, macro policies that lock the circuit of capital within the nation. The Muslim Brotherhood in Egypt negotiated with the IMF a currency-stabilising loan for removal of subsidies on bread and fuel. There is not in the theoretical arsenal of the opposition the faintest idea that capitalism necessarily dislocates and that therefore society must compensate workers as a matter of rights. Such is the crisis of socialist ideology.

The task of revolutionary transformation is implacable within the bounds of the AW itself. Redistributive and resource-retaining policies would resemble the building of socialism in a small country—in an age when retreat in humanist theory was reinforced by the dominant ideology, in part because the threat of a supposedly socialist alternative in the USSR or China has also evaporated as these societies have reprivatised their capital under the control of the Party *nomenklatura*. The crucial moment for development in the AW, as elsewhere, is in reimagining the internationalist socialist project. Even while the capitalist entente on de-developing the AW proceeds, a working-class counteroffensive needs to engage in the struggle for AW working-class security. The AW is central to a global economy organised around finance, militarism and oil. Each of these three constituent elements of capital reaches its apogee in war upon the AW. To deconstruct capital and its encroachment wars, the world working classes must target not the weakest link in the chain, but the most critical one—the formation of working class-led states in the AW.

Chapter Four

THE STILLBORN AND DECOMPOSING ARAB STATE

When the Western colonial powers regrouped the Vilayets and replaced the Ottoman forms of political organisation with modern Arab states, they set the trajectory of what constitutes political activity in the Arab world for years to come. They refounded institutions and organised social relations with the aim of regimenting the labour process. They also kept intact precapitalist despotic social control measures. When, after decolonisation, many of these states weakened under military or neoliberal assaults, they were dubbed 'failed' states. The neoliberal package is not truly distinct from military assaults; in the AW at least, it is an outcome of Arab defeat and waning sovereignty. Neoliberalism in the developing world is the tribute transfer channel to empire. No cohesive social entity represented in a state would tolerate surplus drain under neoliberalism unless it were in a condition of surrender. Military defeats imposed wealth-draining policies by restructuring national classes to consent to the imperialist terms of capitulation. More recently, many of these states have splintered. However, these failures are not a one-time occurrence after which the states are resurrected in better form. Civil wars are fed to make them last a long time. Many Arab states retain the national symbols and borders, but concretely they are steadily collapsing. As agents of national construction, it is not only their effectiveness in development that is receding; it is also health, education, life expectancy, and the social and productive infrastructure. These are the principal repositories of security.

Arab states have come to depend more and more on oil revenues. By ensuring that oil and state revenues devolve in ways that entrench identity-politics divisions in the working class, the ruling alliance ensures the delivery of its political objectives, which are not always related to stability. The state diminishes into something like a sect or tribe and assumes the role of any other institution in civil society. Identity-branded social factions eclipse the state in terms of the authority they exercise over a certain territory. What these weakened Arab states share with the mainstream notion of the state is just the name: 'state'. The new Iraq, for instance, purchased drones to protect its pipelines even as around one million of its orphaned children are abandoned in the streets of Baghdad (Michaels 2012; Al Jazeera 2011). As far as being 'sovereign' is concerned, state sovereignty is shared with US-led capital. In the spirit of colonial times, the US-led class forms part of the ruling-class alliance and partakes in governance. As malleable or collapsing models, Arab states support central capital with resources and, more importantly, by relinquishing control over oil. Prolonged crises at the global centre necessitate an increasing role by US-led capital in laying claim to Arab states, or dismantling even slightly socialising states ('socialising' is used here to mean assuming socialist functions like free healthcare, education and land reform). The NATO bombing and regime change in Libya were a recent case in point of the latter.

Apart from the flow of resources to the centre, conditions of war reinforce global militarism and are themselves principal tributaries of capital. In an organically integrated mode of global wealth making, as social conditions improve in some states, they regress in others in order to restructure value and maintain downward pressure on the costs of certain inputs in production. Social debilitation, especially of Arab and African states, is necessary for the metabolic rate of the reproduction of capital (Mészáros 1995). Capital accumulation as a social process engages preferably undervalued assets, including ideological assets, in the amassing of wealth. Apart from the requisite of strategic control, the degradation of the AW reduces the price of resources to below value—not only resources drawn from the AW itself, but also resources drawn from the rest of the world as a result of the leverage that US-led capital exercises over a very strategic region *qua* the AW. Because the exercise of power in the AW trespasses across national boundaries and affects the entire globe, it undercuts the myth of nation and highlights the significance of cross-border working-class solidarity. In this chapter, I investigate the failure in AW development as a result of unrelenting assault on the sovereignty of Arab states. The Arab state arrived on the historical scene stillborn by colonial design. Under the security cover of Cold War tensions, it arose as a surrogate bourgeoisie and acted in a developmental capacity. The rise of neoliberalism and the fall of the Soviet Union ushered an era of dilapidation, leading to the uprisings.

The Ideal State

The state in international law according to the dictionary definition is 'an association of persons, living in a determinate part of the earth's surface, legally organised and personified, and associated for their own government' (Scruton 1982). This is utterly vacuous. Much like international law itself, the definition is devoid of relationship to anything historically concrete. It can encompass any form of political organisation in history—and for that matter any country club today. Formalised definitions in general transcend history and, at best, exhibit remote reference to reality. Instead of defining, they undefine a subject for insidious reasons. They attempt to abstract from reality a condition so elementary that it applies as a common denominator to everything but explains nothing. They create irreproachable models that cannot be outdone by concrete development.

The state as a broad sociological construct does indeed represent a form of social organisation, but it is a *historically specific* form. A modern nation-state is the principal institution that mediates the class struggles emerging across the landscape of capitalism. The nation-state is the state of becoming, the concrete institutional process by which historically conflicting classes politically realise themselves. The trajectory of its definition at different epochs of capitalist development follows the contours of successive crises and recompositions afflicting the social formation and the levels of organisation of labour and capital, including their history, power and symbolic dimensions. At its inception or in its heyday, definitions of the modern state emphasized its role as guarantor of rights (Hobbes, for instance, or the US Declaration of Independence); but as these states revealed themselves as modes of social control by violent means, definitions increasingly stressed their power. At the peak of idealism, more commentaries favouring the rights aspect emerged— that is, more than those corroborating the power of the state. The nation-state was, in the main, declared to be 'the realisation of the spirit' or 'the actuality of the ethical idea' (Hegel 1952). At the height of rights-based idealisation, the state became for Kant 'an autonomous state, one in which the authority of its laws is in the will of the people in that state' (Allison 1952). However, as working-class slums mushroomed in the late nineteenth century, the perspective in which power is the principal characteristic of the state came to dominate the discourse. The state became 'the institution of organised violence which is used by the ruling class to maintain the conditions of its rule' or, more saliently, 'the organisation that monopolises legitimate violence over a given territory'. These are generic labels from Marxist and Weberian notions of the state respectively. The individual as social being is both an agent and subject of a given social class, and it is the structure of classes shaping the political process that defines the state. In the extreme situation that is the AW, the state, in view of the disarticulation of the labouring classes, is the process by which the ruling classes organise and maintain a subordinate mode of integration into global capital.

The political-economic roots of the social state and its evolution are in its role in regimenting labour and redistributing the share of value in wage goods to the working class. First of all, the wage is in reality social rather than private. Individual productivities do not occur separately from social productivity and outside a structure of power. The reproduction of any single human being involves many people working together. More so in the integrated circuit of capital under financialisation, the reproduction of the wage system involves transnational social classes and implicates the reproduction of global capital itself. The state affords power, time and space for particular capitals to interact and compete.[1] The organised dimension of capital, its political structure of which the state is a predicate, supports the expansion and realisation of value—that is, expanded production and sales. Subject to cyclical movements, capital valorises and revalorises itself by means of its ideological hegemony, and operationally, by measures of control of which the supply of money is central in the financial age. The production of specific types of territorial conditions, state or administration signifies a specific level in the process of the reproduction of capital itself. In a sense, there is nothing too unusual here: the development of capital underlines the development of the state. An organised capital that pursues demand creation and social welfare policies requires a state more inclusive of national labour. Despite being seminally articulated with capital, the state as a result of extensive welfare policies may appear in certain nondecisive aspects distinct and autonomous from it. Capital, however, does not dissipate if it extends more in welfare; it is not demand that makes capital, it is the extraction of wealth via the wage system. Capital withers only as the wage system withers (Rubin 1972; Mészáros 1995).

The subordination of the state to capital arises not only from the dominance of the capitalist class over the state but also from the universality of capital as a social relationship, its hold on modes of social organisation, its ideological hegemony and the struggle that labour undertakes in superseding capital as a social relationship. Wage labour, as the variable component of capital whereby surplus value is created, is as prevalent as capital itself, and the utmost of the socialised states (socialist-like) still derive their wealth simultaneously from their working classes and the power they exercise from tapping into the international division of labour (that is where they stand on the international value ladder). One ought to recall that the historical stage, the traditions and habits of the working class and the rules of the game in general are already set by capital. Capital's passing, therefore, requires more than just the nationalisation of the means of production; it is crucially the

---

1   The initial moment in capital as a result of this interaction, which is private appropriation pitted against social production, grows into the undercurrent of social relations under capitalism.

abolition of the subsumption of labour (Rubin 1972; Mészáros 1995). The real autonomy of the state, or the gradual rise of labour as subject of history, is correlated with capital by the rising share of wages and the flux in the power of labour within the class conflict. Generally, in this continuously unfolding process *cum* crisis, capital's response through the state has been to influence the ranks assigned to each of the social classes through:

a) production relations, in particular class-power and ownership relationships to the social means of production;
b) the social division of labour and the function of each class in material and social reproduction;
c) the distribution of social wealth and the form and amount of revenue to each class; and, consequently,
d) the conditions of the existence of the members of each class.

From a Marxian perspective, wages are *the wages of a social class*—the working class. For Kalecki, as will be seen in more detail in Chapter Eight, the nominal wage is determined simultaneously by the macro conditions of monopoly power and resource leakage abroad. The real wage, in turn, is determined by the power of unions and the working class. In contrast to the neoclassical definition, the wage bill cannot be the sum of the wages of each worker, whose wage is determined by the myth of individual productivity. Nonetheless, the wage share depends on productivity, which is primarily social (and socialized through the mechanism of minimum socially necessary labour and its expression as production price), and ultimately on the power of labour in the state and at the point of production. The wage of each worker is determinedly social because it is his or her share from the social wages of the working class. Where one draws the line between what surgeons receive in salary compared to the wages of cleaning staff is related to divisions within the same working class, but the total wage bill varies in relation to working class power and productivity. Accordingly, here is the root of the political-economic state and its evolution.

But, it is exactly in its outlandish departure from such roots or by the high degree to which the social product was privatised under neoliberalism that the content of the Arab state has to be explained. In its distributive function, the Arab state served as vehicle for the ruling classes to squander resources in a way that has undermined their own existence. The excessive practices of the merchant class have extended far beyond what is necessary for the orderly functioning of the peripheral capitalist formations, over which the state presides (Alavi 1972, 59–81). It is the natural end of merchant grab from the national state to end in the destruction of the state itself as grab turns to speculate on the bigger pie of geopolitical rents arising from the realisation of value by destructive militarisation.

Thus the Arab state has been neither a medium of its own dominant bourgeois class nor a mediator of other national classes. The way state power is arranged vis-à-vis other political institutions and classes—including, no less, the imperialist institutions—is such that any institution of civil society can bypass the state. The state is neither an institution of its own nor an institution of all institutions. Under imperialist assault, the Arab state is either fracturing or being drained of sovereignty. National institutions, those construed by identity politics, do not relinquish their autonomy to the state. Instead, they seize resources by surpassing the state. Always under the purview of a US-led capital whose aim is to incapacitate the national economy, this hollowed-out state leads the assault on the security of labour, which in turn weakens state sovereignty. The share of Arab labour is thus determined not so much by the power that national labour deploys against its own ruling class, but by the struggle it exercises against the monolithic power of US-led imperialism and its regional military presence.

The Arab state, therefore, is condemned to the reign of statism (not *étatisme*) without even the semblance of an autonomous state. Statism is a combination of administrative and repressive practices and contingent arbitration of particular interests, including those of the dominant classes. Excessive Third World statism is often bound up with 'underdevelopment' (Balibar 1991). Balibar extends statism to the modern 'state' in Europe, in view of the rise of new forms of structured and differentiated racisms, in which Muslims are the major group at the receiving end. For him, the European state has ceased to exist as the rights-guarantor state and has assumed the contours of Third World statism: 'But precisely because it is today impossible to trace the frontier between social right and public right—or, if one prefers, "social citizenship" and "political citizenship"—the final conclusion is that there is no "European" law-governed state. Plagiarising Hegel's famous remark, I will therefore risk saying: *Es gibt keinen (Rechts) staat in Europa* [There is no (legal) state in Europe]' (Balibar 1991, 186).

The discrepancy between public and social rights voids the rights-state. In fact, Europe's practice of racism in the colonies would have been ample justification to label European states as statist of the foulest kind centuries ago. The rights-state never existed to begin with. For Hegel to have reached his definition of the state as the actualisation of ethics, he followed the contradictory path of the development of the spirit in time as it oscillated between in-itself mode (the particular) and for-itself mode (the universal), mediating larger and more inclusive forms of social organisations—ultimately, the citizen as species-being influences the state. So, in the Hegelian order of ascendancy, in the despotic Orient, one was not free but all were free; in the slave age, some were free; and in the Prussian state, one and all were free (Hegel 1899, 2007). To counterpoise the same logic of spiritual/bourgeois democratic development onto the modern Arab state, one may aptly conclude that in such states neither one nor all are free (cultural as in humanity's store of knowledge, not folks and mores). That is quite a retrogression in culture; but if one turns Hegel 'upside down' (that is, as per the oft-quoted point from Marx, by standing him on his feet), one sees that the cause of the retrogression is the destruction of the material basis for the reproduction of Arab working classes by imperialist assault.

Hegel aside, although public and social rights tear loose from each other in Arab states, their development cannot be simply filed under 'statism'. As already noted (it is perhaps the single most important theme of this book) the merchant-commandeered Arab state is excessively pliant to imperialism and serves as its conduit. Arab merchant classes have ruled by decree and mediated national labour in relation to the demands of US-led capital. As it has been a middleman in the economy, US-led capital has been also a middleman in Arab state affairs. When the prospects of radical change dawned as in the recent uprisings, US-led capital either stabilised weakened ruling classes with petrodollars where it desired to do so—as with Gulf funding to Egypt—or it fomented violent internal strife where it wished to see social formations set on a course of self-destruction—as in Yemen, Libya and Syria. Gulf petrodollars in American sovereign funds as part of the US's sovereign paper debt are an endless arsenal for effecting imperial control. As discussed in the previous chapter, control is more important to capital than the money form of wealth. In any case, given the puny income of labour in the AW, even a small sum of petrodollars exchanged on the local markets influences events considerably. Roughly, Arab working classes compose 5 per cent of the world population and earn a meagre 0.3 per cent of world income.

Arab states have come to rarely organise class relations around a social contract between national classes. The social contract is one between the ruling merchant class and international financial capital. Whenever the blindness of resource grab leaves a trifle for the national working class, states forfeit their distributive role to a surrogate civil society. As a result, the social person of society is further split from the public person or citizen of the state. The institutions of imperialistically ordained civil society inculcating the narrowness/uselessness of social personhood, woven through with divisive ideological identities sprung from the fertile soil of unemployment, induced scarcity and poverty, which weigh against revolutionary consciousness. The falsity of being as only private being inflicts upon labour the scourge of self-coercion. Merchants in charge of the state seize assets blindly and counteract the organised dimension of national capital. As merchants are set against industrialists, they undermine the vehicle of their own long-term existence within their national territory. It is at this juncture too that one sees the particular form in which Alavi's remark about the self-defeating ruling class/state realised (Alavi 1972). The organised dimension of capital, its docile side, which furnished it with its outstanding resilience, recedes. The state as rejuvenator of capital retreats. The reduction of state action to the action of one section of labour, namely capital's security apparatus, concurrently narrows the state's capacity in development. As the state's ability to transform society is contracted to the requirements of one uncompromising merchant class, whose reproduction actually occurs in international financial circles, national development falls to the bottom of the national agenda. Moreover, the very act of *not* instituting development policy acts as a policy of antidevelopment. Underdevelopment becomes a self-reinforcing totality in which agents and their policies breed ever worsening conditions.

Statism always negates development, but in the AW the process assumes a meaning of its own. It does so, however, not in terms of the 'politics of regime survival' or their impact on institutional development (Migdal 1998). Civil wars of various intensities or outright neoliberalism disable both regime and state. In 'weak' states, it is said in a rather pragmatic tone, one limit on institutional development is the threat of the concentration of power (Migdal 2001). However, the politics of Arab regime survival give rise to the paradox that state leaders usually cripple their own institutions—the very ones that could have assured them the mobilisation capacity required to dominate and transform their societies. But for the merchant class, it is not its own society that matters; it is the fluctuations of the international market. The rate of AW capital flight as calculated in 2008 at times reached a quarter of GDP in some states (UN 2008a). That functional state agencies should counter domestic and international risks is a banality, but the way in which Arab merchant classes are articulated with global capital requires that only the concerns of the leading capitalist partner (US-led financial capital) are met. Between their welfare and repressive functions, Arab state agencies potentially destabilise the rule of their own ruling classes. These national class and value relations are not overlooked by mistake. The instance the concept of cross-border class alliance enters into the analysis of the mainstream, Arab development failure becomes a shared responsibility between US-led imperialist and their partners in the AW. Moreover, strategies of survival are a misnomer in the case of the AW; there are merely strategies for delaying the expiration date of regime and state. In this case, therefore, theorisation of state survivability and institutional development should emerge from an understanding of the class structure, the imperialistically imposed undervaluation of Third World assets, and the ancillary position of an Arab state, in that order.

The Arab state can be defined neither as a case in which the structure of society has prevented the state from politically mobilising clients, nor by the altered priorities of state leaders or the difficulties in implementing policy caused by allowing civil-society actors to capture the state's extensions (Migdal 2001, 93).

There is a US-led imperialist iron wall asphyxiating Arab states and a daunting balance of powers that moulds class formations into malleable constructs for administrating value usurpation at the behest of US-led empire. The iron wall in this particular case is Vladimir Jabotinsky's wall supported by Israel's massive military arsenal and encircles the AW and most of Africa.[2] Political legitimacy and regime power in the AW are today only nominally national. The vortex of power shaping economic inefficiencies and institutional dysfunctions is that of US-led capital. In retrospect, there was less weakness in the Arab states' delivery of domestic policies when they emerged from colonialism in the 1960s and 1970s. In the 1980s, none of the usual hurdles of a decorative parliamentary democracy existed to block development policies. Yet nearly all the policies delivered since have been antidevelopmental. Even in areas of women's education, the indoctrination of autorepressive obscurantist values in (especially) working-class women and girls has hindered their adequate political representation, which is what really matters for gender equality.

And just as an aside, Arab regime security is, for all intents and purposes, the security of the intelligence and repressive apparatus. But the condition of recurrent defeat and ideological defeatism, brought on by direct military assault or by the threat of it, metamorphosed society into a receptor for the terms of surrender. The hegemony of the state over civil society waned, a crisis of rule ebbed, and the merchant class became the henchman of US-led capital. A state holding onto power by the brittle thread of the *mukhabarat* (police repression), is itself brittle.

Thirty years of US-led capital–dictated neoliberalism and lost wars have reshaped the national class structure and the way social classes control wealth creation. One need not dwell on the issue of oil-revenue redistribution when token concessions to the lower strata intensify working-class divisions by objectifying social identities, as in the phenomenal rise of Wahhabism. The failure of national security and the relegation of the national ruling class to an appendage of global capital coincided with the global trend under financialisation. The steering of value away from the working class has gutted state and regime stability simultaneously. Little of the wealth that state and regime earned from national sources could be recycled in productive capacity nationally; the wealth stability potential was always greater abroad. The ruling classes' relationship to their own states became a onetime profit-making game. In hit-and-run situations, the scramble for grab intensifies the war of each against all.

---

2   In reference to Vladimir Jabotinsky pointing out that Israel needs to keep up military pressures on its surrounding Arab neighbours to remain safe, 'The Iron Wall (We and the Arabs)', 1923. Online: http://www.marxists.de/middleast/ironwall/ironwall.htm (viewed 14 February 2012).

That Arab states exhibit many aspects of statism does not prevent the emergence of a developmental state. But a developmental state requires, firstly, an actual state (not a loosely governed territory), and secondly, state autonomy and state capacity. In the majority of cases in the AW, this combination is a tall order. Even if the Arab state exists in some partly autonomous form, its capacity does not feed on national resources to satisfy national appetites for wealth; the merchant-skewed dimension of capital, as mentioned above, allows the state to undervalue its own working class and, hence, the demand for nationally produced goods. Relative autonomy, however, may characterise developmental states and predatory states alike. Yet, autonomy from US-led capital cannot happen, since the merchant class is integrated with it financially as well as in security arrangements. For the most part, in fact, the political security of client regimes is not solely maintained by its own forces, but also by US military support and bases. Nonautonomous states cannot subsume the interests of their own working classes under state policies. As profits get determined before wages, the role of the state in revenue distribution, including the share retained for reinvestment in the national economy, is determined by the priorities of US-led capital. Revenues recirculated into the national economy serve to build patronage safeguards and rarely move past consumption into productive activity. In the AW, the contradiction between regime stability and poor developmental outcomes intensifies to the demands of US-led capital's strategic influence in the region. Where US-led capital cannot be fully in control, it inflicts structural damage through war, neoliberalism and civil war such that the social formation in question edges further away from the state to loose territory. Stabilisation, or not, follows the course of the hegemon.

Although state expenditures may result in welfare-enhancing developmental outcomes when the state monitors investment policies and disciplines private agents (Khan 1994), the Arab state also cannot fit such a model. When the state as the principal constituent of the organised dimension of capital moderates short-term profits for additional regimentation of labour (stabilisation spending), it follows the diktat of US-led imperialism as there would be an interest of keeping things on hold for a while. But more and more this has not been the case in the AW because, as I said above, there is little national commitment left to organise society at home. A state disciplines the private agent, merchant or trader in positive relation to the power of the working class. Because the working class has been disempowered, few state policies discipline the private agent and channel industrial effort to enhance the productive capabilities of society. More of the wealth as a share of value in real and money form, as evidenced by declining subsistence standards (in relation to a historically determined minimum), flows up or out.

The Arab state in its command aspect engenders malformed intermediation between state investment and rising capital output ratios. They invest in non-productive activity. Arab regimes are far less reliant on internal components of developmental security, including the role of security-sensitive sectors such as industry and agriculture in the national economy, because the state draws its revenues from the export of primary products (or is stabilised by geopolitical rents as in the case of Jordan and Lebanon). Political and economic forms of control are combined within the purview of the same ruling class. The point is that stabilisation spending delivers mostly stabilisation—no more, no less.

In times of immediate postindependence autonomy (the 1960s to the late 1970s), state dirigisme, high public investment rates and more egalitarian redistribution characterised all Arab states. A particular set of Arab states followed the path of 'Arab socialism'—that is, nationalised industry and agrarian reform in Egypt, Iraq, Algeria, Libya and Syria—which resulted in significant welfare gains. Two principal military defeats in wars with Israel (June 1967 and October 1973), several open and implicit aggressions against Arab countries, and the 1979 Camp David Accords by which Egypt joined the US constellation, gravely weakened Arab national and joint security. Half-hearted Arab socialist egalitarian processes, initiated from the top down, excluded the working class from participating actively in defending their gains. Under Arab socialism, authoritarian labour-process regimentation remained in place. In due course and under neoliberalism, many of the passed-down working-class benefits were lost to the old ruling classes or their reconstituted variants. At later stages, the Arab ruling class intensified coercion in the labour process and began to gradually reverse the socialisation of assets. Ever since, labour faced the daunting task of combating a local ruling class backed by the powers of US-led imperialism.

Under neoliberalism, welfare reforms, where they existed, have been a sham. Already, Arab states are signatories to nearly all the covenants on economic and social rights: Arab regimes would probably ratify any treaty on human rights. However, it made little difference to the rights of women that the Bremer-designed Iraqi parliament has a quota for women; nor did Lebanon's authorising civil marriage quell sectarianism. Arab social formations are subjugated and non-sovereign class structures. In them, internal industrialisation flounders, the labour force is socialised (private labour is turned into social labour by dispossession) without being engaged in social production, and petrodollars bolster consumption and identity-based divisiveness. Clearly, developing broad alliances in anti-imperialist confrontation may redress the shortfall in sovereignty. However, universal socialist ideological retrogression compounds the difficulties of working-class struggle: without the unifying objective of radical social transformation under working-class rule, workers' struggles tend to remain sectional and culminate either in defeat or in a temporary and often divisive gain. Wagering on imperial powers' contradictions to float the secular democratic forces is also a bad bet in view of the feebleness of the global democratic Left. Labour's success hinges on an elusive internationalism.

In the monarchic Arab states—the Gulf, Morocco and Jordan—regime stability is ordained by the extension of Western security arrangements and the not-so-hidden fact that the monarchs practically own national resources and manage redistribution solely for the purpose of stabilisation. Where there were departures from monarchism, in states such as in Syria, Iraq and Egypt, a weakened national bourgeoisie failed to govern in the immediate postindependence period. In these conditions, the state under Arab socialism acted as a surrogate bourgeoisie in handling capital's private appropriation measures. The state rose as the owner of the principal means of production and appropriator of the surplus. The private sector shrank but still absorbed a significant chunk of the labour force in artisanal and petty farming undertakings. State ownership existed side by side with a constrained private sector. In hindsight, it was inevitable that private sector expansion would recommence when the political climate ripened for 'free market' policies and openness—as happened since the early 1980s.

The key stratum that initiated the conversion from colonial to the postcolonial non-monarchical states, however, was alliance between the military and professionals that commandeered the state apparatus. This state bourgeois class owned the means of production not as individual stakes as the bourgeoisie does, but collectively via the state. The state bourgeois class consisted of party bosses, the upper level of the state bureaucracy, the senior management of economic enterprises, and the top ranks of the military and police forces. This class is what Petras (1976, 439) calls the 'intermediate strata'. Petras defined the intermediate strata as a class-conscious and independent social stratum, distinct both from workers and from traditional landowners, that is horizontally and vertically linked to the salaried middle class. This class has its own political and economic projects, and initially aimed at the fulfilment of egalitarian ends. In its early stages of development, it was anti-imperialist and favoured agrarian reforms that tallied with the aspirations of the peasants and the less property-endowed working class. As ideological and military defeats gripped Arab society, this class underwent a *volte-face*. It promoted free markets under the shadow of state enterprises. At the intersection where state-led development was transmuted into privately led development (the beginning of the neoliberal phase, circa 1980), there was an avalanche of private and state propaganda peddling the soundness of US-like pragmatism as opposed to banality of old-style revolutionary struggle. Pragmatism, the name given by

Charles Peirce to his neopositivist philosophy, became the ideological veneer for submissiveness to imperialist diktat. Behind a surface of calculated risks lurked the subtle politics of a state-restrained bourgeois class itching to grow into the wider financial dollar space. Defeat generated defeatism that served as an alibi for the national bourgeoisie to converge with its international counterpart. Being pragmatic when the alternative of resistance is written off by the ideological vortex of imperialism, means that there is no limit to how much of national assets could be pawned.

As the name implies, a bourgeois class, whether state or private, will maintain a capitalist-defined labour process—the wage system. The degree of egalitarian redistribution was proportional to internal and external power balances and the momentum of populist cant, as in socialist pan-Arabism. However, as the blitzkriegs of US-led imperialism and Israel dealt their blows to these states and the contradiction of working-class underconsumption vs. state capitalist–class conspicuous consumption intensified, the state bourgeois class raised the dosages of repression, thus laying bare the falseness of its populism (Petras 1976). Gulf petrodollars earned by Egyptian and Syrian professionals working in the Gulf propped up the behavioural patterns of consumerism. Wahhabism mixed with oil paid an engineer nearly a hundred fold what socialism's mixed nationalised industry did. In Arab socialist, protected and industrialising economies, much more could be bought on the black market with American dollars than with national currency. Petrodollar spending on luxury goods in these semisocialised economies erected a model of easy earning without effort that many sought to emulate. Under the twin imperatives of defeat and its own capitalistic proclivities, the state bourgeois class transformed itself into a full-fledged private bourgeois class. To justify the ideological transition, the state bourgeois class flaunted the inefficacies of state-supported markets, war fatigue and the futility of anti-imperialist struggle.

The 'Arab socialist' states, as noted, continued to exploit labour via the wage system (Petras 1976, 442). However, USSR-style industrialisation and rising productivity meant that there was more wealth being produced as compared to the colonial era. This additional income was more equally distributed and living standards improved when compared to the neoliberal era (WB 2005; Bush 2002). Moneyed and non-moneyed resources that had been transferred to the colonialists earlier were recirculated in national production. Industrialisation drove up the rate of exploitation, but there were higher wages and reinvestment in the social infrastructure.

This period also saw the introduction of radical social reforms (Amin 1978, Abdel-Malek 1971). While the Arab socialist experience partially reversed the postcolonial debacle, its relative success piggybacked on security relationships with the Soviet Union. However, it is worth noting that fundamental transformations to the mode of production occurred nowhere under Arab socialism. Fundamental transformations require not only changes to forms of ownership, but also a cultural and civilizational transformation whereby ideally social responsibility for social property is manifested in social behaviour. Comparing improvement in living standards under Arab socialism against some utopian condition is to assume that there is an ideal social state that would immediately ensue from socialisation. Insofar, as free health, education, national financing of agriculture and land reforms were concerned, Arab socialist reforms have had a lasting positive impact (Al-Hamsh 2004, 93).

The Class Content of States

By the mid-twentieth century, colonial constraints imposed upon Arab states thwarted the emergence of an effective national industrial class. The puny industrial class that did form could not have assumed the responsibility of leading the debilitated Arab economies through immediate postcolonial transitions. Because this colonially reared class was so short on real and financial resources, the role normally played by the bourgeois class had to be passed to the state. The state bourgeois class, as noted, introduced progressive social transformations (Turner 1984, 61–2; Petras 1976, 440). However, non-military and military aggression on the AW in successive wars incapacitated the state and its ruling class in all its variants. The fanning of war flames around the Arab–Israeli conflict and the strategic role of oil rose to the top of world capital's agenda. The dangers of war, especially in relation to the Arab–Israeli conflict, afforded the Arab bourgeois classes with an alibi to repress national opposition under the pretext of safeguarding national security. As of the 1980s, growing merchant capital heightened this repression to satisfy US-led capital's hegemonic conquests. As the sources of wealth shifted away from national production to co-opting oil and geopolitical revenues into merchant activity, the Arab ruling class came to espouse the objectives of US-led capital. The balance of forces would no longer affect states as somewhat cohesive social entities, but more the particular working classes within states. In the two decades that followed the Second World War, more than half the population were farmers and the industrial working class remained relatively small (Turner 1984, 54). The colonialist-bred bourgeois class diverted investment to commercial endeavours. Under colonialism, the circuit of capital began in money and returned to money without engaging local industry in significant value-added activity. Colonialists, in fact, had groomed a merchant class that circulates money rather than an industrial class that converts money into physical capital in complex production processes.

Profits accruing from commerce alone are effectively a snatching of wealth from of the rest of society to merchants.

In the immediate postindependence period, private entrepreneurial skill remained directed towards trade rather than industry (Turner 1984, 53). The weakness of entrepreneurship stemmed from the fact that the merchants and small retailers comprised a large proportion of the bourgeois class (Berger 1958). It may be that few states anywhere in the developing world (especially in Africa) significantly overcame colonial sediment or the absence of an industrial class. Yet, adding insult to injury, the AW, like sub-Saharan Africa, never escaped the far-reaching hand of colonialism after independence.

While the scope and form of state intervention in economic and social activities varied from one country to another, the trend of the postindependence years towards more public investment was pervasive throughout the AW. The Arab states acted as engines of growth and undertook the task of economic transformation for these economies (Anderson 1987, 11). For instance, aggregate planned investment in eighteen Arab states totalled a substantial $326 billion during 1975–80, or nearly 30 per cent of GDP (Ayubi 1995, 292). The state-owned manufacturing enterprises (excluding the Gulf) accounted for more than 50 per cent of value added in manufacturing. Egypt's state-owned enterprises accounted for about 60 per cent of value added in manufacturing, and Syria's accounted about 55 per cent. The output of these public enterprises recorded an average of 13 per cent of GDP in Egypt and 11 per cent of GDP in Syria (Richards 1990, 192). Land reform resulted in increasing agricultural productivity and slowed the flood of urban migration. With extensive social investment taking place, this era in retrospect was a golden age of development relative to the subsequent neoliberal retrogression in practically all Arab countries. Even leaving aside the recent lag, the rate at which standards of living rose under Arab socialism is said to have been unmatched in more recent experience (Richards 1990, 187, 255 and 416). It really is difficult to prove otherwise, given the quantitative indicators on record.

The private sector, in the initial stages of postcolonial reconstruction, could not have carried out the more egalitarian redistribution needed to align the national forces into a defensive anti-imperialist position. The private sector was engrossed in crisis, its reputation was tarnished by the stigma of a shifty national allegiance, and its central structural weakness, which is its lack of capacity to tap into the substantial resources needed for development, was starkly revealed. Apart from all that, the decisive moment that charted the course of development lay not only in superficial squabbles between party bosses and merchants, but more so in imperialist pressures, foremost the ethnic cleansing of Palestine and the construction of Israel as the colonial settler state. These were kept up in order to drain the capacities of newly liberated or noncompliant Arab states (Abdel-Malek 1971). Under these warlike conditions, unless the state had intervened equitably, it was unlikely that any significant additions to capital stock and technology would have ensued. It is an intractable task to dissociate internal (national) class forces from the forces of international capital in shaping Arab developmental processes—unless of course, everything is 'analysed' to oblivion. At no point in time did the imperialist funding or the weapons stop pouring in to stabilise or destabilise social formations. The latest example of course would be the US's continued channelling of funds to influence events in Egypt during the 2011 uprising. The more the national capitalist class becomes alienated from its national production base and working class, the closer it will gravitate towards the sphere in which its dollarised wealth reproduction occurs. The values of nationalism serve to propel the trajectory of capital only when capital originates or is reproduced through a capitalist social class by nationally retained resources and production. A merchant bourgeoisie, enfeebled by the prospect of state collapse, is socially predisposed to entwine itself with its transnational counterpart.

From its very birth, the nation-state was a constituent of capital's social organisation and assigned a welfare task: the function of reproducing, by coercive and ideological means, a malleable and acquiescent working class. The state became the mediation of the dominant class in the political process. But in militarily weakened or Arab states that are robbed of their resources, social divisions have yawned wide as a result of missing revolutionary labour institutions and the imperialist repression exerted in order to ideologically fragment the social formation. As the state and resources available to labour shrink, the larger the imperialistically funded civil society grows. Here once more, the private person of civil society also exceeds the public person or citizen whose realisation in the state is political emancipation (Marx 1843). Disarticulation on the level of consciousness situates consciousness at odds with the dire conditions of life. This spiritual disconnect is forced upon a poverty-stricken population by a barrage of ideological delusion. With undependable labour organisations, many workers who would stand to benefit from solidarity adopted reconstructed identities paid for by tainted petrodollars (Ali 2002). Even where ballot-box elections were held in the wake of the 2011 uprisings, Islamic parties won in Egypt and Tunisia. The eclipsed citizen voted in a state that is itself eclipsed by imperialistically funded civil society. What remains of these states after the engineered divisions enshrined in rights violating constitutions is the fragmented identity of the working class. In these elections, there was not an individual voting for an individual, there were organisations representing sectarian, tribal, regional orientations and/or ethnicities that picked up the votes of their members. Not surprisingly, these sectional institutions have largely taken over the welfare function that reproduces the working class. Personal livelihood depended on allegiance to sect, regional grouping or ethnic identity. As elsewhere, the crisis of socialist ideology has created a vacuum that reinforces disintegration.

The merchant-capital state of neoliberal years regimented labour and organised the dependent mode of integration with US-led capital. It is not only that the import share of the GDP that was rising; the key sectors of security provision such as food became more import dependent. But the buying and selling of imported goods does not by itself define AW merchant activity. In the condition of uncertainty, real-estate investment in affluent construction that does not redress the housing shortages for the working class became a principal investment activity. Investment in speculative returns on real estate, the service sector and financial speculation is also mercantile in nature. The initial sums invested do not generate much productive activity around them. As in colonial days, money returns back into money, M-M' without deepening production activity or raising productivity. Hence commercial transactions also defined the nature of what should constitute 'industrial' activity of national bourgeoisies as in the rising speculation on the low productivity capital of the real estate sector.

At this stage in the development of Arab states, the national decision making process can be tipped one way or another by the intervention of US-led imperialism. As in the days of colonialism, foreign forces broker national political differences. Cleverly enough, this quasi-colonised state appears independent and without a preponderance of foreign soldiers on national territory. In contrast to the ideal of the state, however, this newly recolonised formation is now a territorial arrangement impersonating a state. Yet in such a territory devoid of self-emanating sovereignty, the idea of reason within the state itself, because in certain features it resonates rights, has once more come under assault. A weakened working class need not enjoy a state with rights but also the embryo of ideas within the state that may resurrect the idea of rights in the future. A similar process occurred in Europe when the crisis of the industrial bourgeoisie required a diminution of the ideas of justice and equality within the bourgeois state. In addressing this attack on the vaguely trailing notions of reason and right within the state a century and half ago, Marx notes the following.

Reason has always existed, but not always in a reasonable form. The critic can therefore start out from any form of theoretical and practical consciousness and from the forms peculiar to existing reality develop the true reality as its obligation and its final goal. As far as real life is concerned, it is precisely the political state—in all its modern forms— which, even where it is not yet consciously imbued with socialist demands, contains the demands of reason. And the political state does not stop there. Everywhere it assumes that reason has been realised. But precisely because of that it everywhere becomes involved in the contradiction between its ideal function and its real prerequisites. (Marx 1843)

The concerted ideological assault on the working classes must include the extirpation of the notion of the *reasonableness* of the state. The state itself now must be rendered redundant. Its mediatory role and responsibility to govern are ideas that may pull together shredded Arab societies. Capital is no longer pursuing the dismantling of socialist states; that was already dismantled. It is even assaulting the state as reason and as an idea, period. Anything to do with reason and the pluralism of the state, its ideal function, is confronting US-led capital.

Before Western colonialism, the forms of political organisation in Arab territory were not deemed 'states' by European standards. According to dominant Eurocentrism, the persons residing in these territories were without their own political history. The fantasy narrative mimicking history then goes on to say that these peoples accepted the generosity of Western colonialism when they were given states. However, whatever name it was given—state, province or Bantustan—as a form of social organisation, the recent Arab state became the nemesis of the Arab working classes. To date, the physical geography of these states did not shift, but their human geography did. They became in some territories the means to effectively annul the working classes as historical agents. But no matter how disastrous these states as forms of social organisation are, it is the *idea* of a state, the reasonable entity that entails political representation that requires demolition. The former Western colonialist regrets the instilling of any form of social organisation in the progeny of 'barbarians'. In fractured states such as Yemen, Iraq, Syria, Somalia, Sudan and Libya, shorter life expectancy, higher child malnutrition and illiteracy abound: 50 million adults, one-sixth of the total population, are counted as illiterates in the AW, but the number could be twice as much this (UNESCO 2012; Mayen 2012). Where there is no war posing an existential threat to the population, the social conditions bred by neoliberalism posed it instead. The existential threats to precolonial populations from a century or so ago, which led to the obliteration of whole native populations in the Americas and Australia, are really as close as they could be to current conditions in Syria and Iraq.

The analytical notion that it is worse to escape exploitation by capitalism than to be exploited by it omits the fact that under global capitalism nothing lies beyond the reach of capital. This notion forfeits the concreteness of colonial history and postcolonial military intervention altogether. Value as a qualitative category is created by the totality of the material available to capital. The dislocated millions in the AW are part of the material of capital. The real and ideological pressures that have pauperised and politically disempowered Arab workers lessen the costs of production in relation to massive unemployment and, more importantly, raise the share of financiers via the power exercised by US-led capital over the Arab region. The pauperisation of Arab workers by war and indirect colonisation resitutes the balance of forces upon which the money form and its associated financial system present themselves as symbols of power. Imperialist power progressively disengages more of the social material in the AW (and much of Africa too) for resource grab. It also appoints itself as a proxy sovereign in Arab states in order to reproduce the terms of trade and price ratios in its favour. The apparent paradox that the cost of imperialist wars exceeds the returns from the colonies in moneyed terms occurs because exchange prices are not set by benign market conditions, but by the fact that a powerless Third World cannot negotiate the price at which it valorises its assets. Wars of recolonisation by fracturing states create the disastrous social conditions that restructure values for global production by the degree of destructiveness wrought upon some corners of the Third World.

The encroachment–accumulation nexus represented the leverage that redresses the market crisis. But development is not only uneven, it is also organically tied together (Mészáros 1995). This means that the rate at which capital metabolises humanity and nature will also rise in inverse proportion to the depth of the crisis. Under the steady revolutionary decline, many more countries may be poised to undergo a transition to a state that is merely the social organisation of militias with the addition of American drones or military bases. Iran, by submitting to desovereignising treaties or by bombardment, is one possible target, which would expand the street-side bomb corridor (car bombs mark Lebanon, Syria and Iraq) from the Fertile Crescent to Afghanistan.

In Western formations where the spoils of colonial plunder bred a nationality bereft of humanist solidarity, capital continues to pollute the cultural discourse with the fetish of nationalism as an eternal social category. Whereas an imam may incantate divisive dogma along the sectarian fault lines using financial wherewithal provided by the Gulf, in Europe the mode of splintering people has become a sophistry to which even philosophers succumb. For instance, in the discussion between Andreas Baader and Jean Paul Sartre, the latter goes so far as to exclude violent forms of struggle from the means of action of working classes in the centre:

> SARTRE: These actions might be justified for Brazil, but not for Germany.
> BAADER: Why?
> SARTRE: In Brazil independent actions were needed to change the situation. They were necessary preparatory work.
> BAADER: Why is it any different here?
> SARTRE: Here there isn't the same type of proletariat as in Brazil (Bohr 2013)

Sartre is here reinforcing the perception that differences between central and peripheral working classes require the former to relinquish certain forms of violent struggle. There is no doubt that different conditions require different forms of struggle, but no form of struggle should be excluded, foremost is violence because it is the twin of capital everywhere. Sartre is implying an essential or permanent difference between central and peripheral proletariats, not making a tactical argument based on current conditions. This distinction requires one to believe that the disciplining of European labour by central capital could have happened without the historical surplus grabbed from the periphery. Capitalist history abounds with violence everywhere and the fact that there is not an infantile Left engaged in organised violence in the present epoch is a mere symptom of European Left complicity. The path of armed struggle is neither an expression of some individual will nor is it merely the result of a committee's administrative decision, but 'armed struggle reflects the nature of the conflict, which is determined by the nature of the enemy' (Habash 1998). A violent enemy necessitates a violent response. Sartre's position tacitly assumes that there can be central capital that grew peacefully and outside colonial relationships, and therefore that central-nation classes exist in isolation and outside value relationships with the Third World. Moreover, under the financialisation phase of imperialism, capital converges globally, and the development of working-class consciousness evolves toward the realisation that the struggle against capital occurs in transnationally. If working-class alliances can develop in a context that prioritises anti-imperialist struggle, and to the extent that central working classes distance themselves from capital, they will begin to steer clear of the domination of one working class by another. That said: in the current state of socialist ideological defeat, conditions for sound internationalist class alliances are more remote than in the times of Sartre. Armed resistance, be it effective or not, when it exists, becomes an indication of the shifts in the revolutionary tide.

Closing Comment

Be it statist, overdeveloped, weak or whatever other form a state takes, it holds power. The state is a principal agent of development to the extent that labouring classes exercise their political rights. It is the one social institution that is capable of influencing the pattern of employment, the production and distribution of goods and services, and the distribution of income and assets at the level of society as a whole. The state, as a sovereign entity, can situate the demands of labouring classes in a political programme and throttle the avarice of profiteers, raise sufficient funds for social investment, and ensure equality of condition prior to equality of opportunity. Equality of condition is a struggle-wrought working-class right. It is about guaranteeing the basic needs of individuals. The state can coordinate economic activity in pursuit of distributive ends irrespective of the formal mechanisms of its involvement in the economy. The state under the struggle-won obligation to establish equality of condition can choose the optimal form of control over property, either through state ownership of specific assets or through redistributing the end products of society (progressive taxation). The state guarantees access to essential material needs such as basic food, housing, health, education and water. An autonomous Arab state can underwrite its own credit expansion, which in turn may mobilise real resources.

These measures were partially carried out under Arab socialism, and their associated state debts were comparatively negligible (WDI, various years). Real development cannot come from oil revenue redistribution in the form of *sadaqa* (Arabic for charity). In the warped social context of neoliberalism, not a single cent of all those petrodollars engenders development. So far, under the merchant mode of organising social life, petrodollars have generated only human and environmental waste. The grotesque separation of the sexes as exercised in Saudi Arabia cannot be development no matter how many glossy high-rises mask the landscape. Economic and social policies that engage the dynamic deployment of resources also rejuvenate the social transformations. Development is after all a civilizational project (Abdel-Malek 1997; Frank 1998).

The reigning cross-border alliance between US-led imperialism and Arab merchant capital is by no means *force majeure*, but it is a major force to deal with. It infiltrates the real and ideological structure of all social relationships. It cripples the effectiveness of working-class struggle and the success of social reforms. Conversely, counter-reforms raise the share of capital, strengthen its means of control and foreshorten working-class people's perspective to immediate survival concerns. Given the puny power of Arab labour, the 'pro-poor' framework introduced by IMF/WB poverty programmes actually raised poverty levels. The neoliberals assumed a fantasy market devoid of power relations and contradictions, in which poverty results from social exclusion or the disengagement of individuals from market processes. But markets are a subset of social relations, which reflect the distorted balance of power between social classes. Market-driven growth cannot be inclusive in the best of circumstances because merchant patrons inherently dispose of resources to upkeep profit rates. Moreover, Arab industrial markets shrank under the neoliberal package and are now incapable of integrating those who were socially disengaged on the advice of the IMF/WB consortium. *This was not a mistake.* Capital accumulation is firstly a social process and only secondly a money accounting framework. In integrated markets, the social means of control of labour, of which unemployment and lower wages are necessary parts, grow harsher with the demands of global capital. These demands include the determination of both market buying power and market costs by making sections of the working classes powerless and abject. Circularly, the fulfilment of these demands lowers costs and reproduces ever more lopsided power relations. The market may act as an engine of growth and poverty reduction in some corners, but it must dislocate in others. In the AW, the process of eroding the state as a power platform that could integrate the working classes cheapens humans and nature as capital inputs. Poverty in the AW results from its war-and-oil subordinate mode of integration into global social and economic reproduction. Unless the Arab state is reconstituted with significant labour representation, value-entrapping mechanisms and radical redistribution, the poverty trap will persist, at the very least because there are too many idle people needing work in too little industry.

Chapter Five

WARS AND OIL CONTROL

Wars are an integral part of the global economy. They reshape the social conditions that produce value, and they uphold the power of the social class that relies on the war economy for reproducing itself. Wars galvanise military technology and civilian spin-offs with public funds, which maintains the US-led capitalist class advantage in technological edge and intellectual property patents. Financially, funding for wars expands US indebtedness in the dollar. US-led wars enlarge the dollarised money supply that has in turn to be underwritten by further military expansion and hegemony over strategic resources, principally oil. In the financial age, the growth of moneyed debt spent on wars also requires higher tax levies and lower social spending on the central working classes: hence the now all-too-familiar austerity. Save the cultural otherness promoted via the war on terror, US-led wars reproduce the social relations by which Arab assets are devalued, including human assets. These wars not only subjugate the occupied or aggressed nations in the Third World; more importantly, they elevate US-led power and classes vis-à-vis other nationalist or advanced capital circles.

Ultimately, wars, as the aggressive facet of capital, generate a most desirable outcome for the bourgeoisie: they commodify human lives. As will be seen in Chapter Eight, where technology and market forces have disengaged billions of working people (recalling that at least 1.1 billion are unemployed by ILO poverty induced standards) the commodification of life or the merging of working people and their labour power implies that by dispensing with some of the working people by means of wars, capital demonstrates the worthlessness of the labour. Unlike the Malthusian model, where welfare measures enacted to help the lower strata later cause the famine that reduces swelling 'surplus' populations so that wages can rise again, in the late twentieth century the surplus of labour power is so huge that by expending human lives, capital destroys unnecessary labour and cheapens already engaged labour. War demonstrates labour's (apparent) irrelevance and justifies its low returns on the basis of its lack of scarcity. Under capitalism, there is no peace, there are different degrees of war. War as a social process restructures power relations and social institutions with the aim (as always) of getting the most wealth for the least costly inputs. It erects the real or symbolic forms of power that grind down the working class. The Arab world is a war 'hot zone' and the incipient ground for the so-called war on terror. It consumes vast quantities of ordnance produced and sold by central countries and foments the conditions for war elsewhere. Combined with the power emanating from oil control, the internalisation of regional conflicts into the core of the world market has long contributed to imperial wealth creation.

Wars in the AW are an integral social process of the world economy, a process with which capital comfortably cohabits. Accumulation on a world scale without wars would lack an essential component, which is the coercive reduction of Third World power and value. For capital to move away from war-making as such would result in a negative shock to the world economy after an indeterminate lag. At least the cheaper inputs would cease to be cheap. But also, somewhat in the way that economies grow from higher rates of raw-material utilisation, the intensity of war itself is foundational to the growth of imperialist riches. Unlike raw-material consumption, however, which immediately raises production, social dislocation revalorises inputs in production after certain lags in time. World capital, in short, has taken on war as part of its reproduction, and income levels are partly determined by this embedded relationship. Not that there ever was a world built around an expanding peace industry disciplining the blind competitive forces of capital: wars of dislocation create the material of capital—that is, the terrorised labour and cheapened raw materials that raise rates of profit.

Like war, oil control is fundamental to capital. Capital as a social relation is inherently a relationship of regimentation, control and hegemony, in which oil control (that is, energy control) figures prominently. Oil control matters much more than just the money earned from the sale of oil grabbed from the poorer Arab countries. What is at stake is not solely the power of the US over smaller nations (in general). Oil control is crucial to maintaining the leading power position of US-led capital within the imperialist centre. In more advanced (developed) financial circles, the conveyor belts channelling the money form of value to US-led capital are significant. The income of the OECD nations is around seventy per cent of global income, and nearly all global financial transactions occur in their designated money space (WDI 2010).

War in the AW may appear to have indigenous causes arising from the tragic farce of resurrected long-dormant Arab sect/clan identity as the sole political form of working-class representation, but in actuality the courses of wars are charted by historical agents at the helm of capitalist development manoeuvring to promote war for its own sake and for oil control. The historical agents are the mediation of US-led class power in impersonal and objective social forms such as the Security Council and the Breton Woods institutions. There is almost no resemblance between the types of political Islam practiced today and past historical forms of Islamic politics. In point of fact, modern-day political Islam shares more in common in its central banks/monetary policy with central conservative parties than it does with the central banks of the caliphs, had they existed!

At any rate, the idea that capitalism expands simply by enlarging the market for commodities implies that crises could be remedied by an appropriate global fiscal policy. This might be so under a social plan in which both quarterly profits and consumerism are regulated and circumscribed, but not in a production system segmented by power structures and organised by an accumulation process that is blind to its own social and environmental consequences. The voracity of capital accumulation continuously shifts forms of 'primitive accumulation' to the developing world, where the acquisitions of cheapened sources of raw material and non-moneyed constituents that go into the formation of value provide the extra margin of profit. It offers capital grabbed and undervalued resources that Eurocentrics consider an entitlement by virtue of Western civilisational and technological advance. Reified nationalism and 'nationally' developed technological advance lend capital, the indivisible global social relationship, a false air of divisibility as it manifests itself in the concrete forms of commodities. The socially constructed international division of labour, its manifestation as a fetish in the national order, divides humanity itself (Verret 1999).

However, capital in the financialisation age, more so than in the monopoly age, steadies its progress by aggressive encroachment, including military aggression, rather than by the simple realisation of commodities in expanding markets. Financial institutions wed themselves closely to the state and militarism, as in the monopoly age, becomes not only in itself a province of accumulation, but also serves through encroachment and dispossession to offset the inherent crisis of accumulation (Luxemburg [1913] 1973). Lenin ([1916] 1966) further emphasised that militarism represented a decisive moment in an accumulation process under imperialism and the principal means by which capital overcomes its crisis.

In this chapter, I explore the war issue in relation to development in the AW and its consequences—abjection and de-development. These outcomes constitute a totality, in which all the moments tell of unspeakable social conditions. From the totality, mainstream literature selects aspects of underdevelopment to obscure the kernel of the process—that is, development dictated by imperialist assault. For instance, the UNDP Arab Human Development Report of 2002 selected three areas of shortfall in the actually unitary condition of underdevelopment—gender, democracy and knowledge—which it called 'deficits'. Later, US-led imperialism, in its attack on Iraq, employed these notions in a racist ideological campaign against Arab working classes under the pretext of their cultural inferiority, making light of the killing of hundreds of thousands (Fergani 2004).

Underdevelopment is overdetermined, and all aspects of existence explain it. Housing, food, employment, environment and all else needed to support a decent existence were deteriorating. The point is to search for the universal (general) social relationship that motivates underdevelopment, which is, as this book argues, the social agency of US-led imperialism. The UNDP strand of Arab capital–funded literature is not only lacking on methodological grounds; it falsifies Arab-world reality by reducing it to few selected cultural images in order to justify wars of aggression. This literature does not mention the class-subordinated alliance of Arab merchant capital with US-led capital and their security arrangements. The real 'Arab deficit' is the waning of the real and ideological power of Arab working classes in opposing imperialist aggression. This chapter investigates the relationship of imperialist wars of aggression to development.

Wars in the Arab World

Since the second half of the twentieth century, the AW has experienced the highest frequency of conflicts globally (SIPRI, various years). It has witnessed numerous wars, civil wars and security threats. The Arab–Israeli conflict, the Gulf wars, intrastate conflicts and civil wars—such as the Lebanese, Syrian, Iraqi, Algerian and Yemeni civil wars, not to mention the disasters of Somalia and Sudan—characterise Arab-world historical process over the last three decades. The impact of these wars has been devastating. Following Iraq's war with Kuwait, the US-led military campaign shattered most of Iraq's economic infrastructure within six weeks (Parker 2007). The sanctions that followed caused the deaths of around one and a half million people, including around five hundred thousand children. The sources for these figures vary; according to Juan Cole, Iraq lost 4 per cent of its population, but the point here is not to play the numbers game (Cole 2013). Two-thirds of Iraq's GDP was lost during this period (Alnasrawi 2001, 214). The occupation and ethnic cleansing of Palestine planted a colonial-settler society armed and backed by European colonialists in the heart of the AW, which to date has been a source of bellicosity and underdevelopment for much of the Third World (Chomsky 1989; Petras 2008). As to the condition of the remaining Palestinians in the occupied territory, 'their poverty had risen substantially, leaving more than 60 per cent of the population below the poverty line of US$2.3 per person a day' (UNCTAD 2006, 6). More than 59 per cent of the total population of Gaza depends on food aid from the United Nations (Roy 2006).

The Lebanese civil war (1975–90) caused around one hundred and fifty thousand deaths. Loss of human life was accompanied by the destruction of capital and infrastructure and the dislocation of a more than a million people. The lost output due to the war was around twelve times the value of Lebanese GDP in 1974 (Eken et al. 1995, 4–5). More recently, the (currently lulled but ongoing) Sudanese civil war and the Somali, Libyan, Iraqi and Syrian civil wars are also appalling manmade calamities. Apart from the longstanding Palestinian refugee situation, the United Nations High Commissioner for Refugees estimated that more than 1.2 million Iraqi refugees have sought asylum in Syria, Jordan, Egypt, Lebanon and the GCC countries. The area is swarming with refugees. Recent estimates of Syrian refugees surpass 1.5 million.[1] In short, it is one big disaster.

Through ideological channels, reasons of propinquity or geopolitical positioning, the impact of war and security threats engulfs the whole region. When regime military stabilisation spending are included in the resources devoted to internal and external security spending, the rates of militarisation are actually far above the reported rates, which are nearly twice the world rate (WDI various years). The Middle East is home to some of the world's most militarised states, with high proportions of armed forces to total population (Tilly 1991; BICC 2012).

As already discussed, military conflicts in the AW reduce the capacity of the social formation to reproduce the working population in relation to the historically determined level of subsistence. Displacement, educational and health degeneration, decrease in income, destruction of capital and productive capacities of the economy, disruption of patterns of economic production, and capital and resource flights undercut the capacity of the social formation to provide for improvements in living standards. Another aside about the historically determined level of subsistence: the notion of Arabs as noble savages or primitive tent dwellers derived from the central-nation TV image of traditional desert nomads does not constitute a criterion for the minimum standard of subsistence. The standard of living itself moves up globally with the progress and wealth produced under capitalism. It is the ideologically inculcated image that assumes that 'noble savages' inhabiting tents should be satisfied with minimum caloric intake, which is too preposterous to be debated. To illustrate, unlike past days, prior to 1980, many Arab cities, particularly Baghdad, Damascus and Beirut, experience long hours of water and electricity shortages when these are currently essential for human development.

---

1   United Nations High Commissioner for Refugees, 'Number of Syrian Refugees Tops 1.5 Million Mark with Many More Expected', UNHCR.org, 17 May 2013. Online: http://www.unhcr.org/519600a59.html (accessed viewed 5 September 2013).

One need not dwell on the impact of de-electrification or these actual physical constraints on the development of revolutionary consciousness.

Conflicts in the AW structurally shift developmental progress onto a lower path. Their consequences persist after conflicts taper down, although none of the conflicts really abated. Mainstream social science does not highlight the importance of the structural value shifts in favour of US-led capital resulting from wars (Collier et al. 2003; Imai 2000; WESS 2008); instead, the impacts of wars in the region, magnified by the perpetual terrorism scare, are accentuated to demonise the whole of the Arab working classes.

The length and high frequency of conflicts also leave little room to investigate whether pauperisation by conflicts presupposes the next war. Unlike Japan, Germany, South Korea and other countries where conflict followed by aid and financing from the centre propelled their economies into more technologically advanced entities, in the AW there is little time between conflicts to rebuild or to stem interests opposed to rebuilding (Koubi 2005). Poor development in this context exhibits a reflex-like relationship with the high rate of conflicts (Humphreys 2003). Poverty, economic decline and economic shocks may or may not trigger internal conflicts, depending on the hold of ruling classes on state power (Lenin 1902; Gramsci 1975; Skocpol 1979, 79–80). It is not inequality or dependence on primary commodities that spark conflicts, for these conditions always exist. The degree of control by the ruling class determines the moment of conflict eruption because in poverty-stricken developing formations, the conditions for violence are omnipresent and are not attenuated by bourgeois institutions. In old-school colonial fashion, destabilisation and jostling to acquire greater influence within the Arab national class structure are important to US-led capital. In the AW, as will be obvious given the facts presented, it is impertinent to dissociate inequality from conflict. However, it is not the functional nature of institutions in charge of managing these inequalities that mitigates conflict (as in Cramer 2003, for instance), because it is unlikely that the conflicts can be mitigated no matter how effective national institutions are. The imperialist assault and the balance of forces favour the imperialist so much, such that it is pointless to discuss this point in the present epoch (more on this in chapter 7). The proposition that there are institutions to allay inequality overlooks the premise that war of aggression qua colonialism is a politico-economic relationship aimed at recomposing classes and their attendant institutional and value relations. It also overly mimics the English accumulation model in its applicability to the Third World. Capitalism as progress or as the re-engagement of socialised labour in social wage activity is not a necessary outcome when crises of overproduction prevail. The world is not the English countryside of primitive accumulation centuries ago. In non-sovereign Arab states, there *are* no mitigating institutions.

Institutions are forms of social organisation that manifest the conflicting forces of class politics; in the Arab context, imperialist intervention is decisive among these class forces.

The mainstream literature further views the relationship of conflict to development in terms of the types of social contracts; their legitimacy, order and fairness; and the capacity of the state to provide services (WESS 2008). As grievances stemming from social inequality rise, 'groups' are said to mobilise, hence increasing the probability of conflict (Stewart 2004). Inversely, the grievances of the poor are met by the greed of the rich who seek enrichment by causing and prolonging the conflicts themselves (Collier and Hoeffler 2000; Collier et al. 2003). To this school of thought, the policy alternative would be an institution that moderates the grievances or simply one that lessens the financial attractiveness of war. But how are these solutions supposed to materialise? The poor nation must negotiate its fate with a 'benevolent' imperialist that pretends to have the poor's best interest at heart. In this add-as-you-go method of thought, there is no departure from a price equilibrium model, and a new institution qua market would clear the excesses and put matters back in equilibrium.

While genuinely legalistic markets exist nowhere, in Arab markets not even the mere semblance of legality surrounds market transactions. The ideological and legal veneer of equal free traders, which at times furnishes some conditions for progress in Western markets, is patently absent in Arab markets. However, in war, as in peace, grievances and greed exist as symptoms of the material mode of organising life. Does this explain anything? Does the changing nature of war from national wars to intrastate wars matter? The new type of war with transnational connections, plunder and criminal activities is said to add something of a novelty to the explanation of conflict (Kaldor 1999). In this line of argument, the collapsing Third World nations in which the political forms of divided classes supplant the state itself are reconstituted in thought, and only in thought, as ideal states responsible for their own fate. A more adequate conceptualisation of the Arab state would stress its changing character under war and neoliberalism to underscore the difference with its concrete structure in the immediate postindependence state. This reification of the state absolves the US-led imperialists from the plunder they have accomplished with their policies. Blame shifts onto the working classes of the Third World, who are supposedly incapable of building good governance or democracy. Much in the same way as the welfare function in central states (supported partially by imperialist spoils) co-opts the central working classes, the aid and geopolitical flows function, structurally channelled via imperialist finance, accentuates identity differences in the AW. As the state has retrenched, imperialistically funded NGOs (the secular missionaries of the modern age) have become the

Trojan horses of sectionalism in the labour movement. Imperialist finance has pitted social classes against themselves and situated sections of identity-bonded labour above the state. Imperialist power positioning in the Arab formation ratchets up the power of the US-led imperialism against other actual or would-be imperialists that will funnel significant capital into US-led financial institutions. In relation to the returns on the power generated by US-led wars that undervalues Third World assets and absorbs immediate money resources from the wealthier moneyed economies, spending on NGOs dims in significance.

> However until now the United States has been able to run up a truly giant national debt for a special reason. Being the world's leading capitalist economy, and a military superpower, its currency has been used for payments between countries. When it needs to pay its debts it merely issues a Treasury bond to which investors from around the world rush to subscribe. Foreign investors buy not only bonds issued by the government but also American corporate bonds, shares, and real estate. These inflows, soaking up as they do the world's savings, ensure that the United States is able to import more than it exports, year after year, without suffering the treatment handed out by the IMF and World bank to countries like Argentina, Brazil, India and so on. This endless supply of golden eggs depends on the United States remaining as the supreme imperialist power and the dollar remaining currency for international payments. However, that is precisely what is now threatened. (RUPE 2003)

The very act of devalorisation is a reassertion of US-led power that draws financial flows on account of its currency as world reserve currency. These immediate money benefits and longer-term ones arising from devastating or controlling the Arab state also offset the costs of interventionist campaigns. This is not a simple case of taking over their oil fields and selling their oil. Compared to US imperial rents, owning an oil carrier at sea to deliver and sell oil is not much of a gain. Arresting oil supplies and owning the global financial channels is the real story. Much more important is the control that diverts resources to US-led capital through manifold financial channels. Under financialisation, the high frequency of financial flows magnifies the contradiction between the high rate of financial earnings and the discipline necessary to clamp down on excessive financier avarice that may loosen the controls of capital in times of crisis, with results like those of the 2007–08 financial crisis. As will be shown below, the intensity of this contradiction becomes itself the impetus for further social deformation of peripheral states by means of war. These disciplining and control processes are the necessary background work for the establishment of the price system and its associated profit rate.

The Price Fetish

When stripped bare of their mystique, prices and the sums of money they amount to are brokered by a structure of power from which the working classes have been excluded. In addition to enforced public-to-private transfers under neoliberalism, wars inflicted upon the Arab formations act as the ultimate instrument of encroachment by which resources and labour are coercively engaged in the formation of value in capitalist accumulation. This real subsumption of labour to capital, in the presence of 'immense surplus population created by large-scale industry in agriculture and the factory system, is exploited here in a way that saves the "capitalist" a part of the production costs of capital, and allows him to speculate directly upon the misery of the workers' (Marx 1863). The double whammy of neoliberally commanded Arab markets that misallocate resources and a US-led imperialism that reinforces abjection by war coercively subsumes Arab resources to capital.

Capital socially binds, represses and harnesses the material available for production including labour power before it engages it. The social category of control as such and the power platforms attendant upon the actual or ideological standing of the working classes precede the formation of prices. Making the Arab working classes more insecure, more vulnerable in the forms of their political organisation, means more profits accruing to central capital—in one facet of this one may envisage that the power-setting influences prices. The pittance spent in money form on control or destabilisation, whether it is the financing of Islamic fundamentalism or the US aid to Egypt, generates value for capital by the degree to which prices of Third World resources fall below value or, more significantly, the degree to which capital exercises control over value-forming processes. By tearing apart old ways of maintaining a living, inflating the ranks of the unemployed and driving people into poverty, capital inexpensively re-engages in production non-money assets (human beings) that had been disengaged by mass unemployment. (Of course, the same measures apply to all other resources—since to the imperialist, Arab working-class people are one more commodity to be devalued). Moreover, the images of dying Arab children, the cause of whose misery is assigned to cultural and identity politics, by 'demonstrating' that Arabs are culturally and nationally inferior, boost racism-laced nationalisms in the centre. Absurd scarcity and lifeboat theories—bringing the Third World poor to First World safe havens—acquire momentum and ideologically bear the weight of capitalist dynamics. The function of these campaigns is to conceal the fact that wars and their consequences in famines and chronic hunger are necessary to reproduce the ideological tools of capital. Deaths in Third World wars, famines and hunger are advertisements for imperialism (Avramidis 2005).

More often than not, diplomatic means of resolving conflicts are doomed to fail in the AW. None worked in the past unless the peace terms exacted more of a human toll than war. Egypt after the Camp David Accords is a case in point: after thirty years of growth, one out of three of its children is malnourished (IRIN 2010). That the empire will not take yes for an answer is not haphazard; war is necessary to circuitously reproduce the international division of labour attendant on accumulation by militarisation. Thus, despite the embargo on Iraq acting as a slow-motion WMD and the capitulation of its leadership, Iraq had to be invaded to crush even its remaining traces of sovereignty (Gordon 2010). Those on the Left who argue that the differences in wages across the globe are primarily derived from degrees of technological advancement, relative to differences in productivity (relative surplus value), forget that productivity in an integrated world is indivisible and that criminally wasted lives have gone into what is being produced. Accumulation and productivity do not start in the factories of the West; they begin in the Congo and Iraq. The concept of socially necessary labour and the reproduction of labour power presumes that wages are not exclusively determined by biological factors but by historical and sociological ones (Emmanuel 1972). The formation of value is an integrated historical process, in which all social moments participate in the realisation of the commodity, and not a statistical exercise accounting for distorted or power-brokered prices. The politics of imperialist aggression grapple with the growing rift between the US-led capital's bloated share of private appropriation and the redistribution of value to a complex global production structure (the shares of other imperialists). In the age of financialisation, this rift is magnified by the fetish incarnate in the dollar-based price system. The more acute the contradictions, the more developing nations have to be stripped of their security before they are deprived of political will and national resources.

Wars trace the outer limits of encroachment in the accumulation process. They are entwined with expansion by commodity realisation—that is, the process by which commodities are brought to market and sold to realise their value. Wars also pre-empt revolutionary consciousness because they delink progressive reforms from their intermediation in revolution. In view of labour's abundance, those who perish in war reduce the number of labourers by so little relative to the huge total (an insignificant reduction of the labour-power commodity) such that they reduce the value of those remaining alive. When central-nation working classes are estranged from their own humanity (the alienated majority vote for the war machine) and under the incessant barrage of scaremongering associated with 'terrorism' and alleged resource scarcity, their initial attitude of compassion for and solidarity with Third World dead or skeletally starved people transmutes into its opposite—deepening nationalisms and other identity forms to the benefit of capital. It is this ideological input of war distorting revolutionary consciousness that lays the ground for new wars. That wars are justified by fabricated information time and again is not a series of gaffes or mistakes; it is, as often said, a systemic calculus of mass crime. Just as wars contribute to the reproduction of social conditions under capitalism, so also they buttress the ideology of capital, which must be continuously reproduced and is never separate from the expropriation of Arab formations. The epitome of war-making ideology was justifying what is utterly unjustifiable under the Charter of the United Nations—launching a war to protect 'a way of life'. During the ideological and media whip-up for the Second Gulf War, the distortion of humanist consciousness became so profound that some ideologues went so far as to quote Hegel's philosophy out of context in a manner that resembled the language of *Mein Kampf*. Here is the snippet from Hegel:

> [Conflict with another sovereign state] is the moment wherein the substance of the state—i.e., its absolute power against everything individual and particular, against life, property, and their rights, even against societies and associations—makes the nullity of these finite things an accomplished fact and brings it home to consciousness. [...] War is the state of affairs which deals in earnest with the vanity of temporal goods and concerns. [...] War has the higher significance that by its agency, as I have remarked elsewhere, 'The ethical health of peoples is preserved in their indifference to the stabilization of finite institutions; just as the blowing of the winds preserves the sea from the foulness which would be the result of a prolonged calm, so also corruption in nations would be the product of prolonged, let alone "perpetual", peace.' (*Philosophy of Right*: 323–24R).[2]

Here is Hitler to illustrate the resemblance and dangers of quoting Hegel or anyone else for that matter out of context:

To those who said that it was war which had sapped the substance of Germany, and that another war would end European civilization, [...]

---

2   Lee Harris drumming up the war at this website: the Tech Central Station: Where Free Markets Meet Technology. http://www.techcentralstation.com (viewed 3 January 2004).

it was only 'eternal peace' which destroyed peoples and that neither the individual nor society could escape Nature's decree that the fittest alone survive.[3]

To do justice to Hegel, who can hardly be quoted in a way that does *not* seem out of context, the above quote is extracted from a treatise in which the state has not yet realised the spirit and, hence, it succumbs to war. The view that Hegel is a totalitarian theorist or fascist ideologue who glorified war as a human achievement is a caricature that has been universally rejected (Stewart 1996). War for Hegel reflects a condition of the underdevelopment of spirit associated with the underdevelopment of the state; therefore it is the by-product of an unethical state. Under the rule of US-led capital, economising with the truth or falsification that promotes war is admitted at decisive levels of the public discourse. That is all the more reason why global working-class differences nurtured by nationalistic wars are an essential proviso of for commanding the social processes that create wealth. The imaginary national rifts splitting worker from worker unknot the organic ties of working classes.

The War–Oil Nexus

In the AW, then, war serves multiple functions; however, it principally bolsters militarisation and abets the control of oil. Discussing the occupation of Iraq, Paul Wolfowitz, deputy secretary of defence under George W. Bush, stated that Iraq's war was about oil (Wright 2003). The process of US-led accumulation rides upon three broad currents: demand-side growth, dollar-expanded financialisation and militarisation. What the American economy cannot generate in *doux commerce*, it generates by war and militarisation. In this duality of republic and empire, argues James Petras, the empire side is deployed to offset the failure of accumulation by commodity realisation/overproduction within the republic (Petras 2011). Not that this analysis changes much; the US republic was imperial from its inception, steadily conquering and colonising territory westward according to Manifest Destiny, displacing or slaughtering native peoples, and importing and then breeding slave labour for primary-goods production (tobacco and then cotton). Here, European wage slavery, as it has been noted in in the mid nineteenth century, needed slavery pure and simple (Marx 1867). War was the republic's instrument from the beginning. Today, the power standing of US-led capital hinges on international consent that the US is in control of oil. Here, the perception of control is as relevant

---

3   Adolf Hitler, *Mein Kampf* (Houghton Mifflin, 1941). Online: http://archive.org/stream/meinkampf035176mbp/meinkampf035176mbp_djvu.txt.

as actual control. Perception of control bolsters confidence in the dollarised financial system, in the sense that dollar expansion is underwritten by oil control. Strengthening control over oil resources provides US-led capital with strategic leverage on most countries. Oil price fluctuations matter less to the US than to others because oil is priced in its own currency: the dollar. US-led capital's share of global income is declining: US GDP is at around twenty per cent, or less than half of what it was by the end of the Second World War; meanwhile, other national capitals are ascending (the BRICs or East Asian Tigers). The US's chronic trade deficit, which is around $700–$800 billion a year,[4] has for some time now incorporated declining competitiveness in areas where the US has been a leader, but the US remains potent in the production of high-tech knowledge (Brenner 2003b; Wallerstein 2000b). That the trade deficit persists partly because of loss of capacity due to deindustrialisation or the outsourcing of manufacturing processes is made less significant because global flows seek the security of the superpower's risk-free dollar assets. US-led capital has maintained its lead via its military might and the technology derived from militarisation that provides an edge over other national industrial capitals. The more the politics of austerity suppresses US national demand, the more that war (in general) or oil wars (in particular) stabilise the dollar pricing of oil, flows of Chinese surpluses and other surpluses into T-bills, and other imperial rents that have propped up long-term US growth (Kohler 1999). In an adjacent manner, the discourse of declining US empire is one thing and declining US-led capital is another. The corporate profit rates exhibit unrelenting growth (growth rates may be lower but also the labour shares), and capital, which assumed a more financialised role centred around the US economy, is not at all in decline.

In Left theories of imperialism, wars emerge from persistent crises in the centre. The more severe the crisis, the more it reduces the role of realisation in the process of capital accumulation and the more it expands the role of capitalist war ventures. Consequently, war is crucial to resolving the difficulties arising from trying to maintain profit rates while balancing the national production and distribution sides. After three decades of neoliberalism, the share of US real wages fell slightly and investment in productive activity (as opposed to finance) is on the wane (Tabb 2007; Brenner 2003a). Dependent Arab oil formations edging towards or experiencing war represent an opportunity to re-empower US-led capital. With US capital wedding itself more closely to financial capital's deflationary policies, central demand is likely

---

4   US Department of Commerce, 'Foreign Trade', US Census Bureau homepage, 2012. Online: http://www.census.gov/foreign-trade/statistics/highlights/annual.html (viewed 12 December 2012).

to remain torpid. The implication of a deepening crisis in the centre would further drive US-led capital to lay claim to oil or to shift the power structure in oil regions in its favour. Imperial rents and dollar seigniorage, the gains of borrowing indefinitely in one's own currency at little cost, here present at the global scale, become attached to oil control and its associated wars, which are nowhere more prevalent than in the AW. The AW functionally redresses the shortfall of capital accumulation and the mercantilist impetus of imperialism by its wars, underdevelopment and security exposure. This reproduction of oil control and war requires the articulation of Arab ruling classes with US-led capital, specifically in how this alliance disempowers the Arab working classes.

There are some nuances that differentiate these wars from previous colonial wars. Unlike the US-led empire, which imports capital by multiple financial channels, colonial Britain exported capital because it also had more serious colonial competitors. It rechannelled its surpluses from the colonies, mainly India, to Australia and Canada. This provided the impression that it was exporting a great share of capital vis-à-vis what it received at home (Patnaik 2009). However, in terms of value for price, the net gains from colonialism remained significant. The deconstruction of indigenous industry and resources around the world produced for Britain an immense historical surplus value (Abdel Malek 1981, 70). The resource flows *to* the US are more significant because its imperialist competitors are doubly subordinated by its expansive power and dollar hegemony. Many separate concrete capitals from around the world merge into the abstract money form of the dollar. US-led capital wars resemble past colonial wars, with the twist that the channels of resource flows to empire are more flexible and intricate as a result of the diluted identities of national capitals. Global wealth is held in dollars, and the world's wealthy become one in the dollar. The billions of dollars wired daily globally involve dollar premiums that are pocketed by US-led capital's financial institutions. The rents obtaining to US-led capital from its imperial standing rise according to the power it garners from the global holders of dollar wealth. US-led capital's national identity undergoes restructuring at the same rate at which financialisation sucks non-American capital into its structure.

Beneath the prices are real values, the blood and toil of working classes. These values are the labour, assets and all other goods required to improve the lives of working classes. They are grabbed and underpriced by imperialist power relationships that short-change the vanquished working population. Colonialism appears more costly to the colonisers, but because of a history of colonialism that already tilted the exchange platforms and enormous real assets are engaged cheaply in production, the actual returns are great. That is once more why the real reason for neocolonising or destroying states is to strip working classes of sovereignty over their resources before their resources are taken away. The balance of forces behind the scenes sets the price of indigenous resources and primary commodities far below the value necessary to reproduce their working populations. As interimperialist rivalry lingers over US financial liabilities and its excessive money grab, US-led capital expands by eroding security-exposed peripheral states and immersing itself as a broker of power within their class structures. This insertion of US representation into the peripheral governing structure is a re-enactment of old colonialism.

For over fifty years, the surfeit money capital of the AW remained unrequited transfers or uncashed cheques. Following the demolition of Iraq, many corners of the Third World are subjected to the full force of a colonial antidevelopment agenda. Libya, Syria, Iraq, Somalia, Yemen, Sudan and Lebanon are now merely plundered territories. Anti-imperialist ideological defeatism, in the form of retreat from secular nationalist or socialist ideologies, correlates closely with military routs. The speed with which Arab wealth evaporates leaves few developmental traces. Most investment is about passively consuming technology and/or the object of investment itself (as in real estate) without knowledge linkages to the local economies. For more than thirty years, the International Country Risk Guide (ICRG) database has pinpointed the AW as one of the riskiest regions globally.[5] The macroeconomic and supposed 'antiwar' policies have merely aggravated conflicts. In the central Arab–Israeli conflict, aid to the Palestinians boosted the Israeli economy because the occupied buy and rebuild with the money and the goods produced by the occupation force. The so-called peace process resulted in more land confiscations. The creation of scarcities in the occupied territories alongside NGOs wielding European or Gulf capital funded fragmentation and the near-collapse of cohesive Palestinian resistance. Not that the instruments of the UN Security Council ever amounted to much, realpolitik superseded international law. Andre Gunder Frank's triangle of oil, guns and the dollar constituted the hinges in the framework of Arab de-development. Through all-out assaults and belligerent international relations, US-led capital created a social existence for the AW that swings between full-fledged conflict and a high level of tension.

In view of the smallness of non-Gulf Arab incomes and per capita incomes in relation to petrodollars, war in the AW is cheap to fund and easy to foment. Wars can be fanned wider by their own heat as a result of already existing hostilities. Even without the deliberately induced oil-control wars, the flames of regional war drive value from around the world into the safety of the US market.

---

5   The International Country Risk Guide nearly always places the AW in the high risk category, (ICRG) various years.

US-led militarisation underwrites the power gap between the US's national production structure and its position in the international division of labour. These interimperialist power gradations are political, social and technological, and they require both wars and the ideological constructs for war to be continued. The emergent consequences are such that if even one conceptually excludes the pursuit of oil from the schema, war making for its own sake would still be a reason for conducting regional wars. The region has not been afforded developmental consideration by the central nations. There is not much to trade with it in value-added merchandise in the Arab region (Arab labour share from global income is around 0.3 per cent). The region simply produces oil and buys manufactured goods and food that are by an historically determined average incapable of reproducing the population at conditions better than those of the past. As such, the AW is the prophylactic used for US-led imperialist positioning and repositioning in international relations.

Only in thought can the reasons for war be separated into war for its own sake as opposed to war in pursuit of strategic resources. Capital accumulation processes, which are class relations mediated through the social agencies of capital, are real, and their primary objective in the AW remains oil and its control. Oil has figured in imperial designs since the early twentieth century under European colonisation (Al Duri 1969). The belligerence of US-led capital in the AW has grown in step with the relevance of oil as a strategic commodity. The commodity itself is strategic because of the world's dependence on it—not solely for energy use and the value-added conversions derived from it (oil), but even more for the hegemony it provides over other major economic entities. Thus, because the perception of oil as a strategic commodity involves control over other (financial) channels of resource flow, its *scarcity* as a commodity is invented and exaggerated. The appearance of controlling something relevant upon which the survival of the global population hinges underwrites the issuance of dollarised money wealth to cover much of the world's future transactions. In an example of oil-scarcity scaremongering language, a few months before the invasion of Iraq, a commentator expressed the hope that the fight for oil would be carried out in cash and not with missiles (Deffeyes 2002). The degree of control itself is a material relationship reproduced over time to leverage a dollar-based monetary system that remains in large part commodity-based (Patnaik 2009; Bagchi 2008). Also, because of high price variations and steadily growing quantities of oil over the last three decades, oil's share of global trade varied between ten and twenty per cent (means of transport rank second at three per cent, using the SITC at the three-digit level).[6] In standard trade theory

---

6   UN, various years, Standard International Trade Classification.

the value of a national currency derives in part from national ownership of a significantly traded commodity priced in that currency. Thus, dollarising the price and exchange of oil is central to US-led capital. Oil's energy share in still-rising powers (China and India in particular) in the developing world is twice that of OECD, making this group more vulnerable to US strategic control of the commodity (UNECE 2005). But it is not only the control of oil itself that counts; control of the oil market also comes into the picture. So what is this oil market, and how is it controlled?

Controlling Oil Markets

Although every market is a process of social and power relationships, the oil market is even more extraordinary than other markets. The struggle to dominate the oil market, therefore, is no ordinary struggle. The degree of control over the oil market translates into some degree of enhanced power in all other markets. But to control an oil market, the principal player, which is undoubtedly US-led capital, intervenes at the source militarily or otherwise, and shunts other players aside while at the same time keeping the financialised transactions of oil under close watch. As already noted, therefore, US-led capital strips oil states of sovereignty over oil and dollarises oil transactions. These two measures represent the collateral needed to lay the foundation of the oil-dollar standard of the world financial system (Patnaik 2009). In this relentless exercise of power, the commodity-based (i.e., oil-based) global monetary system flourishes by the expansion of oil control, which underwrites the dollar.

On the surface, oil prices change in response to a vector sum of economic and geopolitical factors. In recent history, however, the amplitude of oil-price variations has been more typically attributed to growing Iran-related and Gulf-related geopolitical risks and an abundant dollar money supply rather than to narrowed refinery margins (how much more refineries can refine) and smaller cushions (a cushion is the size of the gap between supply and demand). The currently high oil price, which rose from around ten dollars per barrel in 1999 to a current plateau of around one hundred dollars, was partly driven by excess liquidity (easy convertibility of assets into cash) banking on oil futures. Despite the fact that very high international oil prices may hinder an already fragile global recovery from the 2008 recession, US interest-rate policy and US raucous war-on-Iran discourse jitter the market and rattle prices.

Below the surface, oil prices are rarely left to two-dimensional frameworks of supply and demand. As noted, with the oil-dollar standard gripping the international financial system, rising oil prices dampen the performance of all oil-importing economies to a higher degree than they do the US economy, for the obvious reason that the US pays for oil in its own currency. Oil price variations engender shifts in the degree of power enjoyed by the US economy vis-à-vis other economies. In the ongoing lethargic global business cycle since 2008, the US partly reasserts its stature through the demand for dollars arising from higher oil transactions and strategic oil control. Financial capital was contented as a result of expanding US indebtedness and rising *fictitious capital* (the layers upon layers of money claims for which there are no real counterparts in the economy). The rising debts raised the share of real value and wealth acquired by the ruling classes through austerity; for instance, as millions of families whose earners were made redundant were unable to service their home mortgages—or were falsely placed in default— their homes became the property of the lenders, who were able to resell them at higher prices involving new mortgages as the market 'recovered'. Rising debts or fictitious capital have had non-fictitious and in fact dire effects on the working classes of the centre (Bellofiore 2011). But the worst consequences of expanding central debts fall upon working classes in the AW. Wars that underwrite expanding US debts by staking oil rise in intensity as the bond tying oil to the dollar weakens. Much as there were too many dollars for gold, which prompted the US to part with the gold standard, there could be too many dollars for oil or oil control. Hence, propping up the oil-dollar standard involves oil control. Moreover, oil prices have much more to say about the state of the global economy than merely the cost of petrol at the pump.

Crude oil prices exhibit high variability. In the same way, when the AW weakened as of the early 1980s, so did OPEC when in the mid-1980s oil-price determination moved to the Chicago futures market (Mabro 2008). As aptly put by Jayati Ghosh, 'OPEC is more like a club of a minority of oil producers, rather than a cartel that is in command of world oil supply' (2011). More recently, the OPEC Reference Basket price reached US$140 per barrel in July 2008, declined again to US$35 by the end of that year, and in 2013 rose above US$100 once more. Financial speculation, mainly the buying of crude oil futures, was behind the 2008 price surge, and the present hike is driven by speculation around a very geopolitically charged future (UN 2008b). It is worth noting that the much-discussed geological considerations relating to 'peak oil' and extraction cost are not responsible for the oil price rises of either 1973 or 2004. Oil reserves matter in the long run; but current oil *prices* have not been determined by beliefs about the long run (Mabro 2008). These geological considerations have an impact only on the forward-looking or long-term price. But in the internet age, geopolitical problems unnerve the market almost instantaneously and are becoming more portentous by the minute.

Nervousness in the Gulf, past and present, has gained the semblance of permanence and has risen in intensity. The perceived short-term concern influencing oil price relates to a sudden disruption of supply and a higher risk of sagging in the cushion placed beneath the market's ample posterior by Saudi Arabia, which provides the bulk of surplus capacity (Krane 2012).

On the consumption side, demand for oil continues to rise by 1 to 1.5 per cent on average yearly (OPEC 2012). An increase in the rate of growth of China and other parts of Asia over the past two decades has steadily raised demand for oil. Constraints on the production capacity of the cheaply extracted and 'light sweet' crude oil both in the upstream sector (OPEC countries) and in the downstream USA are slowly emerging, but the coming online of shale and tar oils reduce the scope for supply constraints globally. It is relevant to note that oil's strategic status was only minutely a long-term issue. Oil's strategic status arises from short-term considerations, hegemonic control of supply sources or a lockdown of the host regime in relation to oil, and the oil–dollar nexus. Short-term disruptions to shipments or the independence of regimes from US hegemony in relation to the currency in which oil is sold are weighty considerations. To illustrate with proceedings from an actual event, at the conference 'China and the Middle East: Implications of a Rising Political and Economic Relationship',[7] a Gulf scholar addressed a Chinese scholar with remarks that if China continues to support Iran, the Gulf may suspend oil shipments. Not that the scholar's words would make a difference, but in strategic terms that is what shutting off the spigots means. In oil, all it would take to cause major disruptions to real and financial markets is a single short-term fiasco.

However, until 2013, supply constraints have not represented a problem per se because more refineries are accepting sour-quality crude (including so-called 'tar sands' oil or liquefied bitumen) and the cushion has been anything but flattened. One should note that the petroleum market cannot function effectively unless a certain volume of surplus production capacity is available. The extra volume is needed to offset the effects of strikes, storms and smaller wars. No cushion, however, would suffice for a war that resulted in the closure of the Straits of Hormuz. The fear factor developing around this trumped-up story, in particular, is of some significance in pressuring oil price movements, but it is not really threatening. Neither the information sources integrated within the oil market nor central-state intelligence services

---

7   Nurhidayahti Mohammad Miharja, 'Scholars Discuss China and Middle East Relations at Well-Attended Event', National University of Singapore, Middle East Institute, 2011. Online: http://www.mei.nus.edu.sg/blog/scholars-discuss-china-and-middle-east-relations-at-well-attended-event (viewed 27 February 2014).

believe that the Iranian military is capable of blocking the straits. Had Iran's military capabilities been enough to arrest the flow of oil from the straits *and* withstand a massive US assault, the international financial order would be drastically different. Militarism and US control of the eastern flank of the Persian Gulf are what calls the shots and are more relevant as provinces of wealth making than the share of oil revenues obtained by the major oil corporations.

The price of oil is increasingly realised in American futures markets. It rests on an assemblage of futures, spot, physical-forward and derivatives markets where, with expanding liquidity, the futures markets lead. Participants in these markets include major financial institutions such as Goldman Sachs, Morgan Stanley, Merrill Lynch, Société Générale and J. P. Morgan. A large number of hedge funds and individual punters also take part in this market. Hedgers, one may add, are also speculators in view of their fear that the actual price is liable to be less favourable than the price that they are willing to insure. In today's oil market, therefore, the major players are speculators who may more often than not manipulate market outcomes in their favour. The main point to note from this is that the price of oil also moves in response to differential rates of return from investment in other markets and not solely to demand-supply concerns. The presence of dollar liquidity and low rates of return in other markets draw the excess dollar liquidity into the oil market and displace direct producers as the driving forces of this market.

Gulf-related geopolitical concerns and talk of sanctions on Iran are not new and have always filtered into the oil market (Moore 2005). The market has operated with such grim analyses in the background and cohabitated with these conditions for many years. Recently, however, the stakes have risen. The views propagated in the USA by think tanks and the mainstream media about an inevitable strike on Iran elevate the stress level (Ottolenghi 2012). But the more important issue is not the closure of the straits, it is how other powers— China and Russia—will consider the assault. Whoever feeds this information into the market further destabilises, in no haphazard fashion, an already unstable oil price. The power emanating from US geostrategic control of oil areas and high oil-price variability are self-reinforcing elements of the same process by which US-led capital boosts its own clout and negotiation standing relative to other players. The dilemma for importers, specifically China, is to strike a balance between reducing US control in oil areas so as not to become strategically squeezed in terms of strategic supply, and not to weaken the US to the point of loosening the US dollar standard. The latter case may precipitate dollar devaluation and, subsequently, a US debt deflation process. Much of the handling of this fluid relationship depends on the US-led capital establishing hegemony over oil-strategic areas to cover its voracity for money expansion and on how the ripple effect from oil price fluctuation redistributes the shock to its own economy and others.

The oil-dollar standard is not an identity as in $x = y$ or in which the value of a given currency has to be stable in terms of commodities. As such the dollar would, *ex ante*, maintain a stable value in terms of commodities (Patnaik 2009). At no time in recent history has there been a shortage of oil, and at no time have oil prices been even mildly steady in the dollar. The link between the dollar and the price of oil, which is inherently unstable, is (as explained earlier) set by the degree of US power in relation to direct producers and importers. To qualify Patnaik's point, this money system is not only commodity based, it is also power based. The variability of oil prices is partly managed to preserve US imperial stature within a range at one end of which global imbalances press for dollar devaluation while at the other the US uses the threat of such devaluation and debt deflation to blackmail holders of US debts. The concern for US-led capital arises from the rising dollar money supply *qua* liquidity, steady asset prices and low interest rates, which would raise the price of oil to politically intolerable levels. Until shale oil abundance came into play, at such moments the US would speak of releasing strategic reserves—not that shale oil will relieve the pressure on peripheral formations, because the US controls oil in order to pressure competing imperial powers (Winn 2012). The oil-dollar standard is in this sense a power-defined commodity-money instrument both furthering and being furthered by imperialist conquest.

Closing Comment

The oil–dollar nexus varies in strength even as US-led capital's economic power at home wanes. As its share of world industry dwindles, or as it moves labour intensive and environmentally costly production processes to China and India, the US bolsters its mercantilist facet by military enterprise. Despite a sizeable depreciation of the dollar over long stretches of time, the US trade deficit persists for reasons having to do with outsourcing and loss of capacity due to long-standing degradation of intermediate level industry. Since Volker's hike of US interest rates in the late 1970s to partially redress indebtedness by foreign savings, US imports have steadily outstripped US exports. As US social reforms retrenched, US foreign policy mimicked the brutality the US exercised in its own ethnically segregated slums, especially as it bombed away various parts of the Middle East. Its mercantilism follows from the inflow of world resources for T-bills into the US economy. Technological supremacy resulting from militarisation situates US power on apparently unshakeable long-term grounds. I have added the qualifier 'apparently' to underline the fact that 'the

graveyard of history is littered with the shattered claims of chosen peoples'
(Davis 1960), or in a more literary tone:

> And on the pedestal these words appear:
> 'My name is Ozymandias, King of Kings:
> Look on my works, ye mighty, and despair!'
> Nothing beside remains. Round the decay
> Of that colossal wreck, boundless and bare,
> The lone and level sands stretch far away.
>   Shelley, 'Ozymandias', 1819

Years of Arab postindependence development have been written off by wars
and neoliberalism, which freed, in primitive-accumulation fashion, many
social assets either for acquisition or simply to remain idle material for more
central capital. Whereas in earlier times and elsewhere variants of primitive
accumulation led to improvement in economic and social developments, in
the AW, security and development goals parted ways concomitantly with
weakened sovereignty. Wars disengaged social assets, adding to the problem of
an already low production capacity. They served as principal de-development
tools. Whenever short-lived peace ententes prevailed, the weight of potential
defeat restructured social classes into adopting neoliberal policies that usurped
the resources of nations. The terms of peace, as was the case for Egypt, were
worse than war. Such is the grip of capital on history.

The impact of war is not solely physical. It is also ideological, because defeat
and defeatism corrode the sovereignty required in anti-imperialist struggle.
War reshapes the interrelations between security, sovereignty and economic
development in a way that ensures that the terms of war linger on in peace.
Without doubt, sovereignty and security and their requirements impact both
the interrelated processes of the strength of the state, regional integration
and economic development. Wars hinder development or deconstruct states
by imposing a different pattern of political and economic development in
line with the alliance between Arab ruling classes and US-led capital. In this
dynamic, the degree of subordination of national ruling classes to US-led
capital determines development. Development in relation to security emerges
as an outcome of the multitiered power structure, the resultant vector of
which is US-led capital, for which oil and war are essential.

Chapter Six

DISLOCATION UNDER IMPERIALIST ASSAULT

As argued in previous chapters, poor development in the Arab world primarily follows from the politics of imperialist aggression and subordinately from the interface between 'free market' policies and their antidevelopmental outcomes. The stranglehold of free-market ideology is evidenced in the fact that despite the world being mired in a global crisis in which one child under 5 perishes from hunger every five seconds, thirty-five million people die each year from hunger or its immediate aftermath, and one billion people are permanently and severely malnourished (Ziegler 2011), few scholars any longer voice alternative policies such as land and income redistribution, nationalisation and self-reliance. It is probably unprecedented in history that so many people unconsciously share the same belief in the one idea, which is the market dogma. The depth of the schism on the Left is so deep such that even the socialist 'brand names' of the North, Trotskyism and anarchism, which exhibit a puny presence in the South, still mull the issue of why the revolution did not arrive in Weimar Germany when the devastation in the colonies appeared trivial. Where the geographic limits of structural concepts end, the ideological stance masked by social science becomes visible. The presence of a Left organised around the straitjacket of bourgeois democracy, as opposed to the necessity of violent struggle, is all on its own an indication of how detached socialist ideology has become from the working class. The hold of capital's ideology as the social unconscious that distorts the revolutionary consciousness of working classes exceeds the notion of ideology presented by Althusser. In the present epoch, 'people' more than create for themselves an alienated (i.e., imaginary) representation of their conditions of existence, because these conditions of existence are themselves alienating (Althusser 1971). By the fetish of Islamic Ummah and Islam deployed in pro-imperialist mobilisation against the working classes everywhere, Left liberalism converted this virtual reality into something real to justify its collusion with US-led imperial assaults on the Islamic world. Western universities are awash with Islamic studies courses relating present-day developments to the dead ideas of the past with the purpose of othering and demonising Arabs and Muslims. When such a state of consciousness exists, there will only be a slight divergence between what people want and historical outcome. For the first time, historical materialism, the social science that investigates why history happens against people's wishes, stands corrected. Recently, more people make history as they please despite the displeasure of the outcome. Such is the depth of the Left's ideological crisis.

After three decades of Arab developmental failure, there is an indictment neither of past failed policies nor of those who implemented them. In countries where the uprising led to ballot-box democracy (or 'boxocracy'), the new Islamist governments have overlooked past policies and attributed failure to corruption as a moral category. Not, for either the Islamists or the older *nomenklatura*, that the 'free market' inherently channels social wealth into private hands, which is the corruption inalienable from the market; no, it was deviation from the market ethic by those in charge that squandered all those resources. In reality, however, Arab development proceeds in the shadow of an international ideological and power play. It retrogresses according to the degree of interimperialist entente to bolster the US-led capital hand in the Arab region. As US-led capital co-opts other competing capitals in its quest for oil control, the autonomy of Arab states exercised over the execution of their own policies diminishes. To be sure, the AW tested the limits of interimperialist collusion when the US breached the covenants of international security and occupied Iraq, or when it exceeded the Security Council mandate by devastating Libya. The divergence of imperialist opinion over the occupation of Iraq demonstrates the relevance of the AW to imperialism and the extent to which financialisation had diluted the national identity of capital (for those classes piggybacking on US-led financialisation). The nationalism of US capital is related to how it engages the powers of US society in aggression, underwriting the money-value wealth of American and non-American ruling classes that have become united in the dollar. In that sense, US capital's national identity is in form national, but in content, functional and utilitarian. Also in the same sense, the ideological glorification of Western forms of democracy applied to the periphery does not necessarily serve as effective anti-imperialist fronts because they remain a progeny of the mother ideology. Democratic or otherwise, the opposing mode of political organisation in the periphery is effective when it dents capital as it raises intercapitalist antagonisms or destabilises its power structures.

To resume: Arab development does not elude policymakers. It is policymakers who reshape real development into an elusive goal. The scope and scale of coordinated economic and social policy, which augment national productive capacity, are capped off like a used-up oil well by the meagre sovereignty of the Arab state. In the AW, more so than almost anywhere else, nearly all aspects of poor sovereignty and inadequate working-class security ensue in a manner reminiscent of Hobbes weak 'sword of war' from frail national security.[1] The exposure of national security undermines personal, communal and democratic securities concurrently. When battered, these composites of security vitiate any sovereignty substantiated by working-class hegemony over society, and with it, the state as the principal agent of development. In such circumstances, one stands confronted with a self-reinforcing vicious circle.

Sovereignty and autonomy over development policy are necessary but insufficient conditions for the reallocation of resources within national economies. Sufficiency in turn is contingent on the interaction between the choice of policies and their outcomes gauged by social progress. Social and economic processes that involve increasing productive capacity and the freedom of the working class from want (so as to begin to realise their potential) involve reform that favours state-led industrialisation and civil liberties. The burgeoning of civil liberties need not be inversely related to regime stability. When the state itself reallocates value to workers rather than to a minority ruling class, the hegemony of labour over social institutions and the sovereignty rooted in working-class security will prevent state implosion. Labour-determined autonomy, security arrangements and military balance of power demarcate the limits of a development policy that seizes and redistributes the social product nationally. Each *rapport de force* with its concomitant degree of national sovereignty entails a particular pattern of resource allocation that meets (or does not) the sufficiency condition according to the share of value allotted to labour. Ideally, an anti-imperialist front, composed of national classes with vested interests in recycling resources nationally, mobilises assets that build productive capacity. But the subjugated Arab states are far from these ideal conditions: instead of labour representation, the imperialist powers implant themselves into the state structure. The joke circulating among Arab émigrés is that some Arab despots seek the US ambassador's authorisation to use their toilets. As already noted in earlier contexts, the rise of an Arab merchant class integrated with US-led capital in the neoliberal age has obviated sovereignty and sustained a dependent form of integration with financial imperialism. It is this integration, reigning over the AW by military power more than other forms of control, which suppresses development.

---

1   One may note that with compromised Arab national security and lopsided international covenants, Hobbes's remark that 'covenants, without the sword, are but words and of no strength to secure a man at all', can bear significance for these times when covenants are taken to mean international covenants (*Leviathan*, ch. 17).

Circularly, dependency on US-led capital weakens state defences, lowers the costs of imperialist aggression and contributes to the cycle of expropriation by encroachment wars.

The subordinated mode of integration wrenches the developmental decision-making process out of the hands of national forces. The coercion exercised against the working classes by the combined powers of imperialism and merchant/comprador is not coincidental. Politics of repression follow the demands of the leading capital or US-led capital. More and more, the structure of power ruling the development process resembles *force majeure*. The distorted balance of power is also worsened by the unresolved Arab–Israeli conflict. US-led capital hegemony over the AW rests on military superiority, of which Israel's military capabilities are part and parcel. The interconnectedness of US-led capital with Israeli capital is firm. After years of normalisation with Egypt and Jordan, their trade with Israel remains insignificant (IMF, various years). The Israeli trade portfolio is incompatible with the underdeveloped trade demands of the AW (Abou Anaml 2006). Israeli trade targets European markets and Third World armaments sales. Israel's entente with Arab states counters its role in infusing regional militarisation and providing supplementary support for US-led oil control. Not that Israel can ever integrate with its neighbours and remain a principal constituent of US-led capital; from a complementary integration viewpoint, there are few potential markets in the AW with which Israel can engage.

By the late 1950s it became clearer that militarisation and devalorisation of Third World capital alleviate the brunt of central crises and twist the role of reform in central formations away from the revolutionary path to co-opting working classes:

> The leftward-moving labor opposition to capitalism has been counteracted and bought off. Enough benefits of economic imperialism and of systematic waste of capitalism's surplus product have filtered down, or have been wrested from Big Business by unions and other interest groups, so that those potentially dissident elements which count have been harnessed to the chariot of the vested interests. (Davis 1960)

Enter the great recession of 2007–08; the lingering recession as experienced by US-led capital further calls for restructuring of relations with many of the states in the AW—from relations with (more or less) cohesive states to relations with fractured ones. In the Cold War days, differences over the redistribution of resources among the advanced economic powers were, for the most part, mediated through an entente aligned against the Soviet Union. In the post–Cold War era, as rising US debts infringe on the steadiness of the dollar, dollarised money-capital and capitals with national production bases exhibit unease about the sheer avarice of US-led financial grab. It is not that lenders will scurry to translate their paper wealth into real American assets and cause a run on the dollar; rather, under less tension-infused global conditions, other hard currencies would become as desirable as the dollar. Tensions with the potential for militarisation, therefore, specifically those emanating from the Arab region, keep the world on edge and in search of riskless, power-underwritten dollar assets. US-led capital hegemony and the role Israel plays in reshaping Arab states heighten conflicts and impart unease that affords the dollar with its relatively risk-free position. In relative terms, the pressures on other currencies as a result of instability could be greater than that experienced by the dollar.

US hegemony and oil control underwriting the dollar are intertwined with the restructuring of Arab states as satellites and/or their destabilisation and deconstruction. The frustration of other imperial forces over the unfair share of US-led capital from financialisation and unrestrained dollar issuance collides with their apprehensiveness over rising US militarisation, the receding dominion of the dollar, and the potential losses to their dollar-held assets arising from dollar devaluation. Steepening global imbalances remain an element in the aforesaid contradiction; however, they have become secondary in relation to the build-up of fictitious capital—that is, debts that cannot and will not be paid (Hudson 2012). This chapter addresses the history of dislocation in the AW under colonial and imperialist assault in relation to the crisis of capital. Three main areas are covered: a) the mode of integration of the AW with world capital; b) the articulation of nascent Ottoman capitalism with European capital; and c), the dislocation of the neoliberal age, which matches that of the colonial age. The chapter ends with a prognosis of the rise of merchant capital and the road to disintegration.

Structural Aspects of the Mode of Integration

Few countries that enjoy a certain level of security by the extension of superpower defence treaties reap development from the market-expansion side of capital accumulation, as was the case in East Asia. These countries serve as advanced imperial outposts and, on the development side, they are touted as models that all countries can mimic. Paradoxically, by the adding-up fallacy or, realistically, by the logic of blind competition, not all countries can replicate this path. Whatever development may ensue from security ties to the imperial centres only materialises after a degree of autonomous policy space favouring the accumulation of national wealth is acquired. At times, these models also serve an ideological role and are flaunted as paragons of disciplined capitalism—but of capitalism nonetheless. Disciplined or not, capitalism cannot sustain equitable development and remain capitalist. Moreover, it was not because of their moderation of profit rates that they developed. There is a myriad of overdetermined reasons for why they developed, but the primary reason was that they were protected by a Cold War *cordon sanitaire*. By the logic of uneven development, the masses in the security-exposed Third World states could not have exercised sovereignty over their national resources and all develop at the same time. Because on objective grounds as more fall dead when engaged in capitalist production in the AW and Africa, their newly pillaged value exceeds the value accrued from small states (like Taiwan and South Korea) manning the frontiers of the US empire. Here one is assuming the colonially unthinkable, which is that human lives enter as inputs into production processes and are of equal value across the globe.

In the spectrum of Third World developmental experience, somewhere between the conditions of underdevelopment and de-development, states can sometimes detach themselves from an imperialistically dominated accumulation process and adopt a course of self-reliance. This is not an unrealistic detachment, whereby because a developing social entity escapes imperial exploitation, it ceases being an integral part of capital. No developing entity falls beyond the ideological or—closer to the subject—the military reach of capital. The idea that there could be void spaces or islands outside the reach of capital stems from a static perspective irreconcilable with an integrative global history. Even when these Third World states are sucked dry, their abject conditions function as potential material of capital: value grab and ideological goals. With ebbing socialist ideology, their destitution drills fragmentation into labour. In the AW, oil and resources are being sucked dry, and in certain corners such as Yemen, Syria and Iraq, conditions, as is well known, are deplorable.

> What is a realistic prospect, however, is the growing threat to countries, regions and peoples to be marginalized. That is, they may be involuntarily de-linked from the world process of evolution or development. However, they are then de-linked on terms which are not of their own choosing. The most obvious case in point is much of sub-Saharan Africa. There is a decreasing world market in the international division of labour for Africa's natural and human resources. Having been squeezed dry like a lemon in the course of world capitalist 'development', much of Africa may now be abandoned to its fate. However, the same fate increasingly also threatens other regions and peoples elsewhere. (Frank 1996)

Whoever escapes exploitation falls victim to the missile silos of imperialism and is unlikely not to form part of the idle resources available to capital.

These resources are either snatched up or left idle as assets waiting to be directly exploited by capital on demand. Isolated developing formations that ceased to advance on their own terms did so by the incursion of more advanced Western capital. Colonialism deconstructed their national industries. The older colonial ideological line assumed that they were genetically incapable of development. The neoliberal line supposes that they are culturally incapable of progress. These more modern cultural justifications, however, are implicitly genetic. Implicit in mainstream development discourse is the notion that reliance on Western civilisation develops previously undeveloped nations; otherwise, left to themselves, they might as well remain cave dwellers—which of course in reality they were not. In *The Wealth of Nations*, Adam Smith refers to the industrious and rich East (1976, 86).

However, detachment from colonial capital and later US-led capital furnishes the security space for insecure developing states to grow into. When freed, these security-exposed formations evolve their own mode of national capitalism, or better yet, they socialise relations in their own civilisational context. Realistically, however, capitalist metabolic accumulation leaves not a stone unturned. It harnesses world resources, and where it injects prosperity in parts, it must underdevelop other parts. As Rosa Luxemburg puts it:

> The interrelations of accumulating capital and non-capitalist forms of production extend over values as well as over material conditions, for constant capital, variable capital and surplus value alike. The non-capitalist mode of production is the given historical setting for this process. Since the accumulation of capital becomes impossible in all points without non-capitalist surroundings, we cannot gain a true picture of it by assuming the exclusive and absolute domination of the capitalist mode of production. [...] Seeing that the overwhelming majority of resources and labour power is in fact still in the orbit of pre-capitalist production—this being the historical milieu of accumulation—capital must go all out to obtain ascendancy over these territories and social organizations. (Luxemburg 1913)

Recent experience shows no example of successful Arab development. The Gulf's consumption pattern includes industrial establishments that were imported with their know-how and labour. The Gulf industries merely proxy the buying of durable consumption goods, which exhibit no linkages to national industry. These undertakings do not backstop national production or deepen supply chains. In contrast to this model, although the short-lived postindependence Arab development project subdued the liberal notion of citizenship (not that there was or there is citizenship under neoliberalism), it defined a long-term industrial project and a view of the future in which social classes are incorporated within the state. It was not a model of placated hegemony over civil society, but its populist-driven agenda redistributed resources more equitably under controlled trade and capital accounts, hence raising purchasing power and demand for local goods. In the shadow of the nonaligned movement, postindependence Arab states enjoyed a margin of manoeuvre at the critical intersection between national security, sovereignty and the bipolar world order.

As the world transitioned to a US-led unipolar order after the end of the Cold War, the unthinkable happened. The invasion of Iraq, which would have likely resulted in a major transgression on a Soviet area of influence during the Cold War, took place without significant opposition of the great powers. From an unimaginable to an actual condition, the disaster of Iraq and its sectarian fault lines triggered a chain reaction of tension across the Muslim world. It became difficult to distinguish who was more pro–American imperialism: the Iraqi Shia mullahs rooting for American forces or the Wahhabi imams. It was a rare moment in history that denudated the actual political from the imaginary religious. Supposedly opposing sects of Islam objectively allied themselves with the US's and Israel's policy of deconstructing Iraq as part of their factional security objectives. Arab countries further devolved from semiautonomous states into factional states, in these formations, so that it was no longer the state itself that was dependent on imperialism, rather factions within the state. In a manner resembling colonialism, the perverse development that followed was commandeered by foreign capital. The history of development by colonial violence in the AW has not only come full circle, it has also become a downward spiral.

A Synoptic Look Back at History

Although the first shoots of capitalist development were in evidence in the Mediterranean basin by around AD 1500, slowly incubating capitalist relations in the AW picked up speed as a result of direct colonialism in the late nineteenth and early twentieth century. In Ottoman days, neither the grip of the state over its expansive territory nor the level of development in capitalist social relations, technology and production know-how could regiment resources to potentially socialise them. Despite nearly half a million people employed by the Ottoman states in various social functions, the empire's level of development was still lagging in comparison to Europe (Galvin 2004, 80). While the modern nation-state and advances in wage-driven production were on the rise in Europe, the few Arab experiments that attempted to uncap potential wealth via capitalist development—Mohammed Ali of Egypt and the industrial southern belt of the Ottoman Empire linking Tripoli, Aleppo and Mosul—were strangled in the cradle (Al-Duri 1969). The shaping of capitalist development by colonialism selectively reinforced despotic precapitalist relations in the colonies. Colonially bred modes of identity splintered the old social order and regimented the labour process. Outlying resources came within reach of capital. Arab landowning classes tightened their hold on power by a gradual shift to cash crop production, complementing the new mode of integration with colonial Europe. As to the socialisation of the rural areas, the majority of the peasant population remained where they were, working the land to feed themselves and their families.

In contrast to significant export enclaves, principally coastal Algeria and Palestine—the latter exported half a million boxes of oranges to the UK in the late nineteenth century—much of Arab agriculture remained at subsistence level (Scholch 1982). Trade volume with Europe rose, and colonial capital articulated the vast AW of subsistence agriculture with its own mode of production as that world fell under its political jurisdiction. The history of Arab capitalism is said to begin as the high rate of expansion of European capital hitched Arab formations to colonialism (Owen 1969). But a higher degree of integration by trade volume with Europe does not necessarily signify the initiation of capitalism in the AW. The Ottoman Empire was experiencing a dual course of development towards capitalism: firstly by the development of its own capacities, and secondly by its desultory ties to European capital (Lutsky 1975). Capital as a social relationship arose in the AW as it did on much of the planet, via the exigencies of development of productive forces, but its hold over social processes was cemented under colonialism. This differentiation is key because it sheds light on the Eurocentric argument that capitalism was purely a European phenomenon related to its liberal values.

From the redesign of older forms of political organisations into nation-states to the type of civil administrative service, the historical process making the AW became the product of colonialism. True, there were cash crop cultures, vast textile industries and dozens of commercial sea trading posts prior to European colonialism, but the AW lacked two fundamental ingredients: a centralised political authority and advanced weaponry. So advanced was European technology that repeated aerial bombings of Iraqi tribes in the 1920s protesting absentee land ownership could only have been possible under the British (Tarbush 1982). Although the restructuring of precapitalist social relations began under the Ottomans and a momentum was building for a bourgeois transformation conceived locally, colonial forces expedited these changes and their rechannelling. There was no 'precapitalist' Arab formation being assimilated by the Europeans; there was a slowly developing industrial capitalism that was snuffed out by European colonialism (Al-Duri 1969). The colonial *rapport de force* implanted itself in the nascent states as the national power broker. The fact that there are so many Arab states, some small and only viable as outposts of global capital, imply that an Arab industrial structure could not have, *sui generis*, moulded the geographic configuration of today. It is against the *raison d'être* of national industrial capital to fragment its own market.

Not simply because it has more subsistence farmers than wage workers does an Arab region get defined as precapitalist rather than capitalist. Slavery under capitalism was as cruel as if not crueller than past forms of slavery, but it was capitalist. The issue of whether a formation is capitalist or not does not depend on numbers. The size of the reserve army of labour is irrelevant to the definition of capitalism. For a long time, Sudan exhibited a huge unemployment rate while the central pillars of the economy were privately owned, wage-staffed enterprises. Did this characteristic make Sudan precapitalist? It is misleading to constitute a case from these static empirical observations and suppose the coexistence of two distinct modes of production. Sudan and all the other Arab states are within reach of capital—all sorts of reach. Capital after all is a social relationship of control. As a relationship, it has straddled the Arab historical process.

In development under colonialism, it was colonial Europe that determined the metabolic rate of resource utilisation. Gradual infiltrations were followed by occupation and, consequently, the conditions of surplus-value usurpation came to be determined almost entirely by the pace of European capital. Outright colonialism signalled the beginning of 'hegemonic articulation'. The full wrath of Western colonial practice bore down upon the Arab peasantry and working classes. The surplus peasant population, although delinked from capitalist production proper, represented a mass of workers that maintained downward pressure on national and international wages. This population was articulated into colonial capital by violence, which was to overpower impoverished areas. This rather long passage from Lutsky (and Elgwood as quoted by Lutsky) describing the practice of forced labour illustrates how bonded Egyptian labour was made to march in front of British soldiers in the First World War so that the enemy may exhaust its ammunition on shovel-wielding peasants before it reaches British soldiers.

> Egyptians were recruited to the labour corps two or three times a year. Each time, up to 135,000 men were called up. Officially, the recruitment was supposed to be voluntary. [...] In 1917, the voluntary system was abolished and the British recruiting agents began working in the open. What were these labour corps like? Why did the entire adult male population of the villages flee to the desert at the sight of the recruiting agents? Why did thousands of starving people avoid the doubtful honour of becoming 'volunteers'? Why did soldiers and police comb the land for these 'volunteers' who had fled, and deliver them under guard to the barracks?

Because service in the labour corps was the worst kind of penal servitude. [...] They were often the first to come under enemy attack. When the British advanced across the Sinai Desert into Palestine the Egyptian labour corps went in the fore, paving the way with their bodies as well as their work. [...] All told, over one million Egyptian fellaheen and workers passed through this hell. [...] The British used the Egyptian labour corps not only on the Suez front. Egyptian fellaheen with shovels in their hands could be seen in Gallipoli, in Mesopotamia and in far-off Lorraine. According to official data, in 1916 alone, over 10,000 fellaheen were sent to France and over 8,000 to Mesopotamia. (Lutsky 1969)

It is not therefore possible for a hybrid mode of production, half capitalist and half precapitalist, to have emerged when capital is defined as a social relationship as opposed to capital being a pile of commodities or a mass of money. Capitalist relations cemented noncapitalist relations to the extent that social regimentation of labour was possible under prevailing conditions. Deconstructed by European military incursions, national capitalism germinating in the AW prior to its contact with Europe could not pursue its own route to development. Once capital comes into the picture, a capitalist labour process and its associated unemployment and wage system emerge. The wage system transforms precapitalist social relationships, including the shape and substance of the political form of organisation *cum* the nation-state. Despite being seminally articulated with capital, the emerging Arab state under colonialism did not attain even superficial characteristics of autonomy—that is, moderate separation of economic from political interests through the legal system—as occurred at the inceptions of the colonising states. Although Egypt and Iraq have been supposedly independent states since circa 1920, not one major decision in these states has been taken without colonial consent. In one morose incident from the pile of facts indicating their subordination, the Iraqi prime minister (circa 1935) was slapped repeatedly by the British ambassador to Baghdad:

The British Ambassador (circa 1935) relates an encounter with Prime Minister Hikmat Suleiman which, in addition to clearly showing the immense degree of British influence in Iraq, also reflects the weakness of the Prime Minister's character. The Ambassador informed the Foreign Office how he told Hikmat Suleiman very sharply that his manners were bad. [...] When [...] the time came to tell him what was thought about it [the Government's desire to buy arms from-non-British sources] by all in London, I was in some difficulty because I had, as it were, to hold him up with one hand and hit him with the other, I hit him, nevertheless, and the blow was hard—because I took him by surprise. (Tarbush 1982)

In colonised formations, the colonial power chooses the measures of distribution by which value is drawn from the subsumed working class, but more importantly, how the distribution impacts all the joints of social and political domination. The Arab state, gestated socially in a colonial antidevelopmental context, and the forces opposing indigenous development were reinforced by the discovery of oil qua oil control. The proportions of waged to unwaged labour are irrelevant to defining Arab formations as capitalist. The undervalorisation of subsistence farming and the disengagement of peasants from the countryside emerged by colonial diktat despite the fact that the capitalist enclave could not have possibly engaged the massive exodus from the land.

The way conventional explanation treats resource dislocation, including proletarianisation, is to assume that the categories of low technical development and low marginal productivity pre-exist in less-developed formations, and hence resources migrate into areas of higher productivity and returns. These are presented as givens, without historical basis. Little is said of the fact that by the mid-nineteenth century, textile industries flourished in both the Levant and Egypt—silk and cotton respectively. In Mohammed Ali's development project, industry employed nearly forty thousand wage workers (Al-Duri 1969). Then, by the late nineteenth century, European colonialism imposed trade conditions that eroded national industry, which resulted in the first phase of Arab industrial decline. Colonial suppression accentuated an inherent path of uneven development under capitalism by hindering indigenous industrialisation (Al-Duri 1969). More important, colonialism set the exchange price of the local currency in relation to its own currency at levels that undervalued the output of the dominated country, especially the countryside. By the late 1870s, the Ottoman Empire literally pawned Egypt's tax revenue to Britain, and £1 million in taxes had to be excised from the Egyptian peasantry to service Ottoman debts to British banks (Lutsky 1976). Farming areas were condemned to poverty in relation to wealthier small enclaves made up of middlemen and compradors. Looking back at this experience and other similar ones in the Third World, Anouar Abdel-Malik formulated his concept of the historical surplus value: the build-up of central wealth as a result of undermining the production processes of colonised formations (Abdel-Malik 1981). Yet, all the value that formed in the centre in relation to the value snatched from the Third World does not necessarily mean that central working classes exact a toll on peripheral ones. This is not an issue of shares, who gets what and how much. It is an issue of revolutionary consciousness, such that when it comes into bloom, it will reveal the organic unity of working classes as they reappropriate the wealth that is theirs.

As rural abjection and poverty rose, the mainstream addressed it in absolutist terms and attributed it to the peasantry's own technical shortcomings and not to the shifting of value from the countryside to colonialism (Harris 1970). There was little to explain how these low-technology situations came to exist (they were crushed) or why there should be an interconnection between less-developed and more-developed formations. By price motive alone, the price of total capital assets in some Arab countries would not compare to the price of a single luxury street in central cities. In most colonial campaigns, the money cost of wars may outstrip in money value form the benefits from the exploitation of the colonised countries, but not in underpriced value form. If it did so, imperialism ceases to be a politico-economic domain. Yet in hindsight colonisation appears imperative to central capital. As to why there needs be a disengagement of resources in the colonies, or an uprooting from the land and an exchange of labour services for wages, the mainstream claims that an individual makes a choice to engage in waged work. The colonial conditions that create the necessary environment for the dislocation of any resource, including labour, are brushed aside. A more comprehensive view of resource decommissioning would address the impact of the incessant imperialist assault on various social levels that mediate the action of the social class in charge of resource allocation; not the money form, but the interdependent flux of value relations and transfers, which exposes the rationale for colonialism.

In value terms, the reasons to bludgeon the Third World in relation to the social requirements of capital persist. In the AW as in many parts of the Third World, colonialists restructured resources for the picking. The benefits of European capital to the working class in the centre were tardy and skimpy, but altogether they were devastating to the Third World, in which the AW falls on the low end (Baran 1952). By the condition of irreplicable historical time, that is, when comparing capitalist development in relation to itself in real time, one may say that there is nothing progressive about capital now.

The inertia of unequal exchange lingering from colonial days still affords the imperialist forces the authority to dictate the terms of exchange. Here I am using unequal exchange to mean the totality of interactions and value relations and not the narrow declining terms of trade dictum of dependency theory. Following the postcolonial development project, Arab capitalism has relapsed into severe crisis since 1980. Its rate of build-up in productive capacity generated from within has been sluggish. Instead of social transformation and institutions mediating local development requirements with their global contexts—including knowledge exchange and trade that could galvanise local production—the militarised side of global capital seized upon the opportunity presented by social retrogression and unemployment and shattered Arab social entities. In resource-deprived formations, the schism between social being and social consciousness, between what living conditions are and what revolutionary ideas engage people in a development project, gaped wide.

Reinvented forms from the precapitalist past, actually from a non-existent history, were propped up by oil funds to mystify living conditions. Arab ex-pat workers returning from the Gulf to the protected economies of Syria and Egypt in the early 1980s were holding on to high-purchasing-power dollars and the ideals of antisocialist Wahhabism—then fighting to liberate Afghanistan from the Soviets. Between defeats in war and the deployment of antirational religious ways of comprehending reality, the general state of consciousness sank in some aspects to adherence to a schizophrenic mode of perception—which is not so different conceptually from neoclassical economic symbolism.

Working-class solidarity in war-beleaguered social formations is regressed by the destruction of resources, the absence of progressive reforms and the lapse in public spaces meant for socialisation. Instead of ideology as a system that describes real relations which govern the existence of individuals, ideology becomes the imaginary relation of those individuals to the real relations in which they live. The brand of the eternal and unconscious ideology, to employ Althusser's concepts again, promotes abstract and private being and departs from the realisation of social being. In general terms, social being correlates with social ideology, and the latter has receded. At this juncture, an ideology that situates human beings in an existence that is privately rather than socially determined, and which reverts blame for regression onto this imagined private individual, commands the discourse more than at any other time in recent history. As reforms and revolutions go hand in hand, so counter-reforms, arising from lost real and ideological wars, accompany counter-revolutions. Selectively devolved and financed, resurrected traditional structures are given a new political identity through which their share of the social product is determined. Labour divided along religious or ethnic identity lines will be further alienated from the objects required for its survival. In a system structured by capital, a social class as a process realising itself cannot begin to overcome its own internal divisions unless the structure of power is overturned by its hegemony and alliances with other classes—in much of the developing world, chiefly the peasantry. Simply put: working-class struggle requires unity and the situation of class above identity, which is in this era a daunting task.

The slow rate of transforming the reserve labour pool into actively engaged wage labour in endeavours to raise productivity leaves a vast space for petrodollars to develop a system of patronage. In times of crisis of overproduction, the whole idea of employing the majority of workers in high-productivity jobs is simply ludicrous. In the crevice between permanent unemployment and delusional efficiency criteria, the patronage system employs an ideology and promotes selective customs meant to justify the preponderance of idle human resources. The high percentage of Sharia students in the total student body in Saudi Arabia is not a foolish policy that keeps labour from producing actual commodities. The whole purpose of Sharia studentship is to keep labour self-delusional when opportunities for productive work cannot be created. By political Islam, one is reminded of Wilhelm Reich's early work, which among other things analyses the role of both grandiose national myth and the neopatriarchal reduction of women to baby-making machines in justifying Nazi repression and harsh social discipline. The Sharia policy is meant to establish a code of law and conduct so rigid and doctrinaire that even thought outside it, let alone action, is an abomination, because Sharia, which is actually repression in the labour process, is divine will. This stringency in Sharia, by the way, is only true of the modern Wahhabi Sharia. In fact, the many schools of Sharia that were formerly practiced as Islamic jurisprudence, especially during the Abbasid period, varied widely according to the requirements of historical conditions of the times. But since the newly funded Saudi ideology justifies every misery in terms of divine will and the 'mercy' and 'compassion' of the deity, it induces a numbing and even a schizoid dissociation between experience and the enforced conscious interpretation of that experience (Reich 2013). Fantasies built from a falsified history of Islam impose modes of consciousness that attribute politically caused economic and social disaster to divine retribution.

As said above, reinvented identity politics has separated a social mode of being—the working-class experience—from the necessity to struggle in unison against the precariousness of economic conditions caused by the capitalist-induced market. In 'pre-capitalist epochs, class consciousness is unable to achieve complete clarity and to influence the course of history consciously, or because class interests in pre-capitalist society never achieve full (economic) articulation and hence the structuring of society into castes and estates means that economic elements are inextricably joined to political and religious factors, for these manifestations of working-class frailty exist in all societies' (Lukacs 1967, 55). For the Frankfurt school, however, the disarticulation of state of being from state of consciousness is more acute in Western formations' internalising ethos of differentiated racism and invading developing formations. Probably a relatable explanation of the generality of this phenomenon can come from literary sources: Goethe remarked that cultures decay when characterised by the tendency to pure subjectivity, while all progressive periods try to grasp the world as it is (Goethe 1826).

Moreover, the defeatism attendant upon the military crushing of the Arab working class also induces consent to despotism. The futility of struggling against combined US–Israeli military superiority is touted as a 'pragmatic' choice for the masses. In actuality, the main result of this pragmatism is its function for imperial power, which is that of using shortened life expectancy and deaths from wars, generally the abstract labour of Africa and the AW, as inputs in the factories of capital elsewhere.

Because the AW as a condition of primacy to US-led capital serves to undermine other imperialist powers, the political logic explaining the narrow geographical strip so named departs from economic rationales. Imperialism in the AW can be clarified with politics without the economics. Mercantilist-like convictions, such as that US-led capital's ultimate goal is to own all the oil wells by title deed or to trade with the poorer world, conceal the fact that capital is primarily about hegemony and regimentation first and that oil may or may be that lucrative of a deal. When in control, imperialism practically owns the resources anyway. Would a title deed be necessary or is it superfluous? Also, why trade with more than three hundred million working people who earn such meagre wages, when the case may be that the brutalisation and debilitation of Arab working classes pressure larger and wealthier economies to financially concede to US-led capital's own terms? At the most basic level, the issue remains that of capital's insatiable thirst for cheapened resources and the direction of the circuit of capital. At more higher and more complex levels under financialisation, Arab formations are principal pawns in financial rent grab and interimperialist rivalry. It is from this roundabout way of power and finance that the money circuits to US empire begin to surface.

Dislocation under Neoliberalism

Much as under colonialism, under neoliberalism a process of dislocation has gained momentum. Peasants, in particular, have borne the brunt of it as they are increasingly divorced from their previous means and ways of livelihood. Capitalism has as its final goal the destruction of the former modes of production and relations of production all over the world in order to substitute its own mode of production and production relations for them (Rey 1978). However, these substitutions are neither immediate nor complete. Rey adds:

> Capitalism can never immediately and totally eliminate the preceding modes of production, nor above all the relations of production which characterize these modes of production. On the contrary, during an entire period it must reinforce these relations of exploitation, since it is only this development which permits its own provisioning with goods coming from these modes of production, or with men driven from these modes of production and therefore compelled to sell their labour power to capitalism in order to survive. (Rey 1978)

However, in line with Rey's critique of the stages of structuralism, the AW experienced a crisis of transition to capitalism and later became chained to a process of development under persistent crisis. There were no substitutions, rather a process of less industrially evolved Arab formations forcibly complementing more industrial colonialists. The social ruptures in the Arab formations were reinforced at every stage by political and constitutional frameworks designed in a context of national and class wars by the colonialist forces. In the postindependence period, building Arab national economies was arduous to begin with, and precarious when income became more dependent on oil and geopolitical revenues. The social institutions assembled around Arab capital mirrored its powerlessness to fully socialise and engage labour. By 'socialise' here I mean: make the private farmer on the land a social labourer by eviction. By 'fully socialise' I mean: create wage labour that is actively employed in productive industry, not labour that is merely waiting to be employed and that meanwhile ekes out a minimum subsistence in the informal sector—that is, expelling farmers from private lands or socialising them without re-employing them later. At the height of the neoliberal phase, the contradictions between various concrete labour sectors were fuelled by a declining labour share of value and an increasing division of labour (resulting from imported higher technology) and a mode of discipline rooted in feudal despotism. The socially necessary labour and abstract labour are realised in conditions doubly foreshadowed by national merchants and imperialists. The very destruction of the economy from which the merchants circulate their money capital can sometimes be the objective of the US-led imperialist. Because imperialism is in the driver's seat, in the AW socially necessary labour corresponds even more remotely than in other capitalist corners to the necessities of its own society.

Value drain from peripheral agricultural areas in the AW was not restored through exchange with more advanced enclaves. The countryside, the place where the majority lived, slowly perished. Although politically, the less-developed areas of the AW remained under the purview of the central governments, a combination of deliberate underpricing of rural human and agricultural values, highly unequal distribution and rural under-representation entrenched their fringe status. As the state became progressively captured by US-led capital under neoliberalism, the crisis of the rural areas reached tragic proportions. Rural poverty estimates were two to three times the rates of poverty in the urban areas (FAO 2007). Between 1980 and 2010 the share of the rural population from total population in the AW dropped significantly from about sixty per cent to around forty per cent. In absolute terms, an estimated seventy million people moved from the countryside to urban centres within their homelands.[2]

---

2 These are very conservative estimates based on fixed coefficients of population growth and rates of rural–urban migration. These estimates do not include migration outside the AW. A middle-range estimate would put this figure at around one hundred million. Economic and Social Commission for Western Asia (ESCWA), *The Demographic Profile of Arab Countries Ageing Rural Population* (United Nations 2008).

This estimate does not take into account the huge numbers who migrated to the countryside around Cairo and who are still counted as rural area residents. To bring things into focus, this conservative estimate is nearly equivalent to the total number of rural–urban migrants since the beginning of the twentieth century until 1980. In a sense, neoliberalism is competing with old-style colonialism in how rapidly and brutally it dislocates Arab labour and resources.

In addition to war and a ruling class that combined political and economic control without recourse for any conflicting interests, as of the early 1980s the AW entered into inauspicious trade treaties with the rest of the world (nearly all Arab states are signatories to the WTO). These supposedly free treaties also disguised the structural terms of surrender to imperialism. The very word 'free' marks an insidious form of enslavement in waiting for the weaker party. The inflow of cheap imported food drove peasants into poverty as the socialising ideology of resistance waned. Instead of a social ideology that tallies with their social conditions, the mosques of the countryside funded by Wahhabism and Iranian Shiism relegated the causes of the social condition to a religiously tinted positivism of the human condition. By being uprooted they were socialised, but they were deprived of the social, ideological and organisational means to develop a framework that would wrest for them a decent livelihood and more equitable social standards. After the uprisings, the desperate corners of the countryside became poorer and also the sites of Salafi Islamic movements.[3]

While this exodus was occurring, basic food production was decreasing and food imports were rising. The AW is a region where food-price hikes immediately impact the livelihood of the working population. With the exception of Syria (just prior to the 2011 uprising) and Morocco, the consumed food bundle is more than half imported; hence a rise in food prices can reduce income by the exact proportion of national currency spent on food priced in the dollar. As noted in the first chapter, for half of the population, expenditure on food consumes half their income. For countries not experiencing balance-of-payments problems (the GCC countries), importing food is not much of an issue, since they can foot the import bill. However, as agricultural production declined, the poorer economies—Yemen in particular—faced additional debt to cover imports of basic food. As elsewhere, 'free trade' treaties simultaneously undermined domestic agricultural production, food security and national security. Altogether, food consumption per capita in the AW has declined

---

3   'Egypt's Poverty Rate Rises to 26 Per Cent in 2012/13: CAPMAS', Ahram Online, 28 November 2013. Online: http://english.ahram.org.eg/News/87776.aspx (viewed 29 November 2013).

slightly over the past decade (FAO, various years). With conflicts afflicting more countries after the Arab spring, food shortages and malnutrition became more pronounced. In 2012, half a million Yemeni children were at risk of suffering physical and mental damage as a result of malnutrition.[1] Problems of caloric intake deficiency and hunger increasingly plague the working classes in the poorer and conflict-damaged countries.

Arab regimes and World Bank policymakers have deliberately eroded national agriculture and instilled food dependency in the rural sectors by opening up trade unconditionally, designing macro policy that accentuates unevenness and reduces investment in agriculture. On average, by early 2000 employment in agriculture was half its 1970 share, and agricultural contribution to GDP, which was already low, went down by a third (World Bank 2004). Dependence on food imports is rising throughout the AW (FAO stats, various years). 'Free' agricultural trade treaties introduced since the early 1980s have intensified a process of rural–urban migration and, instead of shifting resources from allegedly 'uncompetitive' farming into areas of comparative advantage, as per the neoliberal mantra, they have instead added to unemployment in the urban areas. The national agricultural base is no match for the protected, highly productive and subsidised agriculture of the centre. Depriving people of the independence that comes from self-sufficiency in food production is both necessary to lower wages and also to corrode any potential social base for labour's resistance. In that sense, proletarianisation became inseparable from the process of socialisation under capitalism or the destruction of forms of petty private property, which is a requirement for profit-driven accumulation.

Closing Comment

The Arab uprisings occurred in an era of crisis in humanist theory and its ideological progeny, socialism. This is not at all similar to the position that Lenin expressed to seize state power when faced with the question of the acquisition of state power in semideveloped Russia. At the time, the ideological power of social democracy was sweeping the planet. Lenin's injunction (1917) that the only choice was to seize opportunity and power had behind it an internationalist movement that offered weighty support. As of 1980, the politics of differentiated containment began to show results in Poland, neoliberalism was sweeping the globe, and social-democratic ideals were in retreat.

---

4   'UNICEF Warns on High Rates of Malnutrition among Children in Yemen', UN News Centre, 25 January 2012. Online: http://www.un.org/apps/news/story. asp?NewsID=41037&Cr=yemen&Cr1= (viewed 13 June 2012).

By 1990, the fall of the Soviet Union shattered what remained of the utopia of egalitarianism and ushered in an era of triumphant capitalism. Neoliberal ideology, whose incessant chant was Margaret Thatcher's 'There is no alternative', dominated the social discourse and spearheaded policy. As elsewhere, income inequality in the AW rose at a rate that stripped economic growth of its supposed benefits to the working class. Capital, the social relationship, rose to prominence, and accentuated the symptoms of the private sector's necrotrophic symbiosis with the public sphere.

There are no stages where one waits for a bright future after a stint in social purgatory. Every antisocial reform adopted now influences the future. The more antisocial the reforms become, the more central reforms assume the shape of a bribe to central working class, the further social revolutions retreat. There are two salient cases characterising the countries of the Arab uprisings. The first is the disintegration of the state and its transformation into a territory plagued with violence. These countries are Yemen, Syria and Libya. The second case, comprising Egypt and Tunisia, saw the rise of Islamists to power. Despite worsening social conditions after the uprisings, ideological Islam appears to have lowered the threshold at which people's distaste for their conditions leads to revolt on the one hand, and ratcheted up the power of the ruling class on the other. When one adds to this picture Lebanon, Palestine, Iraq and Sudan, we are confronted with an immense social calamity. In the AW, where one witnesses economic growth and where one does not, the bottom line is: *there is no development.*

The uprisings so far have led to state collapse or to the redomination of old bourgeois ideology. This is only secondarily because bourgeois ideology is far older in origin than variants of socialism, or because it is more fully developed, as Lenin noted in 1902. It is principally because US-led imperialism has supported, organised and disseminated propaganda boosting the Islamic/ Salafi alternative as the sole alternative for social change. Add to that the retrogression in socialist ideology, which has made it all the more effortless for a non-existent phantasm of Islamic history to incarnate the present social discourse. Where Salafi doctrine reins, the spiritual disarticulation it inflicts upon society transcendentally moves consciousness from a concrete comprehension of social processes to an alienation emanating from the money fetishism of modern society, but more so in an Islamic context, it will be cloaked in obscurantism. To shed more light on this, where Herbert Marcuse's one-dimensional man escapes the drudgery of everyday life with modern props that estrange him from others and himself, political Islam provides medieval catechism to do the same for Arab workers today.

Wahhabi versions of political Islam anaesthetise the revolutionary consciousness otherwise destined to spring up in societies undergoing commodification by the forces of imperialist penetration. Not only the neopatriarchal separation of the sexes, but every social measure political Islam implements reinforces the rule of capital. Fundamentalist political Islam à la al-Qaeda is as Chossudovsky (2005) rightly defines it: a US intelligence asset because it acts in favour of capital even when it is supposedly the enemy of the foremost capitalist class, which is the US's. However, nearly all colours of obscurantist versions of political Islam are an ideological asset to capital. Political Islam was purposefully othered by a differentiated structure of racism to make it into the identity of the oppressed. Political Islam was boosted in the Cold War as part of the anticommunist effort and is, more recently, laid out on imperialist grounds as in the shallow differences between Saudi-backed or Qatari-backed colours of political Islam. As such, it is a cultural fetish meant for mobilisation against the Arab working classes. None of political Islam's tenets, as they are today, have existed in the past. It is the mongrelised progeny of Western capitalism. It diverts anti-imperialist resistance into wasteful ends. In a sense, Saudi Arabia, the model peripheral state to imperialism, is being replicated everywhere in the Islamic world and to some extent in the centre as the welfare state withers away. Wealth snatched from the working classes appears to have been bestowed by divine right on merchant capital. Obligations in political Islam obviate rights. The Arab uprisings occurred in the wrong historical moment, one in which the absence of alternative (cooperative, egalitarian) models of social change moved back the historical starting line to the vantage of imperialism.

Chapter Seven

ARAB DISINTEGRATION AND THE RISING POWER OF IMPERIALISM

To resume earlier main points: the Arab world is imperialistically overdetermined (Avramidis 2006a). Imperialist assault, whether militarily or through value-sapping neoliberal policies, explains much of its underdevelopment. After three decades of sustained aggression, the majority of Arab states are decomposing from within. Deterioration in the quality of health, education and nutrition, along with rising food dependency, among many other social variables, indicate receding national security and, conversely, rising US-led imperialist hegemony. Disintegration, both nationally and regionally, has marked the recent path of Arab history. The actual costs of disintegration to working classes in terms of lost lives and living standards are immense. Counterfactually speaking, the costs of an integrative process could have been lighter and the gains in national security (from which many other forms of security follow) could have been significant. The merchant ruling class, which is innately comprador, deploys the cant of pan-Arab or national integration to placate the working classes while implementing policies that have long caused dissolution. It is important to recall that the class pull of world financial capital on the merchant class in charge of Arab development is stronger than its national commitment.

In this chapter, I argue that sovereignty and industrialisation are requisites for integration around a 'social contract' or an egalitarian redistribution-bolstered class entente within a nation-state, and that they also promote cross-border integration with other working class–bolstered nation-states. So far, the elephant in the room is an AW that has deindustrialised and lost wars, both of which processes have vitiated its sovereignty. Also, the industrial mode of development that was gaining ground in the postindependence years ebbed and was replaced by a merchant mode around which social life is now organised. Commerce bereft of industry (the merchant mode) spends on political stabilisation and does not reinvest for development. Merchants tapping into natural or geopolitical resources lose if they integrate with other merchants. They also lose if they integrate their own working class by investing in it.

The merchant mode that came to hold primacy in Arab development therefore predictably severed the umbilical cord tying private to public concerns. The incapacitation of nascent Arab industry under neoliberalism caused the working class to become 'social' (that is incapable of providing for itself by its own means) without being decently employed. Moreover, obscurantist ideology funded by oil revenues has further disarticulated the working masses' state of consciousness. Through ideological channels, overbearing imperialist military power has supported the merchant-class deployment of sectarian and other forms of social divisions that have drained the working class of unity. The struggle for working-class unity and for Arab integration, not necessarily on the basis of pan-Arabism but at least on the basis of anti-imperialism, is crucial to arrest value transfer by neoliberal dispossession and encroachment wars. This chapter concludes that reintegrating the Arab state within itself and integrating the Arab state with other Arab states depends on the outcome of the present struggle and the extent to which the working class grasps power within the state.

Economic integration requires a level of development surpassing the early stages of industrialisation. Past the early stages of industrial development, one expects an autonomous rise in productivity, incomes and, consequently, welfare. As mentioned in Chapter One, the AW exhibits declining productivity growth rates in the presence of underemployment and the highest unemployment rates globally (KILM, various years). In underdeveloped oil states where money capital and absorptive capacity are abundant, national markets are condemned to divest and not to redeploy resources nationally or regionally. The point was made in Chapter Five that Gulf petrodollars have contributed to ideologically shredding and to lessening the competiveness of the national productive bases of many Arab economies. Therefore, the two intertwined conditions of sovereignty and industrialisation that would have laid the grounds for a process of integration are shrivelling in the AW.

Alongside imperialist bellicosity, the merchant mode of accumulation obstructs integrative transformation. Maldistribution and the near-absence of positive intermediation between private and public wealth supplant the welfare base for working-class autonomy and, hence, integration as well. The merchant mode revolves around quick private gains, does not require productive reinvestment in society, and usurps wealth by financial means. It does not rent grab. The notion of rentierism or rent grab is inappropriate to the neocolonial situation of the AW. Often, the critique of local Arab ruling classes as 'rentiers' serves as an *ad hominem* argument meant to conceal the fact that value transfers away from the working class are conducted by the alliance of the Arab merchant and US-led capital classes. Rents are the rightful bread and butter of Arab working classes and it is their theft or the theft of the national wealth that impedes development. As explained in the introduction, the merchant mode of accumulation is a reincarnation of old mercantilism in a modern guise, including the 'backward conditions'. The degeneration in social and political rights, including the status of women, is a vivid manifestation of the social retrogression driven by the ebbing of the cultural spinoffs associated with industrialisation in much of the AW.

Arab mercantilism differs from that of Germany and China. One may recall that present-day exporting industrial superpowers such as Germany and China are dubbed 'mercantilist' in the sense that they often exhibit a trade surplus. But the AW is not and has never been as industrial as Germany. German mercantilism is the commerce of industry selling its products and accumulating a trade surplus consistently over time. The Arab merchant mode is about taking raw or semi-raw products out of the nation-states and selling them. Alongside developing chattel slavery and nationalisms laced with racism and colonial genocide, European mercantilists engaged wage labour in industry and introduced technology and a complex division of labour. They did this under the global pressure of rising trade volumes to meet the demands of the emergent world market. In this way they initiated the wealth-making process of capitalism circa AD 1500. In the AW, however, deindustrialisation, state stabilisation spending derived from oil or geopolitical revenues, and the rise of informal or low-productivity service activity laid the foundation for the new material basis of social relationships. The subjugation of national capital to norms of financial capital, whose activity is centred on money exchange, also imposes acceleration on the duration of the turnover of profits in the national economy. Where Arab industrial and merchant capital did remain tied to each other, the space for their joint activities to produce and sell at home or abroad accounted for a puny portion of total income under neoliberalism. Uneven development, by hindering the homogenisation of labour (the bridging of wage gaps) and value grab by imperialist conquest, also assisted the ascent of merchant capital in the AW. Capital, to be sure, regulates its metabolic rate of reproduction—the consumption of man and nature—by value grab and value creation simultaneously (Lenin 1917). The weaker states of Africa and the AW mainly fall on the grab side of capital. A process of deindustrialisation and fragmentation is the mainstay of their principal historical subject, which is US-led capital.

Imperialist hegemony and the merchant mode are interrelated; they reinforce each other. However, imperialist assault is the underlying historical moment around which all other moments coalesce. The merchant mode of accumulation sets in motion anti-integrationist dynamics. It splinters societies. If a scale of reference serves to illustrate the point, it divides according to the magnitude of its subordination to US-led financial capital.

Furthermore, the merchant mode requires little expansion in productive capacity or synchronisation of human skills with expanding technology. The conventional wisdom posits that oil and geopolitical revenues in the AW are unearned incomes. That is a fallacious and misleading claim. These incomes are earned at tremendous social and environmental costs to the working classes; human losses in war and the demobilisation of resources are incurred by society as a whole. The reified nation-state concept confounds oppressor with oppressed. The joint loot of the Arab ruling classes and their international patrons *is* unearned income; however, the rest of the Arabs—the street vendors, the unemployed, the populations stricken by poverty and war—have more than earned their own shrinking share. As the merchant mode governs social activity, oil and geopolitical revenues are mainly spent on increasing imports, domestic pacification and foreign assets. These measures address US-led imperialist objectives that thrive on the pauperisation and disempowerment of Arab working classes in relation to its hegemony. In the integrated web of global production, national boundaries can no longer disguise the fact that capital draws on a huge pool of global resources. The idleness of Arab resources is closely tied to the central crisis of overproduction. Wealth is humanity's wealth but, conversely, working-class deintegration in the AW is the heavy price paid for the unearned income of the ruling-class alliance. More important, the re-empowerment of Arab working classes could dent the hegemony of the US–Israeli alliance over a region in which they enjoy 'the freedom of action—notably military action—that is almost unparalleled globally' (Levy 2013).

Arab Disintegration in Numbers

The AW exhibits one of the lowest rates of intraregional trade integration in the world. Despite the AW's high degree of openness to the rest of the world, intraregional trade integration remained historically low even after the Greater Arab Free Trade Area (GAFTA) came into effect in 1997. The AW exports significant quantities of raw material (oil) and its competiveness in manufactured exports ranks below the average for least developed countries (UN 2011). Despite an openness rate of 86 per cent (average for the several years before the uprisings) with the rest of the world, the average intraregional trade proportion remained below 12 per cent, and in the case of the GCC intra-trade ratio, it is as low as 6 per cent (UN 2011). In comparison with other regions, the share of intra-Asian trade for instance was 25 per cent and that of intra–Latin American trade was 40 per cent in 2007, while the shares of intra-NAFTA and intra-EU trade were 41 and 66 per cent respectively of their total trade (UN 2011). Historically, the annual average rate of growth of intraregional imports dropped from 14 per cent during the period 1986–89, to 7 per cent during the period 1990–96, bouncing back to 10 per cent during the 1997–2003 period after the GAFTA agreements were ratified, to drop again to 8 per cent during the 2003–09 period (UN 2011).

A cursory look at the share of manufacturing's value added to GDP in Arab countries reveals that on average most of them are low, mostly around the ten per cent mark (LAS, Joint Arab Economic Report 2011, 79). According to the World Bank, the share of manufacturing in investment is declining almost everywhere, and the share of manufacturing in gross domestic product (GDP) is lower than that in all other developing regions except sub-Saharan Africa (World Bank 2011a). However, the share of high-technology exports from total manufactured exports in the AW is at around one to two percentage points, below the rank of sub-Saharan Africa—including South Africa, which is around five per cent (WDI, various years).[1] Historically, the share of investment in GDP, as noted in Chapter One, has been falling and its low output-capital-ratio activity does not hold the promise of conversion to large-scale industry (UN 2008b). The shares of manufacturing value added in Egypt, Syria and Iraq fell significantly, whereas the shares of Gulf countries rose (UN 2007d). Saudi Arabia displays a share of ten per cent in manufacturing value added (LAS 2011). The reason behind this rise is that huge petrochemical plants were 'branch planted' (imported) along with their skilled labour and know-how, tapping into low-paid Asian labour and cheap energy—and therefore generating few positive linkages to the national economy. The jump in this figure led some to argue that Saudi Arabia exhibits traits of a developmental state (Niblock 2007, Hertog 2010). More recently, it is difficult if not absurd to claim that Saudi Arabia has 'developed' when the press carries stories of leading Saudi clerics warning that driving inflicts damage on women's reproductive organs.[2] In any case, with so few tertiary linkages, such rare permutations on oil-value added, and such low employment capacity, the Saudi supply chain remains shallow and the imported petrochemical know-how is incompatible with the broader knowledge base of the economy. Far from signifying development, the inhumane conditions suffered by Asian service labourers in these establishments point in the opposite direction. In any case, the share of industry as a source of the national income remains low (SAMA, annual report, various years). With the rise in oil prices beginning

---

1   It would probably be the same as sub-Saharan Africa's share, but South Africa's exports push Africa's share upward.
2   'Saudi Cleric Says Driving Risks Damaging Women's Ovaries', BBC News, 29 September 2013. Online: http://www.bbc.co.uk/news/world-middle-east-24323934 (viewed 2 October 2013).

in 2002, oil's contribution has also risen as a proportion of national incomes (UN 2009a).

Intra-Arab investments and capital flows have remained steady and low by international standards. However, the economic impact of highly valued cash in pauperised rural areas is significant (UN 2010). The incoming flows restructure rural societies by rewarding the service activity related to the demands of the cash-holding expatriates and undercompensating the productive activity in subsistence areas. Propped up by the exchange rate differential, the wage rate in farming areas climbs, which also makes the labour-intensive production of staple items costly in comparison to the mass produced imported items. This shift away from farming is also supported by the open-ended trade treaties, which altogether overhaul the old social relationships and weaken the traditional support base of farmers.

The AW in general and the Gulf countries in particular remain net exporters of capital to Western markets, as can be discerned from the rates of capital flight and the savings output rates of the oil economies, which exceed the investment output rates (UN 2007). To illustrate with averages for the Gulf states: over the period 2002–10 the average savings rate headed toward fifty per cent, while average investment rate dipped below twenty per cent (WDI, various years).

Intraregional investments mainly went to countries that implemented 'policies conducive to strengthening the operational framework of the domestic financial market, namely Egypt and Jordan' (UN 2011). These are countries whose malleable ruling classes had been fully co-opted in an arrangement favouring US–Israel security. Subtle imperialist considerations dictate the interdependence between Gulf countries and other Arab economies. The expulsions of Palestinians from Kuwait, of Yemenis from Saudi Arabia and of Arab Shiites from the Gulf states recursively illuminate the selective process that determines the numbers of Arab migrant labour and the size of the remittances.[3] The aid intervention of the Gulf states in the successive wars in Iraq, the financing of the First Gulf War, the refinancing of the Second Gulf War, along with the GCC countries' (limited) contributions to the rebuilding of Iraq (not that it was rebuilt), post-uprising aid to Egypt and Tunisia, and their financing the Syrian armed opposition are measures that leveraged US-led capital's objectives.[4] Not only in agriculture, the pressure from petrodollars

---

3   B. Surk, 'Lebanon Shiites Ousted from Gulf as Hezbollah Fans', *Associated Press*, 11 July 2013. Online: http://bigstory.ap.org/article/lebanon-shiites-ousted-gulf-hezbollah-fans (viewed 24 July 2013).

4   According to the Central Bank of Egypt, reserves fell by, on average, around $2 billion a month in October, November and December 2011 and January 2012. Recently, reserves decline by some $600 million a month. They are now at $15.2 billion, half

on locally generated wages mounted in the countries supplying labour to the Gulf, which in turn created a two-tier wage system that contributed to national working-class divisions. For segments of labour, the rise in local wages encumbered nationally bred capital with higher costs uncompensated by rising productivity, production prices or expanding markets. The result was a dichotomy between the two strands of the economy: the economy linked with Gulf petrodollars involved in service and low-productivity endeavours, and the national productive economy, whose competitiveness was dampened by the externally induced boost to wages. Apart from the immediate effects of higher involvement of women in agriculture, the macro effects were commensurate with the size of the labour drain experienced in the labour-exporting economy and its degree of openness.

For a brief period, the events of 11 September 2001 cast doubt on the appropriable nature of Arab money capital abroad. Capital abroad in times of violent regime change or significant political tremors may be withheld by the host country. One ought to note that this argument applies to few individuals, the huge sovereign Gulf funds held against US debt are exactly as sovereign as the small Gulf states are in relation to the US. That said, the sense of insecurity on the part of Arab investors who chose foreign markets may potentially urge them to repatriate their funds, which would impact development prospects in the region. In 2002, the value of Saudi capital transfers abroad fell by approximately two thirds, and many nationals brought back funds to the Saudi or East Asian markets (IMF 2001–02). However, persistent uncertainty at home continued to outweigh the threat of possible confiscation measures by US or European governments, thus limiting the scope of investment for Arab money capital at home. This process of fund repatriation lasted only one quarter, after which the divestiture process resumed its earlier course.

The Integration Literature at a Glance

A vast array of literature covers Arab political and economic integration issues. Inter- or intra-Arab integration would entail political power shifts against US-led regional security arrangements, a point that remains central to Arab integration literature. Under assault and in the grip of merchant capital that controls both economy and state, the ruling-class appropriation

---

what they used to be prior to the uprising. These reserves cover only three months of imports. The Gulf states intervened at every stage to halt the decline in reserves. M. Samhouri, 'Egypt's Hard Economic Choices', *Sada*, 30 January 2013. Online: http://carnegieendowment.org/2013/01/31/egypt-s-hard-economic-choices/f7ib (viewed 4 May 2013).

mechanism predisposes distancing from nearby neighbours. Colonial and postcolonial belligerence in underdeveloping Arab social formations tore the circuits of capital circulation loose from their national valves. The transfer mechanism from private sector to social welfare seized up, the authoritarian and antirational cultural values promulgated by retrogressive reforms rose, and cheap petrodollars sanctioned waste and divisions based on identity politics. Unlike the previous nationalist postindependence period, under neoliberalism, pan-Arab integration was the veneer beneath which disintegration policies were laid. As with the Arab Common Market Accord of 1964, economic integration rose in the accord's early years but soon retreated. Politically, integration fared even worse, as inter-Arab conflicts marred the historical landscape. Integration cant lulls the dispossessed working masses that would benefit from larger markets and stronger Third World political ties. The conditions of recurrent and continual conflict obviate graduated forms of integration created by a sense of security community (Hudson 1999; Deutsch 1957). Security withers and a democracy that engages the working classes fails to materialise.

The standard analytical argument points to three factors that obstruct Arab integration at the regional/international level: troubled intergovernmental relations, the influence of external military threats and the heterogeneity of Arab countries. At the domestic level, the obstacles are the impertinence of intellectual arguments, the rent-based economy and outmoded ways of thinking that continue to be shaped by the heritage of the colonial era. It is also difficult to do justice to the vast literature on integration, but a summary is provided below.

Regional Level

There is to begin with what I think should be called the 'probabilistic' argument, which basically says that both national and external factors divided the AW, but it is the national forces that inflict discord by a higher probability. The persistence of divisions between the Arab states suggests that it is not possible to attribute the present situation in the region entirely to the Arab–Israeli conflict and the political affiliations of different Arab states during the Cold War (Nabli 2007). Pinning probability to social history and allotting significance to national forces reads more like a formalised assessment than an actual study of the development of events. It is baffling that one can lump together national entities whose classes are in a state of war as a single subject of history. The implication of this view is that all the masses that protested their US-backed despotic ruling classes were themselves somehow masters of their own history, and therefore it was they who have taken decisions to drive the AW apart.

That is the absurdity of the argument. Even more astounding is the inference that Arab social classes express their agency in forms of political organisation capable of daunting the military grip of US-led imperialism. There is not an iota of understanding of the terms of military and ideological power with the hegemon in this proposition. Since the detour taken by Egypt at the Camp David Accords, Arab countries have defined their security by the degree of their separateness from each other, while their ruling classes decided to integrate vertically into US-led arrangements, such as the greater Middle East of the Euro-partnership concoctions. The growth in the politics of divisiveness partly transpires from the negligible role accorded to the League of Arab States. This league, by its very constitution, lacks the legal and political authority to override the sovereign autonomy of any Arab state. The preamble to the charter of the league pulled the teeth of this regional arrangement by affording veto power to all states. The sovereignty and independence of member states became inviolable because a unanimous decision is required for any resolution. But the anti-imperialist stance that Nasserite Egypt displayed furnished the league with some consensus in the 1960s and 1970s, which would later taper off after Egypt's moral authority suffered a setback when it ratified the Camp David Accords. Additionally, the following are point-form summaries of some of the explanations of Arab disunity.

1) *External threats:* The strategic importance of the Arab region, in view of its oil reserves and the strategic alliance of the United States with Israel, in particular, inherently foments political and economic divisions (Amin 2007). The frail common-defence agreement among Arab countries lowers the barriers to possible outside intervention (Hassib 2002). Israel opposes Arab rapprochement. Also, it disparages multilateral negotiations with its Arab neighbours, the result of which might link broader normalisation with a restoration of Palestinian rights.

2) *Diversity of Arab social, economic and political systems:* The diversity of the social, economic and political systems of the Arab countries poses a considerable obstacle to regional integration (Hoekman 2002). There are clear discrepancies among Arab societies in terms of human development, education systems, income, participation of women, economic and trade systems, and political and human rights. Putting intraregional free trade before regional capacity building in a diverse environment may result in trade diversion as opposed to trade creation (Naqib 2005). The emphasis on intraregional free-trade treaties may be misplaced in the absence of common investment projects in infrastructure, plant and equipment that would homogenise the diverse conditions.

3) *Domestic discourse:* Arab intellectuals have delivered no compelling argument on integration (Zineldin 1998). Although a vast literature on the virtues of Third World regional blocs was available, most Arab treatises drew on sloganeering to sway opinion. Arguments on both sides are rarely based on sound research. Winners and losers are mentioned; but the game, its payoffs and the social forces that have governed it have not to date been considered. Recently, the exigencies of globalisation have brought back the notion of extended nationalism and regional blocs à la Seers, but these discussions exist on the fringe (Seers 1983). Moreover, a number of the challenges faced by the contemporary AW require a concerted regional response of risk pooling rather than a country-based response. Improving and deepening regional integration and cooperation, through the development of new institutions and the reorganisation of existing ones delivers in terms of security and welfare. Closer integration will not only improve states' socioeconomic situation but will also reduce the likelihood, and thus the costs, of conflict. It is not, however, the difference between those who wish to unite the Arabs within the framework of Islam and those who advocate secular integration that stalls integration. These are virtual historical trends that are used as symbols for the mobilisation of working classes. Content wise, these discussions avoid the class issue and the detection of what it would mean for global financial capital for Arab or African working classes to pool rank. In most cases, these high-handed integrationists are deeply mired into the mystification of nationalism or pan-Islamic models, the latter model acts as a repository of imperialism and ancillary support for the merchant classes. It is not only the anti-imperialist weight of integration that threatens capital. Once the issue of social class enters into the framework of analysis, the priorities of an integrative project also shift from satisfying the profit mechanism (which would be countered by integration) towards the fulfilment of social ends. Working class integration at the social and political levels is a foremost anti-imperialist platform.

Another more concrete facet of disintegration is the failure to enact binding integrative agreements (Azzam 2002). The articles of the many ratified regional transport and trade agreements, for example, are seldom monitored or implemented in full. There are inter-Arab treaties for almost anything that would, if observed, unite Arab states simply by the weight of implemented infrastructure development projects. Devised in the 1950s and 1960s and envisioned as the instruments of Arab integration—the Council of Arab Economic Unity, the Arab Fund for Social and Economic Development, the Arab Monetary Fund, the Arab League Economic and Social Council, and the agreement on the Arab Common Market—became more and more irrelevant with the shift in Arab class structure towards imperialism. Over the past three decades, countless multilateral and bilateral economic and trade agreements have been designed to purposefully overlook any provision for an implementation mechanism.

The Rentier State Argument

A predatory Arab state as opposed to a developmental state overshadows the debate on Arab integration. Societies in resource-abundant countries can be viewed as an amalgam of atomised individuals of whom some band together to prey upon society (Beblawi 1987). Beblawi was the prime minister of Egypt in the military-coup government (July 2013 to March 2014) that is holding its grounds because of geopolitical rents from the Gulf states and its continued commitment to the Camp David Accords. He was previously Under Secretary General of the United Nations in charge of 'democratic' development in the AW, yet the police force was gunning down protestors in the streets during his term in office as prime minister. But societies are historical products of forms of social organisation and relationships powered by the contradictions of various social strata. Societies are more than Hegel's definition of them as mechanical workshops; they are transitional processes. Also, as detailed in Chapter Four, the mode of integration into the global economy reshapes the state presiding over society itself. The rent-grab state under capitalism is not an aberration. Additionally, rent grab is not cultural attribute. It is inherent to a market economy and a by-product of the intertwining of terms of exchange with the global economy and degree of imperialist hegemony over the social formation. The merchant mode of organising social life culminates a process of resource snatch and a ruling class alliance that earns without effort. Yet, fundamentally by referring to rent-grab as a moral category, this discourse assumes that there exists a pristine condition of capitalism in which rent would be absent. That is of course a non-existent historical condition. It never existed because it simply cannot do so in a class system. But underneath these rent *cum* moral indignation arguments, the belief that the US economy represents a sort of perfect moral system to which one and all should aspire lingers. This peculiar belief in the non-existent yet innately perfect world of US democracy, that is either real or on its way to perfection, is what differentiates sober intellectuality from that which adheres to illusory symbolism. The US is inversely democratic to the value drawn from wasted Iraqi and other lives at the gas pumps. In Reinert's remark below, Arab working classes, two-thirds of which are Africans, bear the burden of military assaults as well as of a pejorative discourse that blames the victims for their own underdevelopment.

Africans were not seen as poor because of the colonial economic structure that had been imposed on the continent; Africans were poor because they were black. During a more enlightened era 400 years ago, Francis Bacon discarded race as a factor explaining wealth and poverty. Today the marginally more politically correct version of this type of theory is that Africa is poor because blacks are corrupt. (Reinert 2005)

Some authors confuse integration with exchange-rate or custom unions, a sort of reductionist integration *policy*: the absence of well-defined integration policies in Arab countries constitutes another obstacle to regional integration (Suleiman 2000). In the area of trade integration, governments do not specify medium- or long-term visions of their main foreign trade objectives, and there is a lack of national committees for the coordination of transactions and government policies. Another major barrier to trade development is the lack of cooperation and coordination among Arab countries in transport and infrastructure. The absence of developed land-transport routes, railway lines and shipping routes linking eastern Arab countries hinders regional trade integration. Moreover, the inefficient data systems and large statistical gaps in Arab countries do not allow for meaningful cross-country and regional comparisons (UN 2010). The lack of transparency and uniform disclosure in Arab companies and the absence of uniform Arab stock-market regulations represent another obstacle to regional economic integration (Wilson 1995). Underdeveloped financial institutions in the Arab region further hamper regional trade and economic integration. In particular, domestic credit directed to export-oriented small and medium-sized enterprises in Arab countries is at a low level in relation to the needs of companies and states (UN 2008b).

These are not causes of disintegration but rather outcomes of a merchant mode of appropriation that negates by its very being any form of integration. In fact, money capital and credit expansion cannot promote productive employment of resources in a merchant-based market meant to deprive the working classes of their well-being. Markets are also social institutions with social forces, where in the absence of rights and level playing fields, the transmission mechanisms favour the powerful and ruling social classes. After three decades of neoliberalism and failing Left activism, social classes have been gripped by modes of cultural differentiation that promote versions of social Darwinism. The rising division of labour and a civil society operating under religious guise have overwhelmed the state and pitted public person (the citizen) against private person (the individual in civil society). Currently in the AW, the ideological crisis is far too severe to allow the reconciliation of the citizen as species-being with the person who realises the sovereignty of the state by his or her citizenry (Marx 1844). The religious person supersedes the citizen. Patronage networks under the control of the merchant–imperialist class alliance support the division of classes and immerse workers in imaginary identities drawn from pseudo-historical fantasia. In the agriculturally based precapitalist Islamic empires, full employment was the rule due to the low output per worker and the recurrent crisis of underproduction. Under capitalism, crises of overproduction and profit rates necessitate the permanent disengagement of labour. How does Islamic historical projection on social policy work when such a significant difference in the social order prevails? These fantasia gripping the social imagination by incessant propaganda impede by brutal aggression the initiatives of revolutionaries to realise the working class in the political sphere. More than any other point in history, labour, the historical subject, awaits a reawakening of internationalism. For the time being, networks of families and individuals with parallel stakes in politics and business exercise power such that the contradiction between public and private interests remains recalcitrant.

Anti-integration Imperialism

The overwhelming majority of Arab states can be reduced to the 'merchant US-led capital class' without much sacrifice to content. The schism that separates social personhood from political personhood via racist differentiation in Europe and the USA (where people are legally equal but socially unequal) does the same in the Arab countries by virtue of racism manifest in the heart of the legal structure of pliant Arab states. Revamping of constitutions, as in Iraq, Libya and Egypt, even when they only nominally separate state from religion, is the first measure US-led capital undertakes. Iraq's American-authored constitution splits not only the country but every citizen from the right to belong to the state. To invert Marx's language, every 'worker dissociates himself from the abstract citizen; he has recognised and organised his own powers (*forces propres*) as private powers [Marx says social powers] so that he always separates this social power from himself as *political power*' (Marx 1844). In this state of selective democracy, the only citizen is the representative of US-led capital and his or her subordinate merchant in the ruling nomenclature.

US-led imperialist intervention redesigns the grounds for the expropriation of political rights from the citizen (Shaaban 2003). The record of imperialist intrusion to fragment states and halt any form of Arab integration is lengthy. Integration by way of working-class solidarity strengthens the economic and, subsequently, social and political standing of an Arab political alliance. Common regional objectives, at least those concerned with the retention of a higher portion of the wealth for regional development, can prise loose the grip of the imperialist security arrangement. In the existing arrangement, the anti-Arab balance of forces relies on Israel's superior military capabilities, which assist in maintaining this 'overdetermined' condition of disintegration. Israel and major European powers place the prevention of Arab integration at the top of their agenda. In reference to the only experiment of Arab unity—that between Egypt and Syria (forming the United Arab Republic [UAR], 1958–61), declassified documents from the office of the historian of the US Department of State demonstrate that Arab integration was perceived as posing a more serious threat to European imperialism than communism. Israel and other European powers were willing to tolerate the alliance of Iraqi president Abdul-Karim Qassim with the communists in order to undermine the UAR:

> Israel has consistently encouraged Turkey and Iran to tolerate Qassim lest his overthrow strengthen Nasser.
> (http://history.state.gov/historicaldocuments/frus1958-60v12/d210)

> The West was concerned as to the unions' effect on stability in the area. If the Iraq–Jordan Federation was the only alternative to Jordan's being swallowed up by Egypt then what had happened was the lesser evil from both viewpoints.
> (http://history.state.gov/historicaldocuments/frus1958-60v13/d10)

> *Position.* US policy toward Iraq republic—friendly support for Qassim's declared objective of neutral and truly independent Iraq despite many months of abuse of US and harassment of Americans in Iraq—at last beginning pay dividends. Qassim's earlier suspicions of US and of British as well seem to have been largely overcome.
> (http://history.state.gov/historicaldocuments/frus1958-60v12/d199)

The US's position differed tactically but not substantially from the European–Israeli position. Two underlying assumptions motivated the US stance as it began to crowd out the old colonialists in the Middle East: first, that Arab integration was not serious and that each Arab nation followed its own interests; and second, that Israel should not overindulge in its security concerns because its military capabilities were so superior that it would be able to defeat many Arab armies combined in a very short period. Although these views are expressed in a document that appeared in 1961, it famously took Israel six days to devastate Arab armies in 1967. The following is a selection from the archives on the subject:

> Under-Secretary   McGhee   expressed   understanding   Israel's apprehensions arising from its exposed position but commented

US has great respect for Israel's military competence and estimates it as being match for some time to come for any Arab combination.[5] (my emphasis since it took only six days to win the war of 1967 later)

Because they so completely distrusted Nasser, the British were much more willing to undertake the risks which would be incurred by attempting to follow the third possibility of a Nationalist come-back in Iraq.[6]

Most other governments in the area, as well as some British circles, have shown less concern about developments in Iraq and have hoped that Qassim would provide a useful counterpoise to Nasser. These hopes are fading, and we believe that awareness of the Communist threat will spread. Initially, most of these governments will prefer action to reverse the trend without augmenting Nasser's influence, but if this proves not feasible, there will be increasing willingness to countenance, if not support, Nasser's efforts. Notable exceptions will be Israel and probably the present regime in Jordan.[7]

What is peculiar in Arab political literature describing this period is the language of accusation of treason made by the Arab communists against Arab nationalists. The Iraqi communists, in particular, repeated *ad nauseum* a statement by a Ba'athist leader, Nasser Al-Saadi, in which he says that he had arrived to power in 1963 with the assistance of the US (Yassiri 2006). But in actuality, the position of regional communist parties opposing the UAR played into the Israeli strategy. As such Soviet-prescribed communist politics were less internationalist, because with the power of hindsight these fracturing national positions strengthened the Israeli position at all stages. Iraqi and Syrian pro-Soviet communist parties literally tilted the balance of powers toward Israel by being anti-Nasserite. These communist parties underestimated the necessity of anti-Israeli struggle in the region by bowing to the Soviet strategy of detente with the US.[8]

In Iraq, specifically, Soviet foreign policy assumed a utilitarian anti-internationalist line. First, the communists backed Mustafa Barzani against the monarchy, but as soon as Abdel Karim Qassim took over in a 1958 coup

---

5   http://history.state.gov/historicaldocuments/frus1961-63v17/d275.

6   http://history.state.gov/historicaldocuments/frus1958-60v12/d176.

7   http://history.state.gov/historicaldocuments/frus1958-60v12/d181 (par. 6, 8, 22–8).

8   Nearly half the number of pages of the booklets reporting on the major conferences of the Iraqi and Syrian communist parties contained language copied word for word from the Soviet party conferences in respect to the necessity to quell the nuclear arms race. These parties lacked a personality of their own.

they backed him. According to Tarbush, a shipment of weapons destined for Barzani was diverted to Qassim in 1958, but no sooner had the Soviets backed the Qassim government than Barzani began to side with US regional partners like Iran and Israel (Tarbush 1982). Soon after, in 1959, Barzani launched a protracted guerrilla war against the Iraqi army that would end in its quasi surrender in the 1975 Algiers Treaty. In hindsight, despite its many shortcomings, the pan-Arab nationalist stance was more internationalist and anti-imperialist than the pro-Soviet communist position.

In addition to these regional and extraregional antidevelopment forces, there are specific national appropriation constraints that hamper integration. The bond between 'merchant class' and state represents a social rapport that has so far worked well for its beneficiaries. The unquestionable hold of capital on the state, all by itself, accentuates the rate at which the state siphons resources at the behest of the merchant class. Profits could be made simply by buying anywhere and selling to small monopolised markets or by tapping into oil exports. Forestalling regional market integration is forestalling the sharing of a privately owned asset with others. In the case of the Gulf Cooperation Council (GCC) monetary union, the plans for a single currency are still on hold (Takagi 2012). Not that a single currency matters in this case, given low intraregion trade—as low as six per cent—but this union foisted by the US to strengthen its Gulf allies' security against Iran during the First Gulf War offers proof of two *post facto* conditions: a) merchant capital inherently repels integration; and b) merchant capital lies at the mercy of US-led capital. If any advance in future integration occurs, it will be that which is acquiesced to by US-led capital.

Although there were instances where the immediate postcolonial crisis yielded intermittent socialist or populist reforms, conditions soon relapsed into the colonial-like mode of appropriation. The populism of Arab socialist states did not afford the working class command over the institutions of the reform process. Working classes were incorporated into the state structure. The working class was disengaged from the political process, but not depoliticised. For depoliticisation to occur, the working class must be alienated to the point where it actually becomes in its state of consciousness part of capital. That is, it completely incarnates the imagination of capitalist ideology through war support and consumerism. However, to pin socialist failure on the so-called excesses of faulty policies of the socialist years is to mislead, as the uprisings of 2011 demonstrated later. The 'excesses' of the moderate 'Arab socialist' experience were not the policies of industrial protection, the nationally funded fiscal policies or the macroeconomics of regulation. While these policies were implemented, they delivered dynamic economic and social results. The financing of macro projects was via nationally sponsored credit created within a tightly regulated capital-account environment. Discretionary fiscal and monetary policies under fixed exchange rates and multiple interest rates targeting different sectors swayed little to outside pressures. The transgressions of the Arab socialist period were not the Left macro policies but those of the class in charge of development, which adhered to the terms of victorious US-led capital. Having structurally surrendered, the Arab ruling classes employed the state as a medium for private accumulation. The share of the state bourgeoisie from total wealth rose. With the labouring classes already excluded from political participation, the state capitalists metamorphosed into a class of private capital. Deindustrialisation, as noted, has marked the course of events since 1980. The openness policies constraining national industry were in fact the imposition of war tribute delivered in real assets or value form to US-led imperialism.

The Arab-state opposition to regional cooperation is itself a privately commandeered resource-allocation mechanism. It is a product of internal class articulation neatly nesting in the prevailing international division of labour and deployed to bolster the US-led imperialist security framework. Anti-Arab integration in turn inculcates the merchant mode of appropriation because it actually reduces the geographical space within which a regional industrialisation project may incubate. The scope for an industrial market institution, one that expands by building industrial capacity and disciplining the price system through public participation, is sharply narrowed by Arab disunity. It is this retrenchment of industry that underscores the starting point for national underdevelopment. So far, recent political uprisings have amounted to a change in some of the faces of the ruling class and have accomplished little in the way of class restructuring. Neither the working class nor an industrial entrepreneurial class has taken power. There was neither an industrial-bourgeois revolution nor working-class one.

Unlike what some Arab rentier-class literature posits, the present merchant class does not gain from redistribution of assets pursuant to integrating national markets (Beblawi 1987). Wealth, as things stand, cannot expand by infusing knowledge into production or from integrated regional markets. Despite this *post facto* condition and myriad inter-Arab disputes, the mainstream literature on integration employs catchy phrases highlighting the supposed commitment of Arab governments to integration. 'Regional integration is said to constitute an important element of the international policy strategy of Arab governments' (Hoekman 2010). The very fact that intraregional trade has been low for so long (10 per cent on average, whereas even prior to European integration, intra-European trade represented 60 per cent of total trade) corroborates the view that neither US-led capital nor the regional comprador desires the promotion of cross-border activity. Dividedness reigns despite the fact that being 'small' in a globalising world is a disincentive for capital accumulation. Unless very differentiated production roles are adopted in the international division of labour and export markets are secured, smaller economies may not realise economies of scale. Remaining uncompetitive and small or missing out on the development of technology-based value-added products in an era of globalisation is the furthest any country can situate itself from a strategy of sound development. In the case of the merchant mode of accumulation, industrial capital retrogresses because the bulk of oil or geopolitical revenues flow out of the region in one form or another under the policy aegis of international financial capital. What is more, as a result of dwindling finances, these money flows precipitate real transfers of value, which in turn feed a vicious circle of underdevelopment.

Not only do Arab merchant classes repulse one another, but the retreat in pan-Arabist or socialist ideology left few values in common between working strata within and across Arab states. The material bond between private and public concerns mediated by the state or Arab supranational organisations came undone. Resources devolved via non-state institutions that constitutionally stand over and above the state further accelerate disintegration. For the allocation of resources to be based on social rights and for small, risky market structures to grow into their opposites, the sovereignty of the state has to override the autonomy of sect, tribe or region—the reverse of actual conditions. With the rise of identity over class, these building blocks of integration are in retreat globally as well as regionally.

As can be observed in Sudan, Syria, Egypt, Lebanon and Yemen, the financially lacking Arab social formations (recall that they are financially lacking because of lack of autonomy), national fragmentation is again underway following the uprisings. As socialist ideology has ebbed, counter-reforms have engendered antisocial revolutions. Supported ideologically and financially by 'free market' ideology and Gulf capital, regressive fantasia displaced labour rights ideology. Symbols from the vast experience of Islamic history are refabricated to resolve issues associated with modernity. The needs of forcibly displaced labour under capitalism are dealt with by charity. Regression in development has in turn thwarted social development and widened the gap between civil society and the state. In this crevice, the conditions for the uprising matured. However, as religion is thrown back to the private sphere when the public sphere or the right of active citizenship is denied to private persons, the mix of petrodollars and political religiosity bamboozles vast sections of the peasantry and the working classes. The demystification of real-life processes cannot be formalised. History is a fluid condition in which real time is not an algebraic symbol and variable interdependence is unbounded and mediated through complex social structures. In these structures, revolutionary consciousness defines the ruptures in real time, and power relations reflect the mediation of agency in structure. In the AW, the power is the military power of the US and Israel and revolutionary consciousness seems for the time being fast asleep. However, it is likely that class lines will once again become all too visible as imperialist aggression inevitably mounts.

Despite massive financial wealth earned from oil revenues for over fifty years, the Gulf states—that is, the states that escaped the wrath of imperialist war—remain industrially underdeveloped and, in terms of civil liberties, they are unspeakable (Amnesty International 2009). Underdevelopment is short of capacity by definition. There certainly exists plenty of absorptive capacity for reinvesting oil surplus in the Gulf states. Metaphorically, greening the desert is a possibility. Yet, as mentioned in the first chapter, every measure has been taken to ensure that oil dollars prop up mercantilism, Salafist thought and wasteful consumerism. Under these conditions, oil revenues have dichotomised economies. A highly capitalised oil sector has created few jobs relative to the capital invested in it, while alongside it, some modest job expansion has occurred through patronage in the public sector. However, public-sector underemployment, which is neither socially nor economically effective, merely pacifies. It mitigates unrest and prevents any seepage of knowledge into the productive economy.

To view the situation from another angle: integrating one merchant earning directly from oil revenues through the state or by selling to a captive market can only result in losses to one of the parties because wealth is not expanding from rising productivity so that both parties can expand their profits. They both simply tap into existing assets and resources. The material bases for merchant-sponsored reforms accordingly are lacking, such reforms come to naught socially. Disorderly short-term profiteering forms the basis of one myopic development strategy after another. The drainage of the social value needed to reproduce living standards nationally, however, is determined by the more powerful US-led imperial capital. When the divide between 'private' and 'public' is unbridgeable, and when the exterior dollar safe haven is accessible, investors are likely to play the one-time 'hit and run' strategy and then escape with their cash away from risky zones. For national capital, this transition to merchant/finance capital is a leap from concrete to abstract capital, or from industrial to finance capital—in some cases without ever having passed through the industrial stage, as was the case of the Gulf states. The material structure of accumulation is anti-integrationist within the state and integrationist with US-led financial capital. At the regional level, high-risk markets saturated with money capital and short of labour existing alongside markets with abundant labour and little money capital are the stubbornly persistent state of affairs. At the national level, states with weak sovereignty cannot fuse together their private and public social spheres. Hence the formations of the AW, its states, disintegrate nationally as well as regionally, the supranational Arab League.

The material bases for the deployment of resources necessitate their divestiture from the national economy and the working classes. Reorganising the regional social formation in a way that locks in resources would entail a shift in the class structure that defines the intraregional as well as the extraregional relationships. Complicating matters further, the imperialist hold on the oil–dollar connection and imperial rents defines a key moment in this process. So long as the politics of oil are more extraregional than regional, the anti-development/-integration structure is likely to remain immutable unless the working classes place anti-imperialism at the forefront of the struggle. Inequitable income growth, capital flight and the low rates of investment are indications that the historical subject, which is the imperialist–comprador class alliance, means to replicate these policies time and again.

Closing Comment

When sovereignty, the national manifestation of working-class security, weakens, sovereignty over national resources also weakens. The national ownership of domestic resources would mean that citizens of those nations own those resources and that the international institutional context promotes this process as a right (the second principle of social and economic rights). Instead, US-led capital maintains control of Arab resources by outright military reach, while its dominance in international financial and political institutions promotes usurpation. Internationally sponsored resource-liberalisation regimes, including free capital movement, imply antidevelopment flows. Integration requires sovereignty and autonomy over state and policy space. The idea that for nation-states to integrate, they must be sovereign and be able to partially relinquish sovereignty to a supranational entity in the process is nearly two hundred years old. G. W. F. Hegel (as interpreted by Harris) argues as follows:

> [International law] rests simply on treaty and agreement, subject to the particular wills of the participants, so it cannot regulate treaties or ensure their observance. Its primary principle, *pacta sunt servanda*, as Hegel puts it, 'goes no further than the ought to be'—it is an empty aspiration. The principle cannot be an article of law because the law is itself treaty, which can hardly be the source of its obligatoriness. In consequence the actual situation, as Hegel tells us, alternates between the maintenance of treaty relations and their abrogation. [...] Thus, 'if states were to become members of an international community, their sovereignty would be dissolved and some higher sovereignty would take its place. A community of states is thus strictly a contradiction in terms'. (Harris 1993)

None of the Arab states is sovereign enough to relinquish sovereignty in an integrative process. They cannot give what they do not have. Harris was writing in a Hegelian context, where the 'development of spirit in time' would later result in thought progressively growing out of itself and a communion of nations ensuing. But as envisioned by Marx, a materially grounded picture allows for historical contingency to be reconsidered. Hegel's 'spirit'-cum-cultural development is independent of what social classes do materially to be reproduced. For Marx, the extension of the capitalist mode of production into other areas of the globe is a necessary outcome of the unfettered profit-driven expansion of wealth. These extensions do not always entail progress. Imperialist expansion entails political ententes or subordinations, progress or de-development, always in relation to the metabolic rate of capital reproduction (Mészáros 1994). Capital's reproduction is in increasing crisis, and integration of the AW with the rest of the world through imperialist encroachments subjugates its sovereignty with ever greater brutality.

Imperialistically sponsored regional security arrangements underpin the dynamics of resource allocation to local labour, national and international capital. Trade treaties, European cooperation accords, and scenarios à la the greater Middle East emanating from the centre supplant national technology and purposely erect barriers between Arab states. The impact of this mode of integration into the global economy further widens the gaps—economic, social and cultural—between neighbouring nations and social classes within a nation. The national wealth divide mirrors the extent of linkages to external markets through oil or geopolitical ties. The stronger the merchant-class linkages to Western markets, the higher the social disarticulation. The bellicose mode of expropriation in the AW leads one to Hobbes: 'no room for industry, commodious living, or private property beyond what can be secured via one's own force'. That is an adequate reflection of Arab actuality. The reverse of that case is then a re-empowerment of labour through the state, and to draw from Hobbes again, a state made sovereign by the power of labour and amenable to 'commodious living and the passions that incline men to peace' (Hobbes 1929, 98).

In this epoch, which is rife with civil wars, the hurdle of national integration is proving as elusive as was the regional one. With many Arab states folding from within, it is no longer a question of integrating the AW as an anti-imperialist front but of how to integrate the single state. The course of events appears to be heading toward more violent fragmentation than already taking place in Syria, Libya, Iraq, Sudan and Yemen. The leading strands of world capital, military and financial, seem to be preparing to target Iran either in a bigger war or in some deal, which is similar to the Camp David Accords; and that can be just as devastating as war playing out in slow motion. Instead of building a large anti-imperialist front composed of all cultural variants of society, Iran supported the rise of identity politics, Shiism, in Iraq, Lebanon and Syria with geopolitically devolved rents. In the broader Sunni Islamic world, the US and its allies have used sectarianism to isolate and weaken Iran in its milieu. The weakness of internationalism is such that the anti-imperialist front is Shiite, which also is, as any sect constituting a form of social organisation, capitalist. The problem with a sectarian front, however, is that even if it wins the military war, it loses the social one, unless the day-to-day struggles of the Left mark the labour of history.

Chapter Eight

COMMODIFICATION OF LABOUR

For over a decade prior to the uprisings, the unemployment rate in the AW remained among the highest globally. Despite high growth rates from 2002 until 2011, the official—not the actual—unemployment rate stayed in double-digit territory, between ten and fifteen per cent. This poor job-creation response to economic growth discloses flawed macro policies. If the reason for unemployment's persistence was related to the WB/IMF's 'macro fundamentals', then up to the point at which the Arab uprisings began, these were well positioned. The fiscal accounts were either reduced or in surplus (surplus in the case of oil exporters), the inflation rates were moderate and declining, and reserves covered about two years of imports. Despite that, and as if in defiance of mainstream economic doctrine, unemployment reacted poorly and income inequality gaped wider. The reason is simple enough. In the neoliberal age, the decent job-producing economy had become too small relative to the sheer size of the labour force and most workers had to resort to poverty-wage employment. Value and wealth were extracted by pauperising and disempowering the working class. Consequently, as noted in Chapter One, labour's share of total income declined.

In retrospect, it is apparent that public-sector employment and declining productivity growth enhanced welfare and acted as a social safety valve when job creation was declining and in the absence of unemployment insurance. While the population across the AW was growing at 2.7 per cent annually on average, the capacity of the economy to create decent jobs was dwindling. It was plain to see that the macroeconomic and demographic variables were moving towards an imminent and inevitable collision. There is little room for argument over the unavoidability of collapse; rather, it was a question of timing. The imbalances of an economy whose incremental expansion did not keep pace with demographic growth reached extremes that awaited a weakening in the repressive hold of the ruling class over the state to burst. Under unreformable regimes, gradual political change was never a possibility.

Newly imported labour-saving technology, reliance on oil exports and deindustrialisation were labour shedding. The structural shift from state-led to private-led economies decommissioned much of labour. In contrast, between 1960 and 1980, the rate of population growth was nearly the same as between 1980 and 2010. In the early postindependence period (1960–80), the rate of job expansion nearly kept pace with the rate of population growth. In the second, neoliberal phase beginning in 1980, it did not. So long as accumulation proceeded on the basis of oil- and gas-based revenues and merchant activity, the state did not invest in the skills of the workforce. Not only was labour being deskilled and its labour power cheapened, it was also being commodified. Immiserisation spliced labour with the commodity labour sells for a wage—labour power, its ability to work—such that workers themselves began to be treated as commodities as noted by Meillassoux (1981) and, more recently, by Li (2010). This process of commoditising people has been akin to capitalist development since its early stages:

> It was not merely the products of labourers turned into independent powers, products as rulers and buyers of their producers, but rather also the social forces and the [...] form of this labour, which confront the labourers as properties of their products. Here, then, we have a definite and, at first glance, very mystical, social form, of one of the factors in a historically produced social production process. (Marx [1894] 1959)

It was not merely that another commodity such as oil reserves, which stood over and against labour and dictated its life, it was also the mounting reserves of the working class's own labour that stood against people — the 'surplus population', as Ebenezer Scrooge, quoting Malthus, coldly refers to it. As discussed, wars, civil wars and child malnutrition are parts of a process by which labour is dispensed with to further squeeze socialist ideology and to pressure wages downwards.

Neoliberalism created poorly paid jobs, below subsistence, and demolished the principal link between decent job creation and poverty alleviation. Where neoliberal policy fell short of this goal, wars decimated labour, physically and ideologically. This chapter examines the insurmountable unemployment issue and attempts to chart the policy terrain from a radical policy perspective. Setting aside the threat of US-led imperialism, in the absence of a dynamic rise in productivity in the non-oil sector of the economy, it argues that for the right to work as in article 23 of the Universal Declaration of Human Rights to be implemented, social equity has to precede the mythical individual productivity criteria for job creation. This is not the same as the so-called 'right to work' laws established in many states of the US, which force labour to work for minimal wages and undermine living security (Yates 2013). Article 23 ensures equal pay and remuneration that preserves human dignity. Because it is impossible to achieve full employment and rising productivity measured in moneyed form as a result of the pursuit of profits, the principal thesis for the argument is that a social consideration based on social as opposed to private values must replace the neoclassical efficiency criterion that demands ever lower wages to expand employment.

Foregrounding Unemployment

Judging by official statistics, official unemployment rates responded poorly to the ongoing period of economic growth fuelled by high oil prices, which began in 2002. There was roughly a 2–3 per cent point drop in unemployment over a nine-year period (2002–09) that also saw a cumulative growth rate of around 45 per cent (WDI, various years). Mainstream macroeconomic theory adopts a neo-Malthusian bent and points to a demographic transition as a principal cause of unemployment. Whereas for every person finding a job in the 1980s, there were two newly working-age entrants into the labour market, by the late 1990s, there were nearly four such new entrants to every person finding a job (UN 2004). But contrary to the conventional wisdom, this was in large part because the rate of job creation actually *fell* much faster than the rate at which the labour force grew. Meanwhile, with capital and trade accounts wide open, financial and other resources were fleeing the AW. The exodus of labour, in particular, a resource whose social cost of reproduction was borne by the home countries, was scooped up at cheapened wages. Labour power is not cheap; it is cheapened. Savings were invested abroad or at home into low-productivity, labour-saving areas such as real estate.

While regional and Gulf unemployment was rising, nearly half of the Gulf population (47 per cent) was foreign, of which around fifteen million consisted of expatriate workers from Asia employed at low wages (SAMA various years). This vast Asian labour force aroused attention due to the inhumane conditions in which the workers were employed. The Gulf's excess paper wealth sustains the consumption of its own unemployed in boom times. However, in Saudi Arabia, after a long streak of low oil prices from 1981 to 2002, nearly 30 per cent of the native population lived below the national poverty line in 2002, and many still subsist below that line despite vast wealth.[1] One ought to note that the Saudi state itself was borrowing nearly two hundred billion US dollars at exorbitant short-term interest rates to cover its expenditures in the late 1990s. At the same time, much of the private wealth was held abroad and, in typical financial scheming, the local merchant class that owned the banks was diverting

---

1   'Saudi Arabia's Riches Conceal a Growing Problem of Poverty', *Guardian*, 1 Jan 2013. Online: http://www.theguardian.com/world/2013/jan/01/saudi-arabia-riyadh-poverty-inequality (viewed 30 April 2013).

state assets to itself via these unnecessary loans. In any case, the Gulf policy of paying people to consume and not produce is affordable when oil-generated cash is available, but at the same time it is a disengagement of the human resource from productive activity. Creative workers are reduced to passive consumers. From the demand side, for this situation to be overhauled would require, in line with Keynes' euphemism, a 'euthanasia' of the merchant class and the re-creation of an industrial capitalist class. But such a developmental metamorphosis is prohibited by imperialist diktat. After three decades of neoliberalism combined with heightened political repression, the hard fact remains that there are plenty of idle financial resources, huge numbers of unemployed people and a shrinking productive economy that could hire only a fraction of the reserve army of labour under mainstream (neoclassical) efficiency criteria. These criteria relegate employment creation to a set of wage rates that match productivity growth. When productivity growth is negative, subject to the phantasmagorical world of equal marginal conditions, decent employment creation ceases and poverty wage employment flourishes in the informal sector. The analytics of the neoclassical scheme are straightforward: as productivity growth declines, wages decline and more workers are hired because firms cut costs as a result of lower wages. Yes, there will be employment, but in the absence of industrial or knowledge-based firm expansion, it will be roadside begging employment that contradicts the basics of human living. Still, the reasons for this gap between available financial resources and the low rate of real resource deployment, including labour, fall outside price incentives as an explanation for resource allocation. Merchants gather no additional value from capitalising the national economy, including labour. As per the often quoted phrase of Marx, circulation, or the exchange of commodities, creates no value, and in this context, the greater part of additional value is snatched from the resources by which society maintains itself. Every cent is usurped from schools, hospitals, life expectancy and the basic sustenance of the working class. The merchants' vested interests reach consensus on the point that any serious effort at allocating resources to build national capacity amounts to a transgression against the control of US-led imperialist powers over oil.

Alongside the exigency of placing social equity before neoclassical efficiency in order to create jobs, it may be the role of *demand*, ideally fuelled by productivity gains, that has been purposely overlooked by past and present WB/IMF regional policy. One ought to note that employment creation in a developmental context is not demand derived but development derived. Demand, in view of very low wages, may be insufficient to fuel employment. Nevertheless, the Kaleckian hypothesis that supports the case for demand-led employment is that both unemployment and real wages are demand determined, not price determined. It is not because the wage rate or the price of labour falls that firms hire more labour, it is because there is more general demand for what they produce. Real wages (workers' levels of actual purchasing power) are determined in the product market rather than in the labour market (Kalecki 1972), while money wages are determined in the labour market, where trade union activity takes place. Real wages are little influenced by the conditions in the labour market and are effectively determined by the degree of monopoly and leakages to external markets. Now, in the AW, the leakages are huge and the ruling merchant class monopolises both state and market. So as capital flows out and biased power structures determine market conditions, real wages become determined almost entirely by political stabilisation or destabilisation criteria. That is the closest any economy can come to emulating a planned economy—but in reverse, meaning it is a planned capitalist economy as opposed to socialist. The plan is to stabilise or destabilise via the mediated instruments of capital, that is the institutions falling under its thumb, in relation to imperialist geostrategic interest. The interest of devalorising the colonies, past and present, never ceases under capitalism.

Shrinking Arab industry, rising inflation and regime-sponsored corporatist unionism (where unions exist) have depressed wages. When demand recedes, real wages decline and this in turn causes a further decline in demand *and* output. The neoclassical assumption that firms hire more labour when wages are cheap should not hold, because demand in general is depressed. Keynes held similar views to Kalecki's as he rebutted 'the crude conclusion that a reduction in money wages will increase employment' ([1936] 1964, 261). In reality, a high level of aggregate demand generates higher wages and output. Firms hire in relation to higher profits that ensue from higher economic activity and demand. This does not preclude the fact that each individual firm needs to cut costs. But this is a case of cost cutting in relation to profit making, whose relationship to each other is determined by higher demand. Thus it is demand that determines levels of employment.

Real wages, however, are also affected by the political power of labour whereby trade unions influence money wages relative to increases in general price levels (inflation). When macro measures are taken to lock in resources (regulating capital and trade accounts) enabling the recirculation of wealth within the national economy (preventing leakages), it is the coordinated politics of labour and union activity that ensure a rise in living standards commensurate with productivity growth. Arab regimes have suppressed both autonomous trade unions and the political representation of labour. A 2007 report by the International Trade Union Confederation notes that workers in the Arab region still have fewer trade union rights than anywhere else in the world (ITUC 2007). The mechanism of rising wages, rising demand and rising employment is institutionally jammed by the class in charge of development in the AW—that is, by the ruling alliance of US-led capital and its subordinate partner, the Arab merchant class.

That said, the virtues of the demand side, even if they were to exist in the AW, would be insufficient to drive employment generation. Underdevelopment is essentially a holistic social condition that partly expresses itself in macroeconomic terms as a problem of capacity. The capacity deficit cannot be tackled by supply- or demand-side policies tailored for advanced economies. Western economies already enjoy intricate and complex supply chains and vast real capital assets. Underdevelopment, therefore, amounts to a simultaneous supply and demand side problem. It is also a qualitatively different subject. Consider for example the labour market in the AW. Supposedly it is a place where labour services are exchanged for a money wage. In an Arab labour market, however, the labour share forms around 30 per cent of total income (it is around 65 per cent in advanced economies (KILM, various years); productivity growth is persistently negative; and, if unemployment is assessed more comprehensively by inserting a historically determined living standard into the measurement, since around half the population wallows in abjection, by implication half the labour force could be considered unemployed (Al Mouwahad 2005; Winckler 2005, 102). Also when one considers how little value-added production exists and that compensation to employment is based on unit of labour inputs in 'production', the real unemployment rate would tally with the rates of disguised unemployment, which is also at around half of the employed labour force by virtue of the fact that oil is nearly half of GDP. Most of those remaining employed will be clients of the merchant/US-led capital ruled state: not workers who exchange labour services for a money wage, but who exchange consent or submissiveness for a minimal money-form value—around thirty per cent of the total income, which is the share of labour. Quantitative dissimilarities point to deeper qualitative differences. The social agency that cements the conditions for the hold of the ruling classes on accumulation in the AW requires the immiseration as well as disempowerment of the Arab working class.

For a long time, the WB/IMF framework emphasised supply-side concerns. It advocated reskilling and education even as decent jobs faded away. It unlocked the capital and trade accounts, facilitated the transfer of resources to the centres of finance in dollarised currency, and thereby drained Arab wealth. Not only does the 'free market' not actually exist anywhere; even as an imaginary situation, it is the furthest from a model that might serve as a conduit to development in the AW. Arab markets are qualitatively dissimilar because the merchant class, in its subordinate relationship to US-led capital, must reproduce the conditions that disengage the Arab working population from the production process so as to curb workers' control over their state and natural resources.

Not until the poverty-stricken working class poured into streets in violent protest, did the thrust of the international financial institutions recognise that unemployment was partly a demand problem. For years, the unemployment ranks were swelling, and the principal (WB/IMF) policy advice was supply-sided. This was the case until 2013, when the UNDP and the ILO issued a report entitled *Rethinking Economic Growth: Towards Productive and Inclusive Arab Societies*, which replicates many of the findings of the earlier series of reports entitled *The UN Survey of Economic and Social Conditions in Western Asia* but does not prescribe according to the survey's radical policy frameworks. In any case, faced with huge post-uprising problems, the *Rethinking Economic Growth* report could not help but state the obvious.

1) The report acknowledges that the creation of decent employment in the past had much to do with labour demand, which was determined more by political considerations than competitive market forces. Of course the report avoids the political considerations altogether and alludes to them being locally generated. The report treats 'competitive market forces', which do not exist anywhere, let alone in Arab imperialist backyards with their despotic regimes, as a contingent remedy for unemployment.

2) The report accepts that past economic reforms downplayed the role of public investment on the assumption that it would be replaced by private investment. Private investment, it says, was expected to be more development friendly as it would be driven by profit opportunities on the production side while meeting consumers' and jobseekers' expectations on the social side. These past neoliberal economic policies and reforms were therefore based on purely fictional assumptions. Private investment depends on the nature of the investor. In an Arab context, it would have been easy to see that the major wielders of private funds were the ones with their jails full of prisoners of conscience, their bank accounts abroad and their security apparatus manned by the US. These past policies cannot be a gaffe. No one with the most basic knowledge of the political economy of the AW could be that deluded.

3) The report acknowledges that foreign direct investment (FDI) in the region has been low and favoured resource extraction (oil extraction is the mainstay of capital in the region). For a long time, the neoliberal policy framework advocated dropping the national barrier to foreign investment because its qualitative linkages to the national economic structure will boost performance. Once again, how can a foreign investor place capital in a market of efficiency-seeking FDI when the region is deindustrialising, growing at almost zero per cent, and exhibiting the lowest cost, highest reserve oil extraction in the world?

4) The report acknowledges that trade and capital account openness favoured liberalisation, and were counterdevelopmental. Now, these past reports speak of supply capacity constraints, market access problems, and insecurity at home that may lead locals to shift money capital abroad, yet they recommend openness because it sharpens competition; competition in what? These openness policies were the key policies that brought back colonialism and its tribute under the guise of liberty. Capital became freer to the degree that it usurped resources.

5) The report acknowledges that privatisation paid scant attention to the income-concentration outcomes of handing over management of public goods to private operators. When all the institutions underpinning the performance of the market are under the thumb of the merchant class, including the state and the legal institutions, can privatisation imply anything but the grabbing of public wealth?

Previously, these issues were critically assessed by the surveys submitted to the UN Economic and Social Council. Because of their statutory UN mandate—that is, unlike the UNDP reports, which are financed by private and external sources—the surveys cautioned against adhering blindly to neoliberal policies. However, after admitting the failures of past policies and after some insidious selection of facts abstracted carefully to bridge the somewhat missing confidence divide with the reader, the UNDP/ILO report reverts to trivialising policy, citing everything under the sun as a remedy for an irremediable unemployment situation (irremediable, that is, within the present class structure).

One need not dwell on the details of the report. One particular point, however, undermines the spirit of article 23 of the right to work—that is, 'employment leading to an existence worthy of human dignity'. In the AW, being 'unemployed' is itself a terrible existence, but informal poverty employment is if anything more undignifying. The report says that the employment response to output growth has been significant over the last decade or so and that economic growth in the Arab region has not been 'jobless', because any economic reform that moved countries away from the old social contract towards a greater role for the private sector was likely to increase employment. Setting aside the fact that it is impossible to reduce unemployment when investment rates are falling—as the report itself points out, investment rates fell and hollow growth was generated from rising commodity prices—the report provides an example of the impressive reduction in unemployment. It says, 'The impressive decline in unemployment in Algeria [citing Algeria as an example] was accompanied by an increase in informal employment, at a rate of almost one-to-one' (UNDP/ILO 2012, 59). One wonders, if industry and decent jobs are shrinking and unemployment income is nonexistent, then it only makes sense for a worker to either migrate or eke a living in the poverty-stricken unemployment sector. Algeria may be the top performer still, but creating informal poverty employment is not necessarily proof that market liberalisation works. A state of desperation at work is inconsistent with the dignity of life under universal human rights. Yet these organisations mandated with monitoring the universal declaration are favourably impressed by the creation of desperate poverty employment by the private sector. The most blatant falsification comes to the fore when the report says that there was a one-to-one drop in unemployment and rise in informal employment. This literally means that the people working in the poverty-stricken informal sector were now being counted as employed, and that is why official unemployment fell.

The trouble is not the market, or any other specific feature of capitalism, but capitalism itself. Both Keynesian and neoclassical economists assume that the economy exists as an independent entity, and that as such that entity is intelligible (the premise of 'science'). But Marx argues that this economic castle in the air is simply commodity fetishism, in which 'relations between people take on the fantastical form of relations between things' (*Capital*, vol. 1, ch. 1). Capitalism at its most basic is the selling and buying of labour power in the creation of surplus value and the realisation of that value as profit via circulation. But although central to it, the final buying and selling of goods (which economics refers to as 'activity') is the culmination of social process that begins with the extraction of raw material from faraway places. This activity is only part of capitalist society and therefore subject to multiple social and political contingencies, utterly inseparable from society in its capitalist relationships (Lukacs 1967). The objectification of commodities including labour power, their acquisition of an independent movement and existence of their own entwined with contingency, makes a reading of the reified economy as such an illusion. An illusion, the appearance of commodities exchanged for prices, cannot be reduced to a set of scientific laws because one must look at the social relationships that have led to the exchange and gave to that exchange the power of a fetish in order to conceal its essence. The money-form measure of economic activity clouds many social relations and mediations of contradictions that cannot be discerned from reducing all social reality to final prices and exchange. All the micro assumptions upon which the neoliberal models were built are fantasies meant for ideological delusions to which the ruling structures that fund such science, in their more sober side, do not adhere to or take signal from themselves. When there is a deep crisis, mainstream economists resurrect demand policies and forget all about efficiency and higher output per worker. None of the renunciations of previous assumptions upon which the unsuccessful neoliberal policies were practised would turn the UNDP/ILO report into science because it cites many reified policy instruments as solutions and avoids the question of who did what and why. It fails to investigate the real history or the social forces behind the movement of things and/or to de-reify the social conditions, and therefore it is false. In other words, political economy as practised in the UNDP/ILO report and by the mainstream is fundamentally flawed: the 'economy' of free competition, scarcity and independent price formation they pretend to describe does not exist. One cannot rely on something that does not exist to fix something that does.

Empirical Background

Widely circulated estimates put the overall AW unemployment rate in 2010 at around 13 per cent (KILM, various years). This figure is approximately twice as high as the international average. In the conflict areas of Iraq and Palestine, unemployment rates in 2007 were, respectively, 27 and 29 per cent; in Libya, Syria, Sudan and Yemen the rates are difficult to measure (UN 2007a, 2–5; 2007b, 7; Abrahart et al. 2002, 26). In any case, when in a state of conflict or when nearly half the population spends around half of its income on basic food, official measures of unemployment ring hollow. Naturally, when the bulk of the population is in the youth category, youth unemployment rates will be considerably higher. In Jordan and Egypt, these were 3.6 and 5.9 times (2009 UN estimates) the adult unemployment rates, respectively. Furthermore, female employment averaged a mere 25 per cent of total employment in agriculture, 17.9 per cent in manufacturing and 26.7 per cent in services, nearly half the world averages (UN Development Programme and League of Arab States 2008, 2). When an economy generates too few jobs to keep up with labour force growth, it is predictable that young entrants into the labour market will incur more of the unemployment. Oddly, mainstream literature addressing youth unemployment and the so called 'youth bulge' prior to the uprising treats the issue as a surprising demographic anomaly, or as if some forms of cultural values target the youth for discrimination (UNDP and LAS 2007). How can population growth, the steadiest least variable of social variables, be so unpredictable? The bad faith of this literature is in its ignoring the innate underpinnings of the unemployment problematic under capitalism—particularly in the context of poor job creation, where the creation of idle labour resources chips away at wages globally, and here in the AW in particular, the sovereignty of states.

Also, when national income is rooted in commercial activity that does not require the buildup of knowledge and its transfusion into mass consciousness, dislocation measures institutionalise the disempowerment of youth and women both socially and politically by forcing them into inferior and narrow employment positions. The idle labour of both men and women, although remaining outside moneyed production, buttresses the material of capital, as resources that serve as a reservoir for capital accumulation (Marx 1857). The social regression manifest in the separation of the sexes and the relegation of women to inferior status helps generate the symbolic power structure that undervalues work altogether. Religious obfuscation projects in mystified cultural forms the causes of failed accumulation onto non-existent 'historical traditions' whereby concocted cultural 'laws' ban women from engaging in the total array of productive activity. But with the rise of obscurantist trends in political Islam, the history of women's participation in the economy prior to neoliberalism is completely falsified. In the first half of the twentieth century, subsistence areas in the Arabian Peninsula, as elsewhere in precapitalist working conditions, saw the full employment of women in productive activity, namely non-moneyed subsistence (Mundy 1996). In what could be utterly unthinkable today in Saudi Arabia, a woman, Fatima Al Zamil, was ruler of Ha'il in the Arabian Peninsula from 1911 to 1914. It was not the resurrected ideas of Islam that disengaged women from productive activity, it was the rise of merchant capitalism. As Maxime Rodinson noted, it is rather the historical socioeconomic factors underlying the religious ideology that propel development in the Islamic world and, accordingly, the slow development of capitalism should be ascribed much more to economic distress and political declassing than to religious precepts (Rodinson 1973). Lethargic capital accumulation, which requires the disabling of the state, creates the spiritual underpinnings that reinforce de-development with every aspect of dominant ideology. The issue here is not about banning women from driving, as it is the case in Saudi Arabia, for that is an issue that the monarchy may placate the international community with by removing such a restriction. The crux of the problem is the imposition of idleness upon labour, and subordinately, it is the banning of women from engaging in the full spectrum of productive activity, which is the essence of their disempowerment.

Under pressure from inflation and in the absence of autonomous unionism, real wages in the AW have been falling for the best part of the last two decades (UN 2007). Egypt's nominal minimum wage remained unchanged for 26 years in the face of significant inflation (Maher 2011). Unless one considers the creation of poverty employment as employment, the employment-to-income relationship vanished. According to the faulty official records, it took a 45 per cent growth rate over nine years to bring down the official unemployment rate by 2 or 3 percentage points. With growth generated in commerce tapping into oil and geopolitical revenues, impossible growth rates of more than 15 per cent per annum would be needed to absorb new entrants into the labour market.

It is unlikely that higher (productivity-based) growth rates would be able to absorb the mass of unemployed after such a prolonged and significant period of economic underperformance (UN 2007; Karshenas 1994, 20). Following the deconstruction of Egypt's national economy, the productivity–job-creating nexus represents less a quarter of the actual economy (UN 2009b). Shrinking industry, high capital-to-labour ratios in the oil industry, and labour-saving imported technology account for the low response of employment to growth. The weak internal multiplier of the Arab economies dampened the already limited employment-generating impact of the 2002–2013 oil boom.

Mainstream Views

The kernel of the mainstream argument holds that state intervention and inefficient public-sector employment reduce domestic economic dynamism and accentuate the long-term impact of fluctuations in oil prices (Gardner 2003). Like so much of the mainstream ideology, this is an upside-down view of reality, and especially with regard to the AW. In the Arab postindependence period, the strategy of state intervention delivered some of the highest employment-generating growth rates between 1965 and 1980 (LAS, various years). What is more, the average population growth rate then was not very different from the average rate over the last three decades.

But this is only the beginning of the comprehensive and vicious falsification that is neoliberal economic ideology as it relates to the Third World and to the AW in particular. According to the neoliberal/neoclassical mainstream, state intervention leads to resource misallocation, rent-seeking activities and economic inefficiency; trade or capital account protection accentuates the decline. In due course, public-sector employment declines and unemployment rises. The WB/IMF panacea is for employment to be generated by cutting wages, social insurance and pension contributions along with the enforcement of what are euphemistically described as 'flexible employment conditions' (workers can be sacked at will, for any reason, and their wages and working hours cut on the same basis). These policies are supposed to promote jobs in labour-intensive and low-productivity industries. But the numbers of the unemployed and poverty-wage employed are, to put it mildly, in the majority. Any more downward pressure on wages or flexibility in the labour market may cause them to fall below the minimum caloric intake necessary for subsistence. In plain words, they would starve. But apart from this, the fact that there are so many people living in poverty is the ultimate flexibilisation of the labour market. The vestige of regulation nominally applies to the public sector which employs on average a quarter of the labour force, but the issue of where to throw civil servants when there are no jobs being created is central to policy here.

In reality, low wages attenuate demand and the impact of these structural adjustments is to restructure society into wretchedness. Labour demand derives not only from demand but also from holistic development. Notwithstanding its high rate of import dependency, the most important complex relation explaining the reproduction of unemployment is the rise of commerce under open capital and trade accounts and the concomitant decline in industry.

As pointed out by the mainstream, the transition to employment creation supposedly occurs when 'rigidities' in the labour market and real wages are broken and public-sector employment shrinks. Government intervention *qua* 'distortions' are said to reduce investment and productivity growth and to lead to insufficient job creation in the region. Theoretically, opening the market to international competition, while strengthening the institutions that support markets, encourages investment and stimulates productivity growth. Let us forget about how war drives away development for a moment, in actuality, instead of a positive spillover in employment, flexible labour markets have resulted in higher unemployment rates (in the decent jobs sphere). What end would it serve the merchant class to expand the local demand component by valorising labour when that class enjoys charter-like holds on import markets that satisfy national consumption levels, which rise or fall by the degree of stabilisation spending? Indeed, by making the labour market more flexible, the merchants responded to market signals and hired more unskilled casual labour at below subsistence wage rates in the service sector. The rise in foreign domestic and menial workers underscores the flexibility of the labour market and explains the role of merchants in the rise of intraregional labour flows. For instance, a skilled-labour-exporting economy like Jordan engages low-skilled Egyptian immigrant labour. These economic relationship conceal value transfers from lower-end economies to higher-end ones.

The ratio of imports of goods and services to GDP in the AW went from around twenty per cent in 1970 to about forty-five per cent in 2011 (WDI, various years). Profit margins grew in relation to higher imports, not higher national industrial output (industry shrank). The leakage is significant to the point at which the multiplier of investment, which would create more output per dollar than invested in the national economy, could work in the opposite direction: it creates more output for the exporting economies. Because the merchant class expands by outside production and oil income, it has only a slight interest in the national labour force, which is to keep them purchasing their imported products. Policies like the so-called Saudisation of labour (making labour native-born rather than imported) are ideological placation tools and would only succeed as such. The underlying relationship is that depressing the national service-sector wage serves the purpose of profit maximisation rather than raising productivity.

In the presence of massive poverty employment and a low-productivity informal sector, the labour markets in the AW cannot be rigid. The supply of workers remains elastic. Real wages have dropped sharply and are therefore flexible. Real wages fell steadily in the lost decades of the 1980s and 1990s (El-Mikawy 2002, 82). Real hourly manufacturing wages in the oil-exporting economies fell by almost half between 1986 and 1992, and recovered only slowly by the end of the decade (World Bank 2004, 115). The workers' strikes in Egypt prior to the uprising were in response to high inflation and nonadjusted wages. The public sector spearheaded the process of wage compression and the traumatisation of the working class (a rise in precarious contracts). Predictably, the remaining rigidities in the labour markets, especially public-sector employment, contributed substantially to reducing unemployment or to keeping the ranks of poverty-wage employment from swelling further.

The False Alibi of Population Growth

Although in the 1960s and 1970s, population growth was nearly as rapid as it was in the 1980s, job creation boosted by state intervention was also rapid, and cities absorbed a huge mass of rural migrants into decent jobs. When the transition to neoliberalism occurred, job creation receded while population levels continued to grow at about the same rate. Protected and regulated economies, multiple exchange and interest rates and high public investment were blamed for the shortcomings of the 1960s and 1970s. However, these policies were means to an end, and in comparison to the neoliberal period they performed well. The class behind these nationalistic policies was allied with the working class. Later, as we have seen, the class in charge of development performed a *volte face* and implemented policies of deregulation that reduced job creation. Instead of assigning blame to the class in charge and its insidious policies, mainstream analysts often attribute high unemployment to high population growth in relation to regulatory policies. However, population policy and, subordinately, the politics of reproductive behaviour, provide strong evidence that the state regulates the reproduction of the workforce subject to the demands of capital. To describe the situation schematically: the desired population and labour-force levels are achieved between a lower point at which the ranks of the unemployed do not swell to assist in the formation of a socially cohesive force that threatens the grip of the rule of capital, and a higher point at which labour shortages begin to cut into profits through higher wages. In the AW under neoliberalism, of course, 'capital' is not national capital, but international financial capital. This manipulated equilibrium worsens the plight of Arab working classes because their reproduction is not linked to their own national capital demands but to the demand of US-led capital, for which the commodification of labour serves the purpose of denationalising resources.

In an Arab context, therefore, the absurd consequences of the Iron Law of Wages actually appear to hold—but it is only an appearance, for in actuality it is the workings of the wage system in imperialistically controlled formations that is actually happening. For one thing, as incomes plummeted and wars flared, population levels rose more slowly than what could have occurred in the absence of war and abjection; because of forcible migration, shorter-than-potential life expectancy related to the erosion in basic social services and death related to war. The idea that wars and a below-subsistence wage reduce the workforce is a truism—and like most truisms, it is so true that it conceals its falsity in itself. Firstly, wages vary over much shorter spans than the time it takes to replace working generations, so it is unlikely that wages denominated in money form can suffice as an explanation of the social reproduction of the labour force. Rather, the labour force is reproduced by social value-forming elements that contain both moneyed and non-moneyed components. Secondly, there is a gaping divide between the historically concrete and an analytical mode of reasoning that gauges life by the yardstick of prices (wages being prices). One is hard pressed to find any situation in history where the increase of a surplus population relative to existing capacity does not add to some potentially eruptive social pressure. What neo-Malthusians do not disclose are the class structures and the mode of appropriation that lead to the immiseration of the working class. The subject of history–that is, the class in charge of development—defines the nature of a historical process. Under capitalism, it is the wage system that disposes of labour in relation to an organically regulated mode of capital accumulation that crosses national boundaries. Value relations crossing national boundaries are often missing from social analysis rooted in Eurocentrism. However, two centuries after Malthus, extreme scenarios of the Iron Law linger as ideological scarecrows that posit scarcity as an inherent component of life; but in fact, as even some of Malthus's earliest critics pointed out, scarcity is socially constructed. The fall in the wage rate to below a historically determined subsistence in the AW is a symptom of retreat in state intervention in welfare policy and not the cause of disaster. The class in charge of the state under capital aims to calibrate the rate of population growth to the highest rate of exploitation. This latter condition requires capital to disengage as many workers as possible from a given productive activity and to persistently lower the wage rate making subsistence goods beyond the reach of many. In the AW, the extreme cases of unemployment related to wage depression and the deconstruction of national economies by war and neoliberalism combined with rising population trends boost the ranks of the reserve army of labour. That is why it is not conceivable to speak of supply side considerations when the demand for labour is purposely deconstructed.

The Neo-Malthusian discourse denoted an anti-interventionist macro-policy position. The call for small government is meant to reduce the social cost of the reproduction of the labour force and to boost the process by which labour power is expendable in a shorter or 'cheaper' life span. It is a process by which the cheapening of labour power requires a cheapening of the labourer. That must be viewed globally and not from imaginary European political boundaries. The creation of the value that labour power embodies also generates additional surplus value to the degree to which more grabbed and non-moneyed value-forming components—such as unpaid domestic labour—reproduce human beings. Immigrants on whom the 'host' state did not expend a penny illustrate the point: immigrant labour power was produced by another country, yet it benefits the capital of the country in which it is being used. Capital, in its pursuit of profits, depresses the living wage and extends fewer resources in the reproduction of the labour force. It is under this latter rubric that population growth under capitalism is best understood. Population growth rates are underscored by a specific relationship of surplus value extraction, which is co-determined by the rate of replacement of living by dead labour (technology) in production and by the resulting relative surplus population that depresses wages and thereby augments absolute and relative surplus value (Marx 1867). In weakly sovereign territories, such as the Arab states, the capital that regulates population growth is the sovereign or US-led capital. The deaths or lives of Arab labourers are only relevant in relation to imperialist booty, positioning and control.

In contrast to the politico-economic approach, neoclassical economics frames employment and human reproduction in terms of individual choices. Not only does it hilariously postulate that workers can always choose between leisure and employment, but one of its recent extensions, the 'home economics' paradigm, constructs a theory around an individualistic and one-sided view of childbearing, which maintains that the quality of life to be provided to the child in order to achieve better-quality children is an essential component of family planning (Becker 1973). I must add the qualifier 'hilariously' because for a majority under war and abjection, entertaining the idea of choice is rather outlandish. Backed by the self-evident assumptions that parents seek a high standard of living for their children and that higher quality children in terms of health and education are afforded at higher income levels, it assumes that parents allocate resources for child rearing within a set of preferences and income. That people naturally aspire to better living standards for their children is a platitude too hollow to discuss. However, to lump children in with other commodities is to reduce children to their capacity to labour and to further advance the assumption that a capitalist market redistributes income fairly according to effort (the myth of individual wage based on personal productivity). On the former point: under the Universal Declaration of Human Rights, children are born with inherent rights to decent living regardless of their ability to labour, so it is dehumanising to reduce children to commodities. On the latter: the level of wealth is determined by productivity, which is determinedly social.

The drawback of this approach comes to the fore as the labour process under Arab capitalism is inserted into its framework. Universally, the class position that an individual or family occupies qualifies the behavioural response. A dispossessed individual/family that depends on unsteady jobs and faces an uncertain future behaves not according to fantasy choices but according to necessities imposed by prevailing social conditions. Parents' employment options and their ability to prepare their offspring for earning a decent living are functions of how values are encoded in behaviour in relation to accumulation, class position and wealth. For working-class families in the AW, the 'behavioural response' is determined by the fading farming traditions, which required high reproduction rates and by having to choose between two or three bad options or by finding themselves with no options at all. This is simply because in the AW, expulsion from the countryside, unstable markets, uncertain futures and recurrent crises shape living standards, the path of job creation and reproduction. The drives to broaden the options for work and life choice and to ensure healthy and educated children have both long been central to working-class struggle, and their levels of success are outcomes of that struggle. From a class perspective (which is to say, a dynamic historical one) it is the labour process under capitalism that explains the cycles in population dynamics and not an individual-choice framework situated outside a historical continuum. Recently, the fall in the fertility rates across the AW follows the greater rates of urbanisation and underlines a transition to a mode of reproduction in which lower fertility rates set in. Despite the tapering rates of new entrants to the labour markets, the growth in the ranks of the young unemployed earmarks the persistent incapacity of the economy to create decent jobs. Analytically and historically, it will not be high fertility that causes unemployment, but a policy whose sole purpose is to disengage labour.

Neoclassical formalism, in short, discards the bulk of historical actuality. By transmuting (abstract) social conditions into ideally quantified economic variables, the principal political linkages (the class struggle) that fuse economic conditions with social conditions are thrown away. The appearance of the economy with its price structure is only an epiphenomenon of the social condition. Neoclassical marginal costs and revenues are quantities devoid of social meaning. Neoliberal economic advisors and policymakers and their paradigm, which reduces people to *homo economicus* as opposed to *homo civilis*, the social and political human, applied absurd concepts of productive efficiency and equal marginal rates as policy tools in addressing employment. There can (to put it mildly) be little productive efficiency under deindustrialisation, and marginal/average productivity driving the wage under conditions of malnutrition relegates the labour force to oblivion. As under colonialism, bondage to foreign powers, colonialism, and economic concessions granted to foreigners by virtue of their political and military might still set the context in which working people behave (Rodinson 1973).

A Radical Policy Approach

As we have seen, Arab social formations are developmental failures and are not producing adequate jobs. Mainstream policies do list a variety of reasons for labour-market underperformance and unemployment, but their purpose is to obfuscate the primary reason. For instance, they list in passing, as one reason among many, the cyclical nature of the unemployment problem. Cyclical in the sense that the economy itself does not produce sufficient jobs. However, the mainstream treats all the reasons for unemployment as contributing to it by one or another degree of statistical significance but with equivalent historical weight: factor A, x per cent; factor B, y per cent; factor C, z per cent; and so on. And when it comes to policy, the orthodoxy grotesquely places the accent on educating the right people for the right jobs, when indeed neither the right nor the wrong jobs are being produced.

At its root, accumulation is a social-control process. The roots of the unemployment sickness are in a class and power structure that reproduces it using policies of openness (value drain). It is not discretion on the part of the WB/IMF to exonerate the social agency behind unemployment, but complicity. This subordination of economic theory to the power of capital is the furthest any discipline places itself from the status of a genuine science; and neoclassical economics applied to a Third World context, in particular, represents a kind of paroxysm of pseudoscientific falsification (Lange 1953).

'Apolitical' policies aimed at restoring disengaged labour ring hollow. Labour, as historical agency, has to prioritise its rights. Without upsetting the structures of power and restraining the merchant class, even demand-side policies such as more expansionary fiscal and monetary policies, the building of virtuous linkages between sectors, greater investment in research and development to meet sustainability, increased public investment, public–private partnerships and integration of regional policies into national development strategies—even these will remain mere political slogans. The primary way to restrain the merchant class is to allow its expansion to proceed only in rationed national currency—not dollars. The merchants should not be in a position to handle at will the transfer of national currency through open capital accounts. The principal artery has to be clamped. Multiple exchange and interest rates and partial barter trade shift the rules of the game in favour of the distraught sectors of the Arab economy—that is, the urban and rural working classes and the desperate hand-to-mouth survivors on the lower rungs of the 'informal sector'. When ruling classes strip working classes of their security and sovereignty by depriving them of the medium of the state, they invariably manipulate macro prices—wage, exchange and interest rates—to reinforce a distorted balance of forces. A far cry as this may seem, to even the playing field, the first step would be for labour to seize a modicum of, preferably all, political power within the now merchant-dominated state.

Whether sugar-coated as aid or subsidy, all forms of monetary intermediation from US-led capital aim at further social dislocation. Second-hand 'pro-poor' sentiments conceal the fact that money is *the money form of value* and that value is the creation of class and power relationships. In relation to the soaring industrial sector in which the labouring class is being socially capitalised, there has to be a pauperised sector, socially controlled, to provide cheapened value for higher profits. The agricultural sector, which is the last stronghold of social support for huge parts of the working masses, was being shrunk relative to the economy in order to socialise (that is, uproot and forcibly urbanise) farmers, depriving them of their little property. Since 1980, the share of agriculture in total investment has fallen continuously to reach a low of five per cent by 2009 (Arab Labour Organisation 2010). These were concerted and premeditated efforts aimed at weakening the working classes and reconstituting social value for grabbing by absolute and violent means.

More relevant explications of why capital needs to drive apart the national economy would introduce the role of colonial plunder in mitigating the tendency of the rate of profit to fall. Thus, in a globally interlocked process of accumulation that metabolises capital and labour, there is room for radical reform only insofar as the requirements of accumulation do not raise the standards of living in one corner at the expense of another—uneven development grows by the degree of financialisation (Mészáros 1995). Radical labour reforms imply the antithesis of sectionalism. Radicalism in relation to more internationalised capital requires internationalism. Reform policy is cogent only when the interests of the poorest countries tally with the outcome of reform in any middle or high income country. So far, in the current international division of labour, industrialising middle-income countries are being reprieved from imperialist assault by the extent to which misery and war plagues the lowest echelons such as Yemen, Somalia and Sudan, etc. To illustrate, it is as if Brazil is going to gain grounds in development, imperialism must ensure that social conditions in the least developed countries deteriorate further. Without mention of the centrality of class antagonisms, Keynesian demand-side mantras mask the real objectives of capital and strengthen its ideological hold. Where demand policies work, some other corner of the planet must be socially undervalued to maintain the flow of real wealth— always within the bounds of historically determined wealth and subsistence conditions. Keynesian demand-side policies provide a way for capital to manage accumulation by raising the pauperisation inflicted upon security-exposed countries of the planet; and Arab countries are at the forefront of insecurity. But because value creation is a social process, development policy acquires pertinence when it is made from the standpoint of the forcibly undervalued layers of AW labour.

Conventional policies for job creation such as labour-intensive economic growth are indeed necessary for remedying unemployment; however, they are no longer sufficient to bring back the massive armies of disengaged labour. Now, we are faced with a structural impasse. Given the small size to which the productive Arab economy has been reduced relative to excess labour, intensive growth would require decades before it starts to pay off. This would also have to be an intensive growth that requires at a minimum the adoption of national industrial projects, an import substitution policy and labour-friendly technology. Even then, given the high numbers of the unemployed, low productivity growth will ensue. Low wage growth will follow low productivity growth. The impact on demand that would be needed to kick start the economy may not be significant, unless there is redistribution of wealth. Based on the sheer magnitude of the problem, AW unemployment cannot be solved by standard demand-side recipes.

In the Arab context, equity must precede efficiency in employment creation until the valorisation of socially valuable work begins to pay off at some future date. In any case, full employment under the prevailing global conditions of overproduction is a far cry from the days when low levels of industrial technology were labour absorbing. The socialisation of labour or the fact that people depend on the market for survival should entail actually socialising (as opposed to privatising) the national product by building more egalitarian ownership and distributional structures.

Several further points reflexively arise from the foregoing:

- Firstly, the price system must be reinvented so that it revalorises labour and capitalises the economy with state-generated capital (subordinately, price guarantees and subsidies would be part of that).
- Secondly, property and wealth must be more socialised so that the mode of appropriation also turns back toward the social: social production requires

social appropriation and land reforms, for which state-sponsored industry and financial regulation of major banking institutions are essential steps.

- At the national level, retaining the social product for recirculation within national borders involves multilayered price engineering to ensure that exchange and interest rate policies lock in resources: people, money and capital.
- At a subordinate or sectoral level, leading reform measures include setting guarantees for agricultural output, financing industry and agriculture at concessional rates, and integrating agriculture via increased investment into the economy (in 2012 nearly forty per cent of the AW population resided in rural areas).

Full-employment policies would necessitate a relative delinking of Arab economies through macro-price engineering and partial protectionism. The state has to act as the principal employer and introduce public and social work programmes. As mentioned earlier, development depends on autonomy over policy, resource recirculation within the economy, and adequate interface between social policies and outcomes. These, in turn, depend on weakening comprador links to imperialism, a delinking with globalisation, and a refusal to transfer underpriced social value to the centre (Abdel-Malik 1985; Amin 1990).

Development depends on the nature of the agent of development and on ruling-class predisposition toward capacity building. Principally, the degree of sovereignty over resources, and the class context of the AW will determine whether and how far the various developmental challenges will be dealt with. On the economic side, the contradictions between expansive monetary policy and a vigorous fiscal stimulus, between savings and investments and the absence of automatic stabilisers, must be resolved by confining the issuance of credit to the purview of the state. Attenuating the balance-of-payment constraint through some degree of autonomy furnishes the state with the capacity to focus public investment in job creation. This measure of financial independence is not a novelty; it was the policy framework in the 1960s through the 1970s, and as earlier noted, it outperformed the neoliberal framework.

For macro employment-generating policies to work jointly and interdependently and become developmental tools, Arab countries would have to tackle the imperialist impasse underlying the policy framework. They would have to translate idle financial resources into real resources, introduce a social criterion for employment and link development to working-class security. In none of the Arab countries is there a working class secure from want or a national sovereignty determined by the security of the working masses. At present, steep national income differences and deepening labour force differentiation fuel uncertainty. The short-term relocation of money capital to secure money markets supersedes long-term investment in the national economy. So long as the security apparatus of an Arab country's ruling class depends on imperialist military cover or financing, exploring the interface between employment policy and outcomes is pointless. The only real starting point for discussion is analysis of the US-led imperialist predisposition to underdevelop the AW. The collusion of many other states afraid of oil supply cuts because of US-infused global insecurity incrementally adds to the development debacle. That people of working age are disengaged from productive investment or mainly engaged in exchanging their consent for a token money value is systemic to the AW.

So far, the Arab uprisings have done little or nothing to restructure value transfer in society, and it remains a political face-changing process rather than a social revolution. In places such as Libya where the control of US-led capital was not complete via neoliberal policy, NATO forces and civil wars have accomplished the dereliction of the state. Currently (2014), one group of countries is in open civil war and another has conservative Islamic parties or the US-funded military (Egypt) rising to the helm of power. Elsewhere, Islamic political parties have assumed power through the ballot box; these countries are trapped in the previous regime's policies, further underdeveloping them. The corruption that any revolutionary process is supposed to reverse involves stemming the transfer of value and underpriced resources to the more advanced countries—not the puny dollar bribes that feed the children of underpaid civil servants. So long as the political parties voted into power sanctify property rights irrespective of the degree of maldistribution, ordain a repressive labour process and place obligations before rights, development will continue to wither.

The problem, then, is ultimately straightforward: the majority of the working class has been forcibly dispossessed; the sector of the economy that can employ people in productive activity has been made too small; and hence, Arab economies cannot conceivably re-employ the massive redundant population that was created under war and neoliberalism subject to the mainstream efficiency criterion. Short of a radical solution that revalorises social labour, decentralises the social services of the state and severs the imperialist umbilical cords, little will change. The next uprising awaits not the deplorable social conditions becoming more deplorable, for they are too deplorable already, but the weakening hold of the imperialist-groomed ruling class on the state.

Arab labour is captive to an accumulation structure that is redeployed in time and space through resource divestiture. Reorganising the social formation as a way to lock in resources for development would require a shift in the parameters that define intraregional as well as extraregional class alliances. The looming element of oil control is the determining moment in this historical process. The politics of oil are extraregionally determined. Hence, the structure of accumulation by expropriation will remain unchanged so long as global powers reposition their forces counter to the welfare of the Arab working classes. Politics can always assume primacy—and it always has economic weight—when values and wealth are generated by a class structure organised within the nation-state. For the organised dimension of capital, control takes precedence over immediate money gains. Not that the primacy of politics is peculiar to the pauperisation of the AW, but such primacy assumes new heights here. Arab abjection had to become an end in itself so that maldeveloped Arab formations would act as power and value tributaries to imperialism.

Chapter Nine

COMING TO CONCLUSION IN TIMES OF SOCIALIST IDEOLOGICAL RETREAT

For more than three decades, the dominant mode of analysis in the Arab world has stressed private sector–led development. An enabling environment for the private sector has gradually taken shape, but development has correspondingly retreated. The freer the markets and the flows of trade and finance, the greater the private-property wealth held by the ruling classes became, and the less free and less propertied the working class became. History shows that there are few complete socioeconomic impossibilities; almost certainly, one of them is to achieve development in non-sovereign states that fall on the war-and-oil side of accumulation. In these countries, capital injections and stabilisation efforts resemble filling a sieve with water. Their poor developmental showings should be understood from the standpoint of imperialist power relations and their manifestation in aggression against working classes.

In such a context, primacy is not so much the operational side of monetary or fiscal policy; it is the ownership of such policies. In Arab monetary policy, the history of growth in money supply shows that money expands principally to satisfy foreign-exchange demand or the demands of merchant classes that will convert national funds into dollars. Meanwhile fiscal policy has retrenched: many primary budgets have been maintained in surplus in order to subvent the convertibility of the national currency into the dollar. Had the working classes owned macro policy (that is, driven it by their power within the state) the policies of deindustrialisation, lopsided openness and the rest of the social and economic policies that have so deeply compromised national security would never have been implemented.

As unlikely as it is to get development restarted in non-sovereign war-beset states, it is equally unlikely to find someone with reasonable knowledge of the AW who would think that an unregulated Arab market would not unleash the savagery of the powerful ruling classes. Where bombs and car bombs are not ripping inhabited streets apart, the monopoly of the political and legal system by the ruling few efficiently rubs out anything operating in the interests of the working class. Although in transparency and corruption indices the AW fares badly, these measures are misleading because they overlook the macro-leakage circuits or the efficacy with which the ruling class snatches resources when it practically owns the state (Transparency International 2012). A decent corruption index would measure the power of the ruling class in the state, including the foreign component, and the extent to which the private sector suctions the public sector. Corruption in the AW is not the bribery with a loaf of bread of a Syrian customs officer at the border. The real corruption, that is the usurpation of national resources and not the banal moral category, is the macro policy by which the country's resources hold US debt instruments or assets abroad—or by which Arab labour (that is, working-class human beings) drowns in the high seas in refugee boats seeking work and safety in Europe. At the time of writing in 2013, two boats have recently sunk: one off the shores of Italy and the other off the coast of Australia, both carrying Lebanese, Yemeni, Jordanian and Palestinian refugees; the Palestinian victims were seeking refuge from their bombarded refugee camps in Syria (Al Jazeera 2013a, 2013b).

Moreover, the historical points of departure, which policy should heed, are so near disaster levels that if mainstream economic theory were to set a price of labour intended to clear the market, the 'equilibrium wage rate' would be so low that it would also 'clear away' many human lives. Markets cannot become frictionless by a set of prices clearing the indefinite real hurdles *qua* transaction costs hampering equilibrium. They are terrains of social interaction determined by power structures and interests. However, in neoclassical economics, reality is tailored to fit the fiction of free competition, with earnings based on individual productivity and scarcity. There is never 'free competition', but rather a continual flux of concentrations of power to control markets; and 'scarcity' applies only to the class without purchasing power—scarcity of the basic conditions of survival, like secure shelter and sufficient calories. In the materially enforced neoliberal fantasia, the social human was forced to conform to the symbolic neoclassical human. The end result was that the social human was cast off like any other disused material object. The dynamics of employment and population growth have been shaped by the neoliberal paradigm with the unspoken but evident aim of reducing the value of human life and cheapening the outlays on labour that would generate wealth. This was the policy of the class in charge.

Three years after the uprisings, imports are headed to constitute nearly half of income, unemployment (poverty-determined as explained in the previous chapter) is at around half of the labour force, industrial capacity is at a fraction of what it used to be, and so on. The deconstruction of Arab social formations is nearly complete. Mauritania and Morocco exhibit severe poverty.

Algeria is barely recovering from a civil war in which two hundred thousand lives were lost. Libya is in a state of internal strife. Egypt's children remain malnourished. Yemen, Palestine, Sudan, Somalia, Syria and Iraq are possibly the worst places on the planet. That is the formidable problematic with which we are faced. How to return value—resources, commodities and wealth— that would improve the living conditions of working classes in the AW to those working classes. According to the International Covenant on Economic, Social and Cultural Rights, peoples may, for their own ends, freely dispose of their natural wealth and resources, and in no case may a people be deprived of its own means of subsistence.[1] 'Human rights' interpretations bow to the whims of the principal powers; however, that politically supressed Arab working classes have been denied the right to their own means of subsistence is a *fact*.

Returning wealth to its rightful owner, the working class, is first of all (of course) a political problem. It has to do with the organisational and ideological capabilities of the working class. Working-class solidarity, to begin with, has been fragmented along religious and ethnic identity lines; ideologically, the influence of political Islam grows into the ideological empty space created by global socialist impotence. Cheap petrodollars have inflated Wahhabi doctrine from a marginal cult followed by around a million people in the early twentieth century to a world phenomenon, which in turn has cemented the disarticulation in Arab formations. Although a very small minority in the Islamic world do embrace Wahhabism, its influence in political discourse has left doctrinal and political schisms more pronounced on both national and regional levels. As contradictions within and between Arab countries have grown, the security resulting from class and regional solidarity has waned. Lost also in this fragmenting process are the complementarities that could have arisen between Arab economies with different resource endowments. There are, of course, subtly contributing secondary reasons for the national-level divisions; but the high degree to which regional resources are controlled by a globally integrated merchant minority, including its privately controlled public sector, constitute sufficient *raison d'être* for the divisiveness.

Redistribution as a right has disappeared from the vocabulary of development. The worldly system of capitalism, which destroys nature and human lives to create wealth, funds and resurrects an Islamic civil society to substantiate absurd interpretations of the ongoing Arab disaster—the wrath of god upon evil sinners. Such is the ideological victory of capital.

---

1   UNHCR, *International Covenant on Economic, Social and Cultural Rights* (1966). Online: http://www.ohchr.org/EN/ProfessionalInterest/Pages/CESCR.aspx (viewed 5 October 2012).

It obscures real processes and obstructs the development of concepts that deal with these processes with medieval liturgy. Ideas and the war of ideas are very important. The amount of capital spent to attack concepts like *nationalisation*, *land reform* and *egalitarian distribution*, probably tallies with the amount spent on bombs. The language of demystification is being purged from popular vocabulary.

To sever the ties to imperialism would require protection of national industry, controls on trade and capital accounts, and nationally egalitarian distribution. Now, one asks, if mighty Russia encountered difficulties in that transition at a time of socialist ascendancy, how can a small Arab country at a time of socialist decline attempt it? Not to mention the oil, the strategic value and war economies associated therewith, which would be bound to trigger imperial aggression. To play on contradictions within the imperialist camp, as did Ho Chi Minh in declaring independence in 1945, would not suffice (Ho 1961, 17–21). The 'imperialist camp' of today encompasses nearly the whole planet and the international Left is not so international. Hence the accent in the struggle must be laid on internationalism.

The necessity to practice internationalism is not new. More than a century ago, emancipation was tied to an internationalism that confronted the pillage of the colonies.

If the emancipation of the working classes requires their fraternal concurrence, how are they to fulfil that great mission with a foreign policy in pursuit of criminal designs, playing upon national prejudices, and squandering in piratical wars the people's blood and treasure? It was not the wisdom of the ruling classes, but the heroic resistance to their criminal folly by the working classes of England, that saved the west of Europe from plunging headlong into an infamous crusade for the perpetuation and propagation of slavery on the other side of the Atlantic. [...] The fight for such a foreign policy forms part of the general struggle for the emancipation of the working classes. (Marx 1864)

In the present financial phase of imperialism, the dollar has universalised capital. Capital has become dollarized and has begun to draw profits through financial channels; it has also increasingly become a unified force against global labour. Financialisation and exchange for the sake of exchange do not create value. Values emerge in two ways: from production and increasing labour's average social productivity, and/or from lowering the share of labour in the social product by pauperisation or austerity measures. Hence, the historical surplus value extracted from the periphery continues to buttress the wages of central working classes even as both relatively decline. There is a glut in global output, and investment in industrial activity has long taken a back seat to finance (Bellamy-Foster 2013). Thus, global profits in finance are determined collectively by capital at the expense of the global share of labour. The organised political dimension of capital suppresses labour as the crisis of investment in new production deepens.

The objective grounds that tie labour together also expand by the homogeneity of capital in the dollar because the share of wages will be determined after the share of financialised profits—that is why, among other things, there is austerity. Financialised profits are the sums of money capital that are shared by a multinational bourgeoisie. Wages stagnate or decline across the board as a result of capital's offensive to lower labour's share— now globally determined as a result of rising financialisation. The point of departure in the struggle against imperialism has to also shift from the national to the international terrain; or more appropriately, the national struggle has to mediate the internationalist position or ensure internationalist resonance and impact.

Capital is at its most vulnerable in the AW. Yet if US-led imperialism loses its grip there, the working class in the global crisis that may unfold will only have Left-sentimental sloganeering to rely upon and not an agenda for socialising the means of production. There will be negation without constructivism. Although the objective grounds for the unity of labour have grown, subjectively the social ailments of alienation and commodity fetishism that have spread into every aspect of life and culture in the centre have countervailed the stress of falling wages and the drudgery of meaningless toil (Lefebvre 2003). In much the same way as Islamic politics corresponds to religiously coloured alienation, the central working classes' disbelief in the viability of internationalist alternatives stands for worldly alienation. One may counter with Lefebvre's point that historically, all ideologies have been superseded after a greater or lesser period of unhappy consciousness; but given the collapse of the old working-class movement and the virtual obliteration of socialist ideology and organisation, it is equally likely that more regimenting forms of capital may arise—that is, fascism.

The imposition of Hollywood culture upon consciousness led most to think that history mimics a football series. The losers leave the race. But history is the making of social facts that linger. As Michael Parenti (2003) notes, many of the social achievements of central formations have arisen as a result of competition with the Soviet social-welfare model. The language of socialism, especially the nationalisation of the means of production, must once again clasp the working-class imagination. This is not the communisation of the past; it may be or a variant thereof: the seizure and repurposing of means of production, distribution and communication outside of capital's control by workers' assemblies. This democratisation empowered by workers' reappropriation of the means of production must in advanced capitalism be the very basis for the social revolution, of which the political revolution is the expression and completion. 'The social revolution [...] must draw its poetry from the future' (Marx 1852). In this financialised epoch, a resurgent socialist working-class movement is necessarily an internationalist process.[2]

The absolute general law of capitalist development did not cease to operate. When the mystique of the nation-state is lifted, the Third World unemployed will be revealed as the Lazarus class of capital. As far back as the 1870s, as well as the present time, the dislocated labour in a closely integrated world has contributed to value creation by virtue of its very abjection. 'The relative over-population becomes so much more apparent in a country, the more the capitalist mode of production is developed in it. [...] This is due to the cheapness and abundance of disposable or unemployed wage-labourers' (Marx, *Capital*, vol. 3, ch. 14). Under financialisation, the world has become more integrated than a single country in the mid-nineteenth century. Labour, unemployed or employed, and the very mass of labour, contributes to value directly or indirectly by structurally influencing the production process. In a crisis of overproduction where financialisation has elevated the snatching of wealth in money form to the principal mode of capital concentration, there is even less of a need to engage excess socialised labour in low-return production efforts (Chossudovsky 2003). Here once more the contradiction between the supposedly perennial progressive side of capitalism and its capacity to create mass misery assumes new heights under financialisation—not to mention the environmental crisis.

> The greater the social wealth, the functioning capital, the extent and energy of its growth, and, therefore, also the absolute mass of the proletariat and the productiveness of its labour, the greater is the industrial reserve army. [...] The more extensive, finally, the *Lazarus layers* of the working class, and the industrial reserve army, the greater is official pauperism. *This is the absolute general law of capitalist accumulation.* (Marx, *Capital*, vol. 1, ch. 25)

Capitalism was progressive in relation to precapitalist modes of production, but in relation to itself, that is having been the immanent historical phase for some five centuries, it is not only regressive but also ugly—as per Lukacs. The socialisation of the workforce must entail also socialising the labour process, an arrest of surplus value and accumulation. Socialising production necessarily implies a reinvention of a price system. Capital hides behind the prices it makes

---

2   These remarks were made in discussions with Adam Cornford.

and bestows upon these prices godly qualities and the capability of generating fantasy-like equilibrium and social prosperity. These capital-brokered prices render unnecessary (to capital) much of the social labour of the globe. To revalorise labour and capitalise the distressed sectors, nationalisation, price guarantees and subsidies should equalise the conditions of livelihood.

As I have noted, in the short-lived socialism of the AW it was not nationalisation that went wrong, it was the nature of the ruling class in charge of the national economy. When the class in charge of the state was working-class committed, nationalisation performed well. The outstanding lesson of past experience shows that redistributive policies disconnected from the political empowerment of the labouring classes on the basis of the right to organise politically and to defend working-class achievements lead to disastrous outcomes. Moreover, top-down 'socialism' (redistributive nationalist state capitalism) adopted policies and plans that were less and less congruent with actual social need because they lacked working-class participation. Yet despite the recent uprisings, the class structure and its institutional framework prohibiting the Arab working class from the implementation of an effective development strategy have stayed intact. How might class restructuring favouring the working classes and their development come about?

Reversing Arab Development as an Imperialist Imperative

There are no ready-made answers to the above question. Of the many definitions of development, the one adopted for this work emphasises development as principally the result of incorporating working-class aspirations in the political process—or, more fully, as the outcome of working-class struggle that compels this incorporation. A reversal of de-development is a turnaround in the struggle of Arab working classes to retain and deploy their own resources for their own welfare. Mass political participation must decide social priorities, while bearing in mind the organic linkages of the international working class. The principal contradiction is therefore between the Arab working classes and the alliance of US-led capital with Arab ruling classes.

In this situation, the state of Israel provides US-led capital additional security and buttresses US hegemony. For US-led capital, Israeli capital should grow without integrating with the Arab region commercially or politically, otherwise its gendarme role may falter. As a partner of US-led capital, Israeli capital belongs geographically to the AW, but not economically or socially. Leaving aside the minimal integration implied by the Camp David Accords, it is Israel and the US that viscerally oppose integrative normalisation of Israel into the AW—this is not the selective peace treaties whose purpose is to weaken Arab structures. The whole of the Arab antinormalisation movement places the accent on imaginary conditions. Israel simply cannot normalise relations with the AW, given its *raison d'être* as a gendarme for imperialism implying Arab de-development. Israel only normalises what keeps it apart from its milieu and what keeps the momentum for imperialist aggression ongoing. It is a product of imperialist history and not a maker of it.

In modern times, existential threats do not resemble the massive annihilation inflicted upon Native Americans or Australian Aborigines. The closest one comes to this kind of existential threat is in the Congo war. This war has been recently the subject of peace talks and has tapered down in intensity. However, the war in Syria, as recently in Lebanon and Iraq, has picked up speed and has begun to resemble an existential threat. The Palestinians in particular, and the Arabs of the Fertile Crescent in general, have endured a significant death toll related to imperialist aggression. Michael Neumann likens the Palestinians to the Native Americans and sees as justifiable their violent forms of resistance:

> The Indians had no chance of defeating the whites by conventional military means. So their only resort was to hit soft targets and do the maximum damage. That wasn't just the right thing to do from their point of view. It was the right thing to do, period, because the whites had no business whatever coming thousands of miles to destroy the Indian people. The comparisons with the situation of the Palestinians are beyond obvious. (Neumann 2002)

Seen in reverse, there is an existentialist threat to capital from the working class such that it makes its war against labour a war for existence. In the AW, capital targets social factions that demand the clamping of the open veins of the AW—to borrow the phrase from Eduardo Galeano, nationalisation and socialisation of resources. Its Islamic-coloured foes, however, do not question privatisation and laxness in resource flows; their wars are an asset to imperialism, and as such, they materially compose a pillar of capital.

An immiserated Arab working class imparts much of its immediate insecurity at the national level. Masses residing in underdeveloped conditions would need to sacrifice more heavily in anti-imperialist struggles. The success of their revolutions would be attenuated by their level of underdevelopment, literacy, health, technological capacity and educational attainment. In colloquial terms: the hungry are unable to put up a good fight. Arab development therefore becomes a matter of redressing the regional balance of forces against Israel, the US and their partners, the Arab ruling classes. When all the military defeats to which Arab formations have been subjected are considered, the Israeli factor alone, in as far as it engrains a state of defeat in the social structure, explains much of the desolation of Arab society and its associated failure of development. The way Arab societies have coped with defeat is in how their ruling classes used defeat and defeatism to promote their class interests and implicitly or explicitly impose the terms of tribute transfer and surrender upon the working classes. It is innate to bourgeois ruling classes to pursue wealth making within the context in which they are found. There is nothing sacrosanct about national allegiance to them.

It is not only the crass brutality of the assault on Arab working classes that differentiates the practice of imperialism in the AW from its practice elsewhere in the developing world; there are also distinct politico-economic circumstances for the differences. As pointed out in Chapter Five, the unfair share of US-led capital in imperial rents as a result of the dollarisation of the world reserve currency, together with the dangers of underwriting US debt further by hegemony over the AW, is causing increasing unease and frustration among emerging regional powers. Brazil, Russia, India and China are economies that extract value from national industrial production and are concerned with the expanding dollar debt in relation to real assets. These worries heighten not-so-dormant interimperialist rivalry. US-led capital's insatiable appetite for imperial rents and the expanding volume of dollar-money supply do in fact jeopardise the global financial order to the disadvantage *cum* displeasure of national capitalists that denominate their wealth holdings in the dollar. Hence the presence of US military powers in the AW buttresses US-led capital's hegemony globally as well as supporting its consumption patterns propped up by international inflows.

> The picture is one of consumption without production, dependent on inflows of borrowed foreign capital, which inflows are in turn dependent on American military supremacy. [...] Thus if it does not invade the West Asian region, the United States stands to lose dollar hegemony by losing control of the major oil field development projects in the next decade. (RUPE 2003)

Necessarily but not exclusively, the level of tension in the AW will be contingent upon the degree to which the war/oil-dependent growth of US capital becomes a liability to world capital and warrants a parting with US hegemony and its dollar. By liability I mean here not only in terms of simple economic cost–benefit analysis of the two closed systems of competing imperial rivals, but also in terms of how vital the US and its ally Israel are as a security blanket for the interests of financial capital as whole in the AW. US-led capital also continues to gain from fomenting fanatical ideologies around the Arab–Israeli question. Doctrines of 'the clash of civilisations' and 'cultures of militarism' are inseparable from the actual military superiority that the US displays regionally. Less-developed Arab countries whose national security is exposed will, whether by the demonstration effect or by the actual integrative processes that enable US-led capital to cheapen Third World resources, witness further commoditisation of human life. The price of labour power globally continues to be partially set against the misery of the devastated AW. Imperial booty in the form of the higher share in imperial rent that US-led capital keeps for itself (Amin 2012), the persistent global imbalances, and the potential unsteadiness of the US dollar that endangers wealth holdings combine to keep competitors for the throne of empire unnerved.

In short, US-led capital hegemony over the AW delays the moment at which foreign holders of US debt will convert their US money assets into real assets. This would represent a partial conversion of fictitious capital into real capital—not that anything like a full conversion is possible given the vast mass of fictitious debt—but closing in on that point is the threshold beyond which empire descends (Patnaik 2010). The problem becomes an antinomy. On the one hand, the dollar's very strength as international currency rests on the US securing an underdeveloped AW as collateral against future issuance of its own fiat money; on the other, US-led capital continues its grabbing of imperial rents over and against other productive national capitals. This intractable contradiction leads to varying but nonzero degrees of complicity and even collusion among nations in overlooking the human disasters of the Arab region. How can any nation-state dislodge US imperial standing when part of its wealth is being held in the dollar and against which Arab de-development is its collateral? The brutal embargo on Iraq, which dragged on for many years as an immense tragedy (documented by Joy Gordon [2010]) serves as a recent case in point. None of the upstart nations could afford to defy the threat of oil-supply cuts or still-rising oil prices. At the same time, they do their best to resist US-led capital trespassing on the values of their wealth in the dollar when the US Federal Reserve stretches the dollar supply to satisfy the demands of financialisation.

Wars, 'quantitative easing' and the dynamics of profits extracted by reducing labour's share in financialisation suggest that US-led capital's high-wire act cannot last for too long. The latest positions of China and Russia on the Syrian conflict are such manifestations. The recent financial crisis (2007–08) revealed excesses so egregious that value transfers can no longer be underwritten by growing the dollar-money form without the scrutiny of other nations. US-led imperialist hegemony over the Gulf, including the possibility of an Iran assault or an Iranian deal that will deal to Iran what Camp David dealt to Egypt, are more and more nakedly rackets that US-led capital employs to underwrite the dollar and other imperial rent expansions. The precariousness of the international security arrangement mirrors the unsteadiness of the international financial order. It is because the US is able to heighten insecurity and exercise hegemony simultaneously that capital flows to the US increase. The rise of the dollar after the financial crisis (2007–08) persisted despite the fact that the US economy initiated the fiasco and was itself in dire shape. After the great financial crisis, the resettling of the international financial order into low-intensity currency wars and the calls for a move away from the dollar system unveil the apprehension on the part of many nations in the present US-dominated dollar mechanism that mediates value into money form. In light of the high US debt-to-GDP ratio (around three hundred per cent according to the McKinsey Global Institute)[3] the hegemony exercised by US-led capital would have to intensify to redress weakness in the strategic (military-financial) collateral required to underwrite expanding dollar-denominated money wealth. When this hegemony retreats, the adjustment process will reach a breaking point that may imply significant dollar devaluation. The decision-making space swings between US debt deflation (with a lessening of global wealth holdings in the dollar) and a further exercise in militarism such as laying hegemonic claim to the eastern flank of the Persian Gulf (containing Iran by aggressive military assault or by crippling treaties floating the social classes whose growth depends on the imperialist space—that is, the class partners of imperialism within Iran). Substantial dollar devaluation is an indication of decline, and it protractedly corrodes the status of empire, especially when opportunities for further imperialist encroachments are dashed. It is at this juncture that the crisis of capital, as a crisis in power standing, drags the AW deeper into war and conflict. US-led capital has to command the war-making/deconstruction process on Arab formations and, as such, it grabs new value (imperial rents) from accelerating the debilitation of the Arab states.

There is to be sure a continuous effort by US-led capital to redress its power standing in view of the persistence of the slow credit cycle and precarious financial profitability as of the Great Recession of 2007–08. As mentioned above, US-led capital is eying the containment of Iran to ensure hegemony over the eastern flank of the Persian Gulf. However, global capital is split on the issue of aggression against Iran. Rising national capital in China and other nationalist economies are strategically opposed to the amalgam of US-led financialised capital on this issue. The tacit collusion of 'capital-account constrained' Chinese capital with the US's aggressive stance over Iran may hold only to the point at which its strategic losses in oil areas begin to critically destabilise its national economy, and the same holds true for other rising industrial nations. They would also be especially concerned over losses sustained to their dollar-denominated wealth holdings. US-led

3   McKinsey Global Institute. Online: http://www.financialiceberg.com/jan_30_in_us_debt_we_trust.html (viewed 10 September 2013).

capital, in particular the financialised classes and institutions that share in the grab resulting from increased financialisation (free riders upon US imperial ventures) know well that a stable dollar and dollar rents rely heavily on US control in oil areas. Financialised and free-riding capital circles will continue to support the US unconditionally in laying stake to the eastern side of the Gulf (Iran), or at least weakening the sovereignty of the Iranian state, such that US hegemony expands. As to more nationally based capitals, keeping their wealth steady in the dollar is one thing, but forfeiting the real source of their wealth, which is their hold on their national economies, is another (these would result from strategic imbalance). In one indication of the growing dissatisfaction over the US's bellicose stance towards Iran, China, which has sparingly used its veto power in the past outside its own vicinity, twice vetoed the UN Security Council resolution over Syria, which is the gateway to Iran. The struggle within China between the 'left and right wings or nationalist vs. financialised capital' can be detected from the way capital controls have been settled so far in favour of the national capitalist (regulated account supporters still exercise much influence in China and it is this channel which would, if opened up, permit US capital to further co-opt Chinese capital [Xiao 2006]). China has been the main force breaking the embargo on Iran. The way an alternative petro-renminbi is forming in Asia to pay for Iranian oil is disconcerting to US-led capital. This embryonic shift from a unipolar to a multipolar world is a window of opportunity within which smaller, insecure nations may exercise the right to reown their policies and the right to develop.

De-development in Context

As has been pointed out all along, the defeat of national forces necessarily restructured Arab society into the pliable political formations they have become. The redistribution of wealth to the ruling classes in a context of capitalist despotism imposed scarcity in basic needs on the working class over which it competed internally and splintered as socialist ideology moved back. The rise of Islamic obscurantism had nothing to do with recreating the past. The past cannot be recreated anywhere. It was wholly a product of present-day defeatism and petrodollar cronyism. Political Islam is the infused ideological obsequiousness necessary for the Arab merchant and US-led capital alliance to demobilise the working class and disengage Arab resources. Disarticulation or the massive disconnect between peoples' real demands and the ideas and forms of social organisation with which they seek to fulfil these demands, is not an exclusive condition plaguing Arab formations, but over the last thirty years, the rift has severely deepened. The discord that has formed along politically instituted cultural lines grew as a result of shifting from industrialisation to merchant modes of reproduction. It was not only the ghosts of an (in any case fictionalized) Islamic past whose pressure transformed resistance into submission, so that redistributive capacity devolved to the newly formed religious identity institutions; the US-led imperialist alliance choreographed this working-class fragmentation at every stage. The historical agents were wars and the International Financial Institutions. It is highly improbable that any of the existing Arab ruling classes can draw legitimacy from nationally mediated working-class positions for one simple reason: no effort is being spared to dismantle the working class as a historical agent. It has become a working class without a working-class consciousness and thereby pitted against itself. Ironically, not much money value is extracted from absolute surplus value creation (extending the working day or intensifying labour without raising the wage) or from immiserating the Arab working class. There are really not many valuable working hours by which the working class could be short-changed. Generally, much of Arab working classes and resources lie in a state of suspended animation as material of capital. They are part of the labour force by their very waiting to be engaged in value production whenever capital calls and they exert downward pressures on the improvement of living conditions on a planetary scale. This state of being is a result of three major factors: the global overproduction crisis, the way the developing mode of production is articulated with the developed (in the case of the AW it is principally a military force that imposes articulation), and the way in which peripheral crises are part and parcel of the formation of value in the centre. Labour power and resources exist as use-values for capital.

> When it is said that capital is 'accumulated (realised) labour (properly, *objectified* [*vergegenständlichte*] labour), which serves as the means for new labour (production)', then this refers to the simple *material of capital*, without regard to the formal character without which it is not capital. This means nothing more than that capital is an instrument of production, for, in the broadest sense, every object, including those furnished purely by nature, e.g., a stone, must first be appropriated by some sort of activity before it can function as an instrument, as means of production. (Marx 1857)

In more particular terms, although much of the Third World can be classified as geostrategic, the hyped worth of oil to humanity and the location of around half of the world's known (cheaply extracted) oil reserves attach substance to the claim of Arab strategic importance. Add to that claim the fact that around a third of the world's seaborne oil supply passes through the Straits of Hormuz (20 per cent of total world supply), the threats of expanding wars that keep the world on edge, and the AW's geostrategic position becomes clear through the ideological fog. In these circumstances, the concept of primacy of politics implies that imperialist positioning in the region cannot be explained solely in terms of the money-form value extracted from the Arab formations proper—as in the general condition above. The AW matters more for how US-led imperialism secures control of the regional resources to leverage its imperial position in relation to the rest of the world. That is why Arab national economic relations and policies do not nurture national development, but rather supplement the position of US-led imperialism globally by their very underdevelopment. The degree of imperialist coercion suffered by the Arab working classes is not coincidental. It is an outcome of the necessities of US-led imperialism and the specific characteristic of a region carved up and reshaped by continual imperialist aggression. Arab oil and Arab local wars, by virtue of their contribution to value and by being means of imperialist global control, are requisites of capital and fall within the purview of US-led imperialism.

Overcoming the Impasse

How then does one mobilise real resources? Put differently, how can the AW develop? The present work has argued that in order to assess policy options available to the AW, one must better understand its class structure as mediated through its political framework. In more illustrative analytical wording, it is the resultant balance of class forces that will drive and shape the task of development. General policy prescriptions that claim to provide a panacea for development, like the motto 'Free the markets!' are just platitudes used by merchant regimes in alliance with US-led capital to inculcate the discipline of a market that is anything but free. Development, after all, depends on the nature of the agency of development. The class substance of Arab institutions—that is, the actual decision-making context of the AW—will determine whether its countries will be able to deal with the various developmental challenges.

The principal challenge is to recirculate value nationally: to close the spigots of real and financial transfers to the centre. This means a revalorisation of national values by what is socially necessary for the working class in the resisting nation. It means making your own prices with which to value your own resources. In the golden age of postindependence Arab growth, monetary policy followed a vigorous fiscal stimulus plan, regional savings tallied with regional investments, redistribution superseded automatic stabilizers, and the state's capacity to intervene in productive investment was socially linked to the health of the state itself. These measures were possible because the economy was regulated and trade and capital accounts were tightly controlled. Money was partially de-fetishised and financing growth could not be done at the expense of the working class. Real wages and employment were the crux of the development strategy. The manipulation of exchange and interest rates cushioned international pressures on national currency. When the decision makers were bound to the working class, these measures worked. In fact, the deficits and debt levels were insignificant when compared to the present era's indebtedness rates (WDI, various years). That is why incomes policy and redistribution countervailed the absurdity that the rich save to invest at home or to invest, period. Simplifying reality to a set of almost platonic forms—the Nation, the Leader, the True Faith, and inevitably, the Subhuman Enemy—in order to promote an aggressive agenda is what fascism does. One is hard-pressed to find historical examples of a bourgeoisie whose class interests were subdued by its nationalism, unless of course nationalism was itself an instrument in its capital accumulation. The tenets of the postindependence projects emphasized noninflationary growth accompanied by fair redistribution and rising wages (Gosh 2008). The intensification of the class struggle to temper profit motivation and promote egalitarian state policies will clash with the bourgeoisie. Such reforms call for state intervention and planning investment, which cannot materialise without an egalitarian redistribution and a significant weight for labour in the state.

However, in the AW the grip of phantasmagorical ideology has become so strong such that many realities have just turned upside down. When in 2008, the global financial crisis overtook the planet, the interlocutor of the ruling social class in Syria announced that their economy was spared and that some US\$ 11 billion in investment was forthcoming from abroad.[4] This was at a time when malnutritional stunting in children under five years old had reached 28 per cent.[5] Not long after, that country witnessed an uprising and a civil war that is ongoing at this writing in 2013, leading to the exodus of over a million refugees—the largest migration in such a brief period in recently recorded history. When one contemplates the brassy fanfare of claims by Arab countries wallowing in severe social crisis that they have weathered the global financial meltdown and are successful economies, one is witness to the monolithic power of capital's ideology. These are countries with high malnutrition rates and poverty employment, some are in a state of war, and yet they speak of fiscal and monetary contraction as if their capitals were London or New York. Even worse, the Arab intelligentsia is still co-opted and peddles the neoliberal fairy tales *ad nauseum*.

---

4   http://www.alwatan.sy/dindex.php?idn=128939&fb_source=message(viewed 2 March 2012).

5   'At a Glance: Syrian Arab Republic', UNICEF. Online: http://www.unicef.org/infobycountry/syria_statistics.html (viewed 27 October 2012).

In its 2012 conference, the Economic Research Forum rehashes the old terminology of state rebuilding and eliminating corruption.[6] According to this worn-out and empirically vacant rhetoric, states were not deconstructed and the macro accounts did not divert resources to antisocial ends as a result of neoliberal policies; rather, the cause is the inherent immorality of an Arab population incapable of adhering to Western liberal democratic standards. To reiterate: Arab states have been dispossessed of their sovereignty and they do not possess the tools of development. Whenever an imperialistically induced disaster happens, it becomes an 'unintended consequence'. In the AW, all social disasters are the *intended* consequences of the ruling class mediating its position in an ideological vortex of complex forms of organisation and decision making. The avalanche of capital's ideological victory, its power vortex, creates downstream the imagery, the institutions and structures from which the interest of capital are served intentionally or unintentionally in relation to its capabilities. At this stage in socialist ideological retreat, it may be safe to say that not a single disaster can escape the steel tentacles of capital.

When idle resources and unemployment figures in the AW exceed those of the Great Depression, it may be best to paraphrase Chekhov: even an imbecile can cope with a crisis—it is everyday life that exhausts us. To imply that the AW has weathered the financial crisis is to say that the AW was not in crisis to begin with. But the AW was and is in severe social crisis, including (from the working-class viewpoint) acute economic crisis; and the fact that damage from the 2007–08 meltdown was minimal owes more to the disconnect between the financial and the real sectors as in any underdeveloped economy, or to the abundance of financial wealth accrued from oil rents, than to the effectiveness of macro policies.

Ideal policies mediate the divide between economic growth and development. In the AW, however, constraints emerge at every juncture in the policymaking space. Merchant capitalists commandeer institutional arrangements and treat public policies as extensions of their vested interests. Whereas expansionary fiscal policies require a progressive taxation system and a reconstitution of several exchange rates protecting the national consumption bundles and currency from balance of payment pressures, AW state tax revenues are derived from indirect consumption taxes levied upon the working classes, and the capital accounts remain open. The region's import gap reduces the effectiveness of fiscal policies by dissipating public expenditures via leakages and weak multipliers or accelerator effects, but the trade account remains wide open. Similarly, the effectiveness of monetary

---

6   ERF's Eighteenth Annual Conference, 2012. Online: http://www.erf.org.eg/cms. php?id=NEW_publication_details_books&publication_id=1670 (viewed 1 June 2013).

policy is weakened by the pegging to the dollar and the rift between the financial and real economies, limiting price effects to areas that attract speculative attention; yet there are virtually no regulatory frameworks. These structural issues require resolute political power capable of shutting off the capital and trade account leakages.

After years of market liberalisation, uncertainty has also risen with the growing inequity in the ownership structure. The recent real estate bubbles fuelled by central bank policies drove further apart the wealth of real estate owners from that of non-owners. The sheer magnitude of privately owned assets relative to the huge mass that does not hold assets is in itself a seminal contributor to uncertainty. The steepness of the divide, keenly supervised by US-led imperialism, hinders the formation of development-mediated social forms of organisation. In view of the strength of the merchant-class hold on economic returns and/or of the ambiguity surrounding ownership that mixes private and public sectors, any national redistributive strategy can be perceived as harmful to the haves vis-à-vis the have-nots. There is no Keynesian 'widow's cruse' whereby entrepreneurs earn what they spend and workers spend what they earn. Arab investors mostly earn what the state expends on labour and only marginally earn what they spend at home. They are mainly merchants and not industrialists investing in the knowledge economy or plant and equipment. The usurpation of surplus, which depletes the economy of the capacity to regenerate itself, would cease under equitable-*cum*-industrial reforms. Another way to look at this is that the severed social intermediation of private with social interests, combined with imperialist intervention, lays the terrain for the reproduction of de-development.

In theory, the AW stands to learn from the successes and failures of other regions in buttressing their positions vis-à-vis their underdevelopment crises. It could, for instance, partially model its institutions on the basis of the East Asian experience, where rent-seeking and security objectives were aligned in parallel with developmental activities. It could steer away from the very causes of the recent financial crisis in the centre: namely, neoliberal policies that have compressed wages and demand for more than two decades, and allowed short-term profiteering from financial speculation to boom at the expense of socially driven economic activity. It could also learn from the EU model of integration, whereby nation-states relinquished part of their sovereignty in order to expand output. But none of these strategies can be mimicked by the AW because the AW simply is not a world for the Arab working classes. While the rest of the world was anxiously eyeing the steady rise in the unemployment rates of the more developed economies in the aftermath of the international financial crisis, unemployment rates in the AW had been the highest globally for more than a decade and no one paid attention. In 2009, the principal statutory publication submitted to the UN Economic and Social Council (ECOSOC) warned:

> Crisis or not, in a conflict-affected developing context in which the rate of unemployment —a key measure of welfare and development—holds nearly steady at the double-digit level and responds poorly to fluctuations in growth rates, the vast majority of the lower strata, who are already in dire need, could likely sustain little more harm than they have already suffered. [...] Already a huge part of the region's savings do not get funnelled back into national or regional investment, unequivocally implying that this leakage is underpinned by an articulation of various levels of security that has for long undermined the potential for development. [...] It is for that reason that security and sovereignty become interrelated goals and form necessary, albeit insufficient, conditions for sound economic development. Sufficiency will require [...] the establishment of a domestic coalition for a pro-poor and rights-based development policy (UN 2009a).

The crisis of the AW is not one that can be merely quantified with economic measures. It is a deeply rooted social crisis that is continually fed and reproduced by social dislocation, artificially stimulated religious and ethnic conflict, and a vortex of international powers emboldened by US military excursions and Israel's superior military capabilities. The regional dynamic of development is, plainly put, *oil and wars*, together and apart. That is why it is difficult to replicate the experience of others in the AW. That is why, in addressing the nearly intractable task of exposing the process of development, it is advisable to focus on the single most fundamental issue underlying the AW's feebleness in all capacities, which is the power deficit of the working class in the state. It is inevitable that the ideological illusions will come undone. The state that the Arab working classes will want to seize will be a continuation of their former national liberation struggles; it will also likely involve the immediate and forcible mass resocialisation of the means of life, starting with the financial sector, distribution, transport and communications, that is increasingly also the only open path of anticapitalist/communising action in the centre. In these struggles, 'history has proved and will go on proving that people's war is the most effective weapon against US imperialism and its lackeys. All revolutionary people will learn to wage people's war against US imperialism and its lackeys' (Lin 1966, 58). This struggle is not an Arab problem alone. As capital becomes ever more rapacious in its destruction of human life and the biosphere, the struggle of the international working class will be the struggle of the Arab working class.

REFERENCES

Abadie, A., and Gardeazabal, J. (2003) 'The Economic Costs of Conflict: A Case Study of the Basque Country', *American Economic Review*, vol. 93, no. 1.

Abdel-Malek, A. (1967) 'The Crisis in Nasser's Egypt', *New Left Review*, vol. 45.

Abdel-Malek, A. (1968) *Egypt: Military Society; The Army Regime, the Left, and Social Change under Nasser* (New York: Vintage Books).

Abdel-Malek, A. (1971) *The Army and National Movement (Al-jaysh wa-al-harakah al-wataniyah)*, translated from Arabic (Beirut: Dar-Ibn Khaldoun).

Abdel-Malek, A. (1981) *Social Dialectics: Nation and Revolution*, vol. 2 (New York: SUNY Press).

Abdel-Malek, A. (1985) *Taghyir Al'alam* ('Alam Alma'rifa).

Abderrezak, A. (2004) 'Colonisation's Long-Lasting Influence on Economic Growth: Evidence from the MENA Region', *Journal of North African Studies*, vol. 9, no. 3.

Abed, G. T. (2003) 'Unfulfilled Promise: Why the Middle East and North Africa Region has Lagged in Growth and Globalization', *Finance and Development*, vol. 40, no. 1.

Abrahart, A., Kaur, I., and Tzannatos, Z. (2002) 'Government Employment and Active Labor Market Policies in MENA in a Comparative International Context', in H. Handoussa and Z. Tzannatos (eds), *Employment Creation and Social Protection in the Middle East and North Africa* (Cairo and New York: The American University in Cairo Press).

Abou Anaml, H. (2006) *Alikstad al Israeli* (Beirut: Markaz Dirasat al-Wahda al-'Arabiya).

Abu-Bader, S., and Abu-Qarn, A. S. (2003) 'Government Expenditures, Military Spending and Economic Growth: Causality Evidence from Egypt, Israel and Syria', *Journal of Policy Modelling*, vol. 25.

Abu-Qarn, A. S., and Abu-Bader, S. (2007) 'Sources of Growth Revisited: Evidence from Selected MENA Countries', *World Development*, vol. 35, no. 5.

Adams, R. H. Jr., and Page, J. (2003) 'Poverty, Inequality and Growth in Selected Middle East and North Africa Countries, 1980–2000', *World Development*, vol. 31, no. 12.

Agosin, M. R., and Tussie, D. (eds) (1993) *Trade and Growth: New Dilemmas in Trade Policy* (London: Macmillan).

Al-Duri, A. A. (1969) *Muqaddimah fi al-tarikh al-iqtisadi al-Arabi* (Beirut: Dar al-Taliiah).

Al-Hamsh, M. (2004) *al-Fiqr al-Iqtissadi fi al-Khitab al-Siyassi al-Souri fil al-Karn al-Ishreen* (Economic thinking of Syrian political speech in the twentieth century) (Beirut: Bisan).

Al Jazeera (2011) 'Iraq's Abandoned Children', 10 May, viewed 17 August 2012. http://www.aljazeera.com/video/middleeast/2011/05/201151041017174884.html

Al Jazeera (2013a) 'Death Toll Hits 28 in Indonesian Boat Sinking', 28 September, viewed 4 October 2013. http://www.aljazeera.com/news/asia-pacific/2013/09/more-refugees-found-drowned-off-indonesia-20139296152682599.html

Al Jazeera (2013b) '32 Palestinian and Syrian Refugees Drown, 212 Survive Another Sinking Incident Near Coasts of Malta and Italy', 17 October, viewed 20 October 2013.

http://www.aljazeerah.info/News/2013/October/17%20n/32%20Palestinian%20 and%20Syrian%20Refugees%20Drown,%20212%20Survive%20Another%20 Sinking%20Incident%20Near%20Coasts%20of%20Malta%20and%20Italy,%20 October%2017,%202013.htm

Al-Kanaani, K. I. (2002) 'The Integration Attempts in the Fourth World: The Case of the Arab World', *(DRUID) Academy Winter 2002 PhD Conference*, 17–19 January, Danish Research Unit for Industrial Dynamics, Aalborg.

Al-Khafaji, I. (1986) 'State Incubation of Iraqi Capitalism', *Middle East Report*, no. 142.

Alavi, H. (1972) 'The State in Post-Colonial Societies: Pakistan and Bangladesh', *New Left Review*, vol. 1, no. 74.

Alesina, A., and Rodrik, D. (1994) 'Distributive Politics and Economic Growth', *Quarterly Journal of Economics*, vol. 109, no. 2.

Ali, T. (2002) *The Clash of Fundamentalisms: Crusades, Jihads and Modernity* (London: Verso).

Allison, H. (1990) *Kant's Theory of Freedom* (New York: Cambridge University Press).

Alnasrawi, A. (2001) 'Iraq: Economic Sanctions and Consequences, 1990–2000', *Third World Quarterly*, vol. 22, no. 2.

Althusser, L. (1971) *Lenin and Philosophy, and Other Essays* (New York: Monthly Review Press).

Amin, S. (1976) *Unequal Development: An Essay on the Social Formations of Peripheral Capitalism* (Hassocks: The Harvester Press).

Amin, S. (1978) 'The Arab Nation: Some Conclusions and Problems', *MERIP Reports*, no. 68.

Amin, S. (1990) *Delinking: Towards a Polycentric World* (London: Zed Books).

Amin, S. (1992) 'Contribution to a Debate: The World Capitalist System and Previous Systems', *The Arab World: Nation State and Democracy* (London: Zed Books).

Amin, S. (2012) 'The Surplus in Monopoly Capitalism and the Imperialist Rent', *Monthly Review*, vol. 64, no. 3.

Amsden, A. (1997) 'Bringing Production Back In: Understanding Government's Economic Role in Late Industrialization', *World Development*, vol. 25, no.4.

Amsden, A. (2001) *The Rise of the Rest: Challenges to the West from Late Industrializing Economies* (Oxford: Oxford University Press).

Anderson, L. (1987) 'The State in the Middle East and North Africa', *Comparative Politics*, vol. 20, no. 1.

Arab Labour Organisation (2010) Workshop on Agricultural Rebirth, Damascus, 23–5 November.

Arab Organization for Agricultural Development, *Statistical Abstract*, no. 29.

Arab Monetary Fund (various years) *Joint Arab Economic Report* (Abu Dhabi: Arab Monetary Fund).

Arestis, P., and Sawyer, M. (2003) 'Reinventing Fiscal Policy', *Journal of Post-Keynesian Economics*, vol. 26, no. 1.

Arestis, P., and Sawyer, M. (2005) 'Inflation Targeting: A Critical Appraisal', *Greek Economic Review*, forthcoming.

Argitis, G., and Pitelis, C. (2001) 'Monetary Policy and the Distribution of Income: Evidence for the United States and the United Kingdom', *Journal of Post Keynesian Economics*, vol. 23, no. 4.

Arraf, J. (2011) 'Iraq's Abandoned Children', Al Jazeera, viewed 3 July 2012. http://english.aljazeera.net/video/middleeast/2011/05/201151041017174884.html

Aschauer, D. A. (1989) 'Is Public Expenditure Productive?', *Journal of Monetary Economics*, vol. 23.

Avramidis, S. (2005) 'Articulation by the Power of the Gun', *Towards a Cosmopolitan Marxism*, 4–6 November, Historical Materialism Conference, London.

Avramidis, S. (2006a) 'Articulation by the "Barrel of a Gun": Development under the Threat of War in the Near East', *New Directions in Marxist Theory*, 8–10 December, Historical Materialism Conference, London.

Avramidis, S. (2006b) 'Famines Are an Advertisement for Imperialism', *International Development Economics Associates*, viewed 26 June 2012. http://www.networkideas.org/news/jul2006/news03_Famines.htm

Ayubi, N. N. (1992) 'Withered Socialism or Whether Socialism? The Radical Arab States as Populist-Corporatist Regimes', *Third World Quarterly*, vol. 13, no.1.

Ayubi, N. N. (1995) *Over-Stating the Arab State: Politics and Society in the Middle East* (London: I. B. Tauris).

Azzam, H. (2002) *The Arab World: Facing the Challenge of the New Millennium* (London: I. B. Tauris).

Bagchi, A. 'Money under Capitalism: Domestic Universal', *International Development Economics Associates*, viewed 15 March 2013. http://www.networkideas.org/ideasact/sep08/amiya_bagchi.pdf

Baker, D., Epstein. G, and Pollin, R. (eds) (1998) *Globalisation and Progressive Economic Policy* (Cambridge: Cambridge University Press).

Balibar, É. (1991) 'Es Gibt Keinen Staat in Europa: Racism and Politics in Europe Today', *New Left Review*, vol. 1, no. 186, viewed 17 August 2013. http://www.newleftreview.org/?view=1627

Baran, P. (1952) 'On the Political Economy of Backwardness', *Manchester School of Economy and Social Studies*, vol. 20, no.1.

Baran, P. (1973) *The Political Economy of Growth* (Middlesex: Penguin).

Batatu, H. (1986) 'State and Capitalism in Iraq: A Comment', *Middle East Report*, no. 142.

Bauer, B. (1843) *The Jewish Question*, viewed 17 August 2013. http://www.marxists.org/archive/marx/works/1844/jewish-question/

BBC News (2013) 'Saudi Cleric Says Driving Risks Damaging Women's Ovaries', 29 September, viewed 2 October 2013. http://www.bbc.co.uk/news/world-middle-east-24323934

Beblawi, H., and Luciani, G. (eds) (1987) *The Rentier State* (London: Croom Helm).

Becker, G. S., and Lewis, G. (1973) 'Interaction between Quantity and Quality of Children', *Journal of Political Economy*, vol. 81, no. 2.

Bellofiore, R. (2011) 'A Crisis of Capitalism', *Guardian*, 21 September, viewed 6 November 2012. http://www.theguardian.com/commentisfree/2011/sep/21/crisis-of-capitalism

Berger, M. (1958) 'The Middle Class in the Arab World', in Walter Z. Laqueur (ed.), *The Middle East in Transition: Studies in Contemporary History* (London: Routledge and Kegan Paul).

Bianchi, R. (2012) 'Egypt's Revolutionary Elections', *The Singapore Middle East Papers* (Singapore: National University of Singapore).

Binns, P. (1986) 'State Capitalism, Marxism and the Modern World', *Education for Socialists*, no. 1.

Binns, P., and Hallas, D. (1976) 'The Soviet Union: State Capitalist or Socialist?', *Marxist Internet Archive*, viewed 11 December 2011. http://www.marxists.org/archive/hallas/works/1976/09/su2.htm#top.

Bohr, F., and Wiegrefe, K., 'The Philosopher and the Terrorist: When Sartre Met RAF Leader Andreas Baader', *Spiegel Online International*, viewed 3 January 2013.

http://www.spiegel.de/international/germany/transcript-released-of-sartre-visit-to-raf-leader-andreas-baader-a-881395.html

Bottomore, T. (1993) *Elites and Society*, 2nd ed. (London: Routledge).

Bracking S. (2004) 'Neoclassical and Structural Analysis of Poverty: Winning the "Economic Kingdom" for the Poor', *Third World Quarterly*, vol. 25, no. 5.

Braverman, H. (1959) 'The Nasser Revolution', *American Socialist Internet Archive*, viewed 23 July 2012. http://www.marx.org/history/etol/newspape/amersocialist/amersoc_5901.htm

Brenner, R. (2003a) 'On the Crisis in the US Economy', *London Review of Books*, vol. 5, no. 3.

Brenner, R. (2003b) 'Towards the Precipice: The Continuing Collapse of the US Economy', *London Review of Books*, no. 5.

Bruno, M. (1995) 'Does Inflation Really Lower Growth?', *Finance and Development*, vol. 32, no. 3.

Bruno, M., and Easterly, W. (1996) 'Inflation and Growth: In Search of a Stable Relationship', *Federal Reserve Bank of St. Louis Review*, May–June.

Buick, A., and Crump, J. (1986) *State Capitalism: The Wages System under New Management* (London: Macmillan).

Buliř, A. (2001) 'Income Inequality: Does Inflation Matter?', *IMF Staff Papers*, vol. 48, no. 1.

Bulmer-Thomas, V. (2003) *The Economic History of Latin America since Independence*, 2nd ed. (Cambridge: Cambridge University Press).

Burnham, J. (1945) *The Managerial Revolution* (London: Penguin).

Bush, R. (2004a) *Civil Society and the Uncivil State: Land Tenure Reform in Egypt and the Crisis of Rural Livelihoods* (Geneva: United Nations Research Institute for Social Development).

Bush, R. (2004b) *Poverty and Neoliberalism: Persistence and Reproduction in the Global South* (London: Pluto Press).

Bush, R. (2004c) 'Poverty and Neo-liberal Bias in the Middle East and North Africa', *Development and Change*, vol. 35, no. 4.

Calvo, G., Leiderman, L., and Reinhart, C. (1993) 'Capital Inflows and Exchange Rate Appreciation in Latin America: The Role of External Factors', *IMF Staff Papers*, vol. 40, no. 1.

Cammack, P. (1989) 'Bringing the State Back In?', *British Journal of Political Science*, vol. 19, no. 2.

Campbell, R. H., and Skinner, A. S. (eds) (1976) *Glasgow Edition of the Works and Correspondence of Adam Smith*, vol. 2, *An Inquiry into the Nature and Causes of the Wealth of Nations* (Oxford: Oxford University Press).

Castells, M. (1992) 'Four Asian Tigers with a Dragon Head: A Comparative Analysis of the State, Economy, and Society in the Asian Pacific Rim', in R. P. Appelbaum and J. A. Henderson (eds), *States and Development in the Asian Pacific Rim* (Newbury Park: Sage Publications).

CBB (Central Bank of Bahrain). (various years) *Economic Indicators* (Bahrain: CBB)

Central Bank of Bahrain (various years) *Economic Indicators*, viewed 21 June 2013. http://www.cbb.gov.bh/page-p-economic_indicators.htm

Chandler, D. (2006) *Empire in Denial: The Politics of State-Building* (London: Pluto Press).

Chang, H.-J. (1993) 'The Political Economy of Industrial Policy in Korea', *Cambridge Journal of Economics*, vol. 17, no. 4.

Chang, H.-J. (1994) *The Political Economy of Industrial Policy* (London: Macmillan).

Chang, H.-J. (2000) 'The Triumph of the Rentiers?', *Challenge*, vol. 43, no. 1.

Chang, H.-J. (2002) *Kicking Away the Ladder?: Policies and Institutions for Economic Development in Historical Perspective* (London: Anthem Press).

Chang, H.-J. (2003) *Globalisation, Economic Development and the Role of the State* (London: Zed Books).

Chang, H.-J., and Grabel, I. (2004) *Reclaiming Development: An Alternative Economic Policy Manual* (London: Zed Books).

Chomsky, N. (1983) *Zionism, Militarism, and the Decline of United States Power* (Cambridge: South End Press).

Chossudovsky, M. (2005) *America's 'War on Terrorism'* (Quebec: Global Research, Centre for Research on Globalization).

Chossudovsky, M. (2006) *The Globalization of Poverty and the New World Order* (Québec: Global Research, Center for Research on Globalization).

Chouman, A. (2005) 'The Socialist Experience in Syria, the Consequences of its Movement towards the Market Economy, and the Impact of Restructuring and Globalization' (unpublished paper).

Cliff, T. ([1955] 1974) *State Capitalism in Russia* (London: Pluto Press).

Cole, J. (2013) 'The American Genocide Against Iraq: 4% of Population Dead as Result of US Sanctions, Wars', *Informed Comment*, October 17, viewed 27 October 2013. http://www.juancole.com/2013/10/american-population-sanctions.html

Coleman, I. (2012) 'Reforming Egypt's Untenable Subsidies', *Council on Foreign Relations*, viewed 18 June 2013. http://www.cfr.org/egypt/reforming-egypts-untenable-subsidies/p27885

Collier, P., and Anke, H. (2000) 'Greed and Grievance in Civil War', *World Bank Policy Research Working Paper*, no. 2355.

Collier, P., Elliott, V. L., Hegre, H., Hoeffler, A., Reynal-Querol, M., and Sambanis, N. (2003) 'Breaking the Conflict Trap: Civil War and Development Policy', *World Bank Policy Research Report*, no. 26121.

Commission on Human Security (CHS) (2003) (New York: Communications Development).

Cooper, M. N. (1983) 'State Capitalism, Class Structure, and Social Transformation in the Third World: The Case of Egypt', *International Journal of Middle East Studies*, vol. 15, no. 4.

Coopération Internationale pour le Développement et la Solidarité (CIDSE) (2006) 'CIDSE Study on Security and Development', CIDSE Reflection Paper, January.

Coulomb, F., and Dunne, J. P. (2008) 'Economics, Conflict and War', *Real-World Economics Review*, vol. 46.

Cramer, C. (2000) 'Inequality, Development and Economic Correctness', *SOAS Department of Economics Working Paper*, no. 105.

Cramer, C. (2003) 'Does Inequality Causes Conflict?', *Journal of International Development*, vol. 15.

CSB (State of Kuwait Central Statistical Bureau). (2011) *Annual Statistical Abstract* (Kuwait: CSB).

Dagdeviren, H., van der Hoeven, R., and Weeks, J. (2002) 'Poverty Reduction with Growth and Redistribution', *Development and Change*, vol. 33, no. 3.

Dahl, R. (1971) *Polyarchy* (New Haven: Yale University Press).

Daily News Egypt. (2011) 'US Gives Egypt $150 Million to Help with Transition', *Daily News Egypt*, February 18, viewed 3 July 2012. http://www.dailynewsegypt.com/2011/02/18/us-gives-egypt-150-mln-to-help-with-transition/

Dal Lago, A. (2006) 'The Global State of War', *Ephemera*, vol. 6, no. 1.

Dasgupta, D., Keller, J., and Srinivasan, T. G. (2002) 'Reform and Elusive Growth in the Middle-East: What Has Happened in the 1990s?', *World Bank Middle East and North Africa Working Paper Series*, no. 25.

Davis A. K. (1960) 'Decline and Fall', *Monthly Review*, vol. 12, no. 5.

Deffeyes, K. (2002) *Hubbert's Peak: The Impending World Oil Shortage* (Princeton, NJ: Princeton University Press).

Department for International Development (2005) *Fighting Poverty to Build a Safer World* (London: Department for International Development).

Dornbusch, R., and Fischer, S. (1991) 'Moderate Inflation', NBER Working Paper, no. 3896.

Duri, A. A. (1969) *Muqaddimah fī al-tārīkh al-iqtiṣādī al-`arabī* (Beirut: Dār al-Ṭalī'ah).

Durlauf, S. N., and Blume, L. E. (2008) *The New Palgrave Dictionary of Economics* (New York: Macmillan Press).

ESCCHR (Economic and Social Council, Commission on Human Rights) (2004) Open-Ended Working Group on the Right to Development, 5th Session, Geneva, 11–20 February, viewed 5 October 2012.http://www.ohchr.org/EN/Issues/Development/Pages/WGRightToDevelopment.aspx

ECLAC (Economic Commission For Latin America and the Caribbean) (2011) *Social Panorama of Latin America* (Chile: United Nations Publication).

Economic Research Forum (2012) *ERF's Eighteenth Annual Conference: Selected Papers*, viewed 1 June 2013. http://www.erf.org.eg/cms.php?id=NEW_publication_details_books&publication_id=1670

Eken, S., Cashin, P., Erbas, S. N., Martelino, J., and Mazarei, A. (1995) 'Economic Dislocation and Recovery in Lebanon', IMF Occasional Paper, no. 120.

Eken, S., Helbling, T., and Mazarei, A. (1997) 'Fiscal Policy and Growth in the Middle East and North Africa Region', *IMF Working Paper*, viewed on 23 November 2013. http://www.frpii.org/english/Portals/0/Library/Fiscal%20Policy/Fiscal%20Policy%20and%20Growth%20in%20the%20Middle%20East%20and%20North%20Africa%20Region.pdf

Eken, S., Robalino, D. A, Schieber, G. (2003) 'Living Better: Improving Human Development Indicators in MENA Will Require Different Approaches to Health, Education, and Social Protection', *Finance and Development*, March.

El-Erian, M. A., Bisat, A., and Helbling, T. (1997) *Growth, Investment, and Saving in the Arab Economies* (IMF).

El-Erian, M. A., and Fennell, S. (1997) *The Economy of the Middle East and North Africa in 1997* (IMF).

El-Erian, M. A., Fennell, S., et al. (1998) *Growth and Stability in the Middle East and North Africa* (IMF).

El-Ghonemy, M. R. (1998) *Affluence and Poverty in the Middle East* (London: Routledge).

El-Mikawy, N., and Posusney, M. P. (2002) 'Labor Representation in the Age of Globalization: Trends and Issues in Non-Oil-Based Arab Economies', in H. Handoussa and Z. Tzannatos (eds), *Employment Creation and Social Protection in the Middle East and North Africa* (Cairo and New York: American University in Cairo Press).

Elbadawi, I. (2004) *Reviving Growth in the Arab World* (Washington, DC: World Bank).

Elias, D. (2005) 'Riot Highlights Gulf Working Conditions', *AP Online*, 25 April, viewed 18 March 2012. http://www.highbeam.com/doc/1P1-107841644.html

Emirates 24/7 (2010) 'Lawyer Wants Jinn to Testify in Court', 23 October, viewed 20 November 2012. http://www.emirates247.com/news/region/lawyer-wants-jinn-to-testify-in-court-2010-10-23-1.307686

Emmanuel, A. (1972) *Unequal Exchange: A Study of the Imperialism of Trade.* Trans. Pearce, B. (New York and London: Monthly Review Press).

Engels, F. (ed.) (1847) *Wage Labour and Capital*, viewed 12 January 2013. http://www.marxists.org/archive/marx/works/1847/wage-labour/index.htm

Engels, F. (ed.) (1894) *Capital*, vol. 3: *The Process of Capitalist Production as a Whole* (New York: International Publishers), viewed 12 January 2013. http://www.marxists.org/archive/marx/works/1894-c3/

Epstein, G., Grabel, I., and Jomo, K. S. (2004) 'Capital Management Techniques in Developing Countries: An Assessment of Experiences from the 1990s and Lessons for the Future', G-24 Discussion Paper Series, viewed 28 August 2012. http://unctad.org/en/Docs/gdsmdpbg2420043_en.pdf

Epstein, G., and Yeldan, E. (2004) 'Alternatives to Inflation Targeting Monetary Policy for Stable and Egalitarian Growth in Developing Countries: A Multi-Country Research Project' (unpublished manuscript).

Everhart, S. S., and Sumlinski, M. A. (2001) 'Trends in Private Investment in Developing Countries, Statistics for 1970–2000 and the Impact on Private Investment of Corruption and the Quality of Public Investment', International Finance Corporation Discussion Paper, no. 44.

Fasano, U., and Wang, Q (2001) *Fiscal Expenditure Policy and Non-oil Economic Growth: Evidence from GCC Countries* (IMF).

Feldstein, M., and Horioka, C. (1980) 'Domestic Saving and International Capital Flows', *Economic Journal*, vol. 90.

Fergany, N. (2004) 'Critique of the Greater Middle East project: The Arabs sorely need to refuse a reform from abroad' (in Arabic), *Al-Hayat*, 19 February.

Fine, B. (2006) 'The Developmental State and the Political Economy of Development', in K. S. Jomo and B. Fine (eds), *The New Development Economics: After the Washington Consensus* (New York: Zed Books).

Fine, B., and Saad Filho, A. (2004) *Marx's Capital* (London: Pluto Press).

Fine, B., and Stoneman, C. (1996) 'Introduction: State and Development', *Journal of Southern African Studies*, vol. 22, no. 1.

Financial Iceberg, *In US Debt We Trust: The Transfer from Private to Public Debt*, viewed 3 March 2012. http://www.financialiceberg.com/jan_30_in_us_debt_we_trust.html

Fischer, S., Sahay, R., and Végh, C. (2002) 'Modern Hyper- and High Inflations', *Journal of Economic Literature*, vol. 40.

FAO (Food and Agriculture Organization) of the United Nations (2001) 'A Special Agricultural Safeguard: Buttressing the Market Access Reforms of Developing Countries', *FAO Geneva Round Table on Selected Agricultural Trade Policy Issues*, Geneva, 21 March, viewed 4 September 2012. http://www.fao.org/trade/docs/Safeguard_en.htm

FAO (various years) *CountrySTAT*, viewed 10 July 2012. http://www.fao.org/economic/ess/countrystat/en

Foucault, M. (1980) *Power/Knowledge* (New York and Toronto: Pantheon Books).

Forder, J. (2003) 'Central Bank Independence: Economic Theory, Evidence and Political Legitimacy', *International Papers in Political Economy*, vol. 10, no. 2.

Foster, J. B. (2013) 'The Epochal Crisis', *Monthly Review*, vol. 65, no. 5.

Frances, S. (2004) 'Development and Security', CRISE Working Paper, no. 3.

Frank, A. G. (1966) 'The Development of Underdevelopment', *Monthly Review*, September.

Frank, A. G. (1991) *Third World War: A Political Economy of the Gulf War and New World Order*. http://www.rrojasdatabank.info/agfrank/gulf_war.html

Frank, A. G. (1996) *The Underdevelopment of Development*. http://rrojasdatabank.info/agfrank/underdev.html

Frank, A. G. (1998) *ReOrient: Global Economy in the Asian Age* (Berkeley: University of California Press).

Gardner, E. (2003) *Creating Employment in the Middle East and North Africa* (Washington, DC: IMF).

Garuda, G. (2000) 'The Distributional Effects of IMF Programs: A Cross-Country Analysis', *World Development*, vol. 28.

Gereffi, G., and Wyman, D. L. (eds) (1990) *Manufacturing Miracles: Paths of Industrialization in Latin America and East Asia* (Princeton, NJ: Princeton University Press).

Gelvin. J. (2004) *The Modern Middle East: A History* (New York: Oxford University Press).

Ghosh, J. (2008) *Growth, Macroeconomic Policies and Structural Change* (Geneva: United Nations Research Institute For Social Development).

Ghosh, J. (2011) 'Global Oil Prices', *International Development Economics Association*, July 13, viewed 10 September 2013. http://www.networkideas.org/news/jul2011/news13_Oil_Prices.htm

Gindin, S. (2013) 'Beyond the Economic Crisis: The Crisis in Trade Unionism', *Socialist Project E-Bulletin*, no. 878.

Gongora, T. (1997) 'War Making and State Power in the Contemporary Middle East', *International Journal of Middle East Studies*, vol. 29, no. 3.

Gordon, J. (2010) *Invisible War: The United States and the Iraq Sanctions* (Cambridge, MA: Harvard University Press).

Gramsci, A. (1971) *Selections from the Prison Notebooks* (New York: International Publishers).

Gramsci, A. (1978) *Selections from Political Writings (1921–1926)*, Quintin Hoare (ed.) (London: Lawrence and Wishart).

Griffin, K. (1970) 'Foreign Capital, Domestic Savings and Economics Development', *Bulletin of the Oxford University Institute of Economics and Statistics*, vol. 32, no. 2.

Grossman, G. M., and Helpman, E. (1990) 'Comparative Advantage and Long-Run Growth', *American Economic Review*, vol. 80, no. 4.

Habash, G. (1998) Interview by Free Arab Voice, viewed 5 December 2012. http://www.freearabvoice.org/EL-Hakim.htm

Hakimian, H. (2001) 'From MENA to East Asia and Back: Lessons of Globalization, Crisis and Economic Reform', in H. Hakimian and Z. Moshaver (eds), *The State and Global Change: The Political Economy of Transition in the Middle East and North Africa* (Richmond: Curzon).

Hakura, D. S. (2004) 'Growth in the Middle East and North Africa', IMF Working Paper, WP/04/56.

Halpern, M. (1962) 'Middle Eastern Armies and the New Middle Class', in John J. Johnson (ed.), *The Role of the Military in Underdeveloped Countries* (Princeton, NJ: Princeton University Press).

Halpern, M. (1963) *The Politics of Social Change in the Middle East and North Africa* (Princeton, NJ: Princeton University Press).

Harris, E. (1993) 'Hegel's Theory of Sovereignty, International Relations, and War', in L. S. Stepelevich (ed.), *Selected Essays on G. W. F. Hegel* (Atlantic Highlands, NJ: Humanities Press).

Harris, J. R., and Todaro, M. P. (1970) 'Migration, Unemployment and Development: A Two Sector Analysis', *American Economic Review*, no. 60.

Harris, L. (2004) The Tech Central Station: Where Free Markets Meet Technology, viewed 3 January. http://www.techcentralstation.com/

Hegel, G. W. (1952) *Philosophy of Right* (Oxford: Oxford University Press).

Hegel, G. W. (2007) *The Philosophy of History* (New York: Cosimo).

Henningsen, P. (2012) 'Strange Bedfellows: How the U.S. and Egypt Control the Destiny of the Region', Infowars.com, 19 March, viewed 3 November 2012. http://21stcenturywire.com/2012/03/20/strange-bedfellows-how-the-u-s-and-egypt-control-the-destiny-of-the-region/

Henry, C. M., and Springborg, R. (2001) *Globalization and the Politics of Development in the Middle East* (Cambridge: Cambridge University Press).

Hertog, S. (2010) 'Defying the Resource Curse: Explaining Successful State-Owned Enterprises in Rentier States', *World Politics*, vol. 62.

Heston, A., Summers, R., and Aten, B. (2002) 'Penn World Table Version 6.1', *Centre for International Comparisons at the University of Pennsylvania*.

Heydemann, S. (2000) *War, Institutions, and Social Change in the Middle East* (Berkeley: University of California Press).

Higginbottom, A. (2005) 'Human Rights, Globalisation and Dependency' (unpublished manuscript).

Hilferding, R. (1981) *Financial Capital: A Study of the Latest Phase of Capitalist Development* (London: Routledge and Kegan Paul), viewed 12 January 2013. http://www.marxists.org/archive/hilferding/1910/finkap/

Hinnebusch, R. (2001) 'The Politics of Economic Liberalization: Comparing Egypt and Syria', in H. Hakimian and Z. Moshaver (eds), *The State and Global Change: The Political Economy of Transition in the Middle East and North Africa* (Richmond: Curzon).

Hitler, A. (1941) *Mein Kampf* (Boston: Houghton Mifflin Harcourt).

Ho, C. M. (1961) 'Declaration of Independence, Democratic Republic of Vietnam', in *Selected Works*, vol. 3, pp. 17–21 (Hanoi: Foreign Languages Publication House).

Hobbes, T. ([1651] 1929) *Leviathan* (Oxford: Claredon Press).

Hoekman, B., and Messerlin, P. (2002) 'Initial Conditions and Incentives for Arab Economic Integration: Can the European Community's Success Be Emulated?', World Bank Policy Research Working Paper, no. 2921.

Hoekman, B., and Sekkat K. (2010) 'Arab Economic Integration: The Missing Links', Global Entrepreneurship Monitor Working Paper Series.

Hudson, M. (1999) 'Arab Integration: An Overview', in M. Hudson (ed.), *Middle East Dilemma: The Politics and Economics of Arab Integration* (New York: Columbia University Press).

Hudson, M. (2012) *The Bubble and Beyond: Fictitious Capital, Debt, Deflation and the Global Crisis* (ISLET).

Humphreys, M. (2003) *Economics and Violent Conflict*, Program on Humanitarian Policy and Conflict Research (Harvard College).

Hussein, M. (1971) *La Lutte de classes en Egypte, 1945–1970* (Paris: Maspero).

Ianchovichina, E., Loening, J., and Wood, C. (2012) 'How Vulnerable Are Arab Countries to Global Food Price Shocks?', Policy Research Working Paper, no. 6018.

ILO (International Labour Organisation) (2003) *Key Indicators of the Labour Market* (Geneva: International Labour Organisation).

ILO (2013) *ILO in the Arab States*, viewed 15 September 2013. http://www.ilo.org/public/english/region/arpro/beirut/downloads/events/qatar/skills.pdf

Ilyenkov, E. V. (1961) *The Dialectics of the Abstract and the Concrete in Marx's Capital* (Rome: Feltrinelli Publishers).

Ilyenkov, E. V. (1974) *Dialectical Logic, Essays on its History and Theory* (Moscow: Progress Publishers).

Imai, K., and Weinstein, J. (2000) 'Measuring the Economic Impact of Civil War', Centre for International Development Working Paper, no. 51.

International Workingmen's Association (1864) 'Inaugural Address of the International Working Men's Association: "The First International"', viewed 3 May 2013. http://www.marxists.org/archive/marx/works/1864/10/27.htm

IMF (International Monetary Fund) (2002) *International Financial Statistics (IFS)* (Washington, DC: IMF).

IMF (2006) *World Economic Report* (Washington, DC: IMF).

IMF (various years) *Direction of Trade Statistics* (Washington, DC: IMF).

ITUC (International Trade Union Confederation) (2007) *Annual Survey of Violations of Trade Union Rights* (Brussels: ITUC).

Islam, M. Q. (2000) 'Fiscal Policy and Social Welfare in Selected MENA Countries' in: W. Shahin and G. Dibeh (eds), *Earnings Inequality, Unemployment, and Poverty in the Middle East and North Africa* (Westport, CT: Greenwood Press).

Jabotinsky, V. (1923) *The Iron Wall (We and the Arabs)*, viewed 14 February 2012. http://www.marxists.de/middleast/ironwall/ironwall.htm

Johnson, Chalmers (1999) 'The Developmental State: Odyssey of a Concept', in M. Woo-Cumings (ed.), *The Developmental State* (Ithaca, NY: Cornell University Press).

Jomo, K. S., and Reinert, E. S. (2005) *The Origin of Development Economics: How Schools of Economic Thought have Addressed Development* (New Delhi: Tulika Books).

Jones, C. I. (1995) 'Time Series Tests of Endogenous Growth Models', *Quarterly Journal of Economics*, vol. 110, no. 2.

Kadri, A. (2008) *A Regional Unemployment Strategy* (Qatar: Arab Labour Organisation).

Kakwani, N., and Son, H. (2001) 'On Pro-Poor Government Fiscal Policies: With Application to the Philippines', *Asia and Pacific Forum on Poverty: Reforming Policies and Institutions for Poverty Reduction*, 5–9 February 2001, Asian Development Bank, Manila.

Kaldor, M. (1999) *New and Old Wars: Organised Violence in a Global Era* (Oxford: Polity Press).

Kalecki, M. (1935) 'A Macrodynamic Theory of Business Cycles', *Econometrica*, vol. 3, no. 3.

Kalecki, M. (1943) 'Political Aspects of Full Employment', *Political Quarterly*, vol. 14, no. 4.

Kalecki, M. (1965) 'On Paul Baran's Political Economy of Growth', *Monthly Review*, vol. 17, no. 6.

Kalecki, M. (1972) 'The Structure of Investment', in M. Kalecki (ed.), *Selected Essays on the Economic Growth of the Socialist and the Mixed Economy* (Cambridge: Cambridge University Press).

Kalecki, M. (1976) *Essays on Developing Economies* (Hassocks: Harvester Press).

Kaplan, E., and Rodrik, D. (2000) 'Did the Malaysian Capital Controls Work?' (unpublished manuscript).

Karl, T. L. (1997) *The Paradox of Plenty* (Berkeley: University of California Press).

Karshenas, M. (1994) *Macroeconomic Policies, Structural Change and Employment in the Middle East and North Africa* (Geneva: International Labour Organization).

Karshenas, M. (2001) 'Structural Obstacles to Economic Adjustment in the MENA Region: The International Trade Aspects', in H. Hakimian and Z. Moshaver (eds), *The State and Global Change: The Political Economy of Transition in the Middle East and North Africa* (Richmond: Curzon).

Kautsky, K. (1914) 'Ultra-imperialism (Editorial Note)', *Die Neue Zeit*, September.

Kelly, T., and Alpa, S. (2006) 'Introduction: A Double-Edged Sword: Protection and State Violence', *Critique of Anthropology*, vol. 26, no. 3.

Keynes, J. M. (1937) 'The General Theory of Employment', *Quarterly Journal of Economics*, vol. 51, no. 2.

Keynes, J. M. ([1936] 1964) *The General Theory of Employment, Interest and Money* (Cambridge: Cambridge University Press).

Khan, M. (1994) 'State Failure in Weak States', mimeo, University of Cambridge.

Khuri, F. (1982) 'The Study of Civil-Military Relations in Modernising Societies in the Middle East: A Critical Assessment', in R. Kolkowicz and A. Korbonski (eds), *Soldiers, Peasants and Bureaucrats: Civil-Military Relations in Communist and Modernising Societies* (London: George Allen and Unwin).

Kinninmont, J. (2013) 'Qatar's Delicate Balancing Act', BBC News, 6 January, viewed 3 June 2013. http://www.bbc.co.uk/news/world-middle-east-21029018

Koechlin, T. (1999) 'The Limits of Globalization: An Assessment of the Extent and Consequences of the Mobility of Productive Capital', in S. D. Gupta (ed.), *The Political Economy of Globalization* (London: Kluwer Academic Publishers).

Kohler, G. (1999) 'Global Keynesianism and Beyond', *Journal of World Systems*, vol. 5, no. 2.

Korzeniewicz, R. P., and Smith, W. C. (2000) 'Poverty, Inequality, and Growth in Latin America: Searching for the High Road to Globalization', *Latin American Research Review*, vol. 35, no. 3.

Koubi, V. (2005) 'War and Economic Performance', *Journal of Peace Research*, vol. 42, no. 1.

Krane, J. (2012) 'The End of the Saudi Oil Reserve Margin', *Wall Street Journal*, April 3, viewed 10 September 2013. http://online.wsj.com/article/SB100014240527023038165045773195717322274 92.html?mod=googlenews_wsj

Kroegstrup, S., and Matar, L. (2005) 'Foreign Direct Investment, Absorptive Capacity and Growth in the Arab World', Graduate Institute of International Studies Working Paper, no. 2.

Lange, O. (1953) *Scope and Method of Economics: Readings in the Philosophy of Science*, H. Feigl and M. Brodbeck (eds) (New York, Appleton-Century-Crofts).

League of Arab States (2005) Ataqrir al-Arabi Almouwahad (Cairo).

Leca, J. (1988) 'Social Structure and Political Stability: Comparative Evidence from the Algerian, Syrian, and Iraqi Cases', in A. I. Dawishi and I. W. Zartman (eds), *Beyond Coercion: The Durability of the Arab State* (New York: Croom Helm).

Lefebvre, H. (2003) *Key Writings* (London and New York: Continuum).

Leftwich, A. (2005) 'Politics in Command: Development Studies and the Rediscovery of Social Science', *New Political Economy*, vol. 10, no. 4.

Lenin, V. I. (1961a) *Lenin's Collected Works*, vol. 5: *What is To Be Done* (Moscow: Foreign Languages Publishing House).

Lenin, V. I. (1961b) *Lenin's Collected Works*, vol. 25: *The State and Revolution* (Moscow: Foreign Languages Publishing House).

Lenin, V. I. ([1916] 1963) *Imperialism, the Highest Stage of Capitalism*, viewed on 12 September 2013. http://www.marxists.org/archive/lenin/works/1916/imp-hsc/ch07.htm

Levy, D. (2013) 'Maximum Bibi', *Foreign Policy*, 27 September, viewed 2 October 2013. http://www.foreignpolicy.com/articles/2013/09/27/the_obstructionist_benjamin_netanyahu_israel_iran

Lin, B. (1966). *Long Live the Victory of People's War! In Commemoration of the 20th Anniversary of Victory in the Chinese People's War of Resistance Against Japan* (Beijing: Foreign Languages Press).

Lindgren, G. (2006) 'Studies in Conflict Economics and Economic Growth', *Department of Peace and Conflict Research*, report no. 72.

Lockman, Z. (ed.) (1994) *Workers and working classes in the Middle East: Struggles, Histories, Historiographies* (Albany: State University of New York Press).

Lucas, R. E. (1988) 'On the Mechanics of Economic Development', *Journal of Monetary Economics*, vol. 22, no. 1.

Lukacs, G. ([1920] 1967) *History and Class Consciousness* (London: Merlin Press).

Lutsky, V. B. (1969) *Modern History of the Arab Countries* (Moscow: Progress Publishers).

Luxembourg, R. (1913) *The Accumulation of Capital*, viewed 5 July 2012. http://www.marxists.org/archive/luxemburg/1913/accumulation-capital/

Mabro, R. (2008) 'The Oil Price Conundrum', *Oxford Energy Forum*, no.74.

MacEwan, A. (2003) 'Debt and Democracy: Can Heavily Indebted Countries Pursue Democratic Economic Programs?', paper presented at the symposium 'Common Defense Against Neoliberalism', Istanbul.

Maher, S. (2011) 'The Political Economy of the Egyptian Uprising', *Monthly Review*, vol. 63, no. 6.

Maiju, M. P. (2003) 'Persistence of Underdevelopment: Does the Type of Natural Resource Endowment Matter?', WIDER Discussion Paper, vol. 2003/37.

Martinussen, J. (1997) *State, Society and Market: A Guide to Competing Theories of Development* (London and New York: Zed Books).

Marx, K. (1843) 'Marx to Ruge', *Letters from the Deutsch-Französische Jahrbücher*, viewed on 4 September 2012. http://www.marxists.org/archive/marx/works/1843/letters/43_09.htm

Marx, K. (1857) *Grundrisse: Outlines of the Critique of Political Economy*, viewed 22 November 2012. http://www.marxists.org/archive/marx/works/1857/grundrisse/

Marx, K. (1867) 'The Value-Form', appendix to the 1st German edition of *Capital*, vol. 1, viewed on 6 September 2012. http://www.marxists.org/archive/marx/works/1867-c1/appendix.htm

Marx, K. (1887a) *Capital: A Critique of Political Economy*, vol. 1 (Moscow: Progress Publishers).

Marx, K. (1887b) *Capital: The Law of the Tendency of the Rate of Profit to Fall*, vol. 3 (Moscow: Progress Publishers).

Marx, K. (1937) *The Eighteenth Brumaire of Louis Bonaparte* (Moscow: Progress Publishers).

Marx, K. (1958) 'Marx's Economic Manuscripts of 1861–63, Part 3, Relative Surplus Value, Formal and Real Subsumption of Labour under Capital, Transitional Forms', *MECW*, vol. 34.

Marx, K. (1969) *Theories of Surplus-Value*, vol. 3 (London: Lawrence and Wishart).

Mayer, J., Butkevicius, A., and Kadri, A. (2002) 'Dynamic Products in World Exports', United Nations Conference on Trade and Development (UNCTAD) Discussion Paper, no. 159.

Mayen, N. (2012) 'Yemen Battles Hunger, Child Malnutrition', *Al Arabiya News*, 11 June, viewed 17 August 2013. http://english.alarabiya.net/articles/2012/06/11/220010.html

McKinley, T. (2003) *The Macroeconomics of Poverty Reduction: Initial Findings of the UNDP Asia-Pacific Regional Programme* (New York: UNDP).

McKinley, T. (2004) 'MDG-Based PRSPs Need More Ambitious Economic Policies', Draft Discussion Paper, UNDP.

McKinley, T. (ed.) (2001) 'Introduction', in *Macroeconomic Policy, Growth and Poverty Reduction* (London: Palgrave).

McKinsey Global Institute. 'US Debt Composition % of GDP', in Financial Iceberg, viewed 10 September 2013. http://www.financialiceberg.com/jan_30_in_us_debt_we_trust.html

Meillassoux, C. (1981) *Maidens, Meal and Money: Capitalism and the Domestic Community* (Cambridge: Cambridge University Press).

Mészáros, I. (1995) 'Beyond Capital: Toward a Theory of Transition', *Monthly Review Press*, viewed on 17 August 2013. http://monthlyreview.org/press/books/pb8812/

Michaels, J. (2012) 'Iraq Buys U.S. Drones to Protect Oil', *USA TODAY*, 20 May, viewed 17 August 2012. http://usatoday30.usatoday.com/news/world/story/2012-05-20/iraq-oil-drones/55099590/1

Migdal, J. S. (1988) *Strong Societies and Weak States: State-Society Relations and State Capabilities in the Third World* (Princeton, NJ: Princeton University Press).

Migdal, J. S. (2001) *State in Society: Studying How States and Societies Transform and Constitute One Another* (Cambridge: Cambridge University Press).

Miharja, N. M. (2012) 'Scholars Discuss China and Middle East Relations at Well-Attended Event', *Middle East Institute*, April 6, viewed 15 August 2013. http://mei.nus.edu.sg/blog/scholars-discuss-china-and-middle-east-relations-at-well-attended-event

Milanovic, B. (2002) 'True World Income Distribution, 1988 and 1993: First Calculation Based on Household Surveys Alone', *Economic Journal*, vol. 112, no. 476.

Milanovic, B. (2003) 'The Two Faces of Globalization: Against Globalization as We Know It', *World Development*, vol. 31, no. 4.

Minh, H. C. (1960–1962) *Selected Works*, vol. 3: *Vietnamese Declaration of Independence*, viewed 3 July 2012. http://www.marxists.org/reference/archive/ho-chi-minh/works/1945/declaration-independence.htm

Miniesy, R. S., Nugent, J. B., and Yousef, T. M. (2001) 'Intra-regional Trade Integration in the Middle East: Past Performance and Future Potential', in H. Hakimian and J. B. Nugent (eds), *Trade Policy and Economic Integration in the Middle East and North Africa: Economic Boundaries in Flux* (London: Routledge).

Moore, M. (2005) 'European Sanctions against Iran Could Raise Oil Prices', *Canadian Press*, viewed 10 September 2013. http://newsmine.org/content.php?ol=war-on-terror/iran/nuclear-posturing/european-sanctions-against-iran-could-raise-oil-prices.txt

Moses, R. L. (2011) 'Right, Left or Centre in China', *Diplomat*, 9 May, viewed 18 June 2013. http://thediplomat.com/2011/05/09/right-left-or-centre-in-china/

MRZine (2009) 'Egypt: Nearly a Third of Children Malnourished', 8 November, viewed 11 March 2012. http://mrzine.monthlyreview.org/2009/irin081109.html

Mundy, M. (1996) *Domestic Government, Kinship, Community and Polity in North Yemen* (London and New York: I. B. Tauris).

Nabli, M., and Véganzonès-Varoudakis M. (2007) 'Reform Complementarities and Economic Growth in the Middle East and North Africa', *Journal of International Development*, vol. 19, no. 1.

Nabli, M. K. (2004) 'Long-Term Economic Development Challenges and Prospects for the Arab Countries', Conference of the Institut du Monde Arabe, World Bank, Paris, 12 February.

National Science Foundation (2012) *Science and Engineering Indicators 2012* (Arlington: National Science Foundation), viewed 22 May 2013. http://www.nsf.gov/statistics/seind12/c0/c0i.htm

Neumann, M. (2002) 'Israelis and Indians', *Counterpunch*, 9 April, viewed 24 March 2012. http://www.counterpunch.org/2002/04/09/israelis-and-indians/

New York Times (2013) 'Text of Obama's Speech at the UN', 24 September, viewed 4 October 2013. http://www.nytimes.com/2013/09/25/us/politics/text-of-obamas-speech-at-the-un.html?_r=0

Niblock, T., and Malik, M. (2007) *The Political Economy of Saudi Arabia* (London: Routledge).

Nurkse, R. (1952) 'Growth in Underdeveloped Countries: Some International Aspects of the Problem of Economic Development', *American Economic Review*, vol. 42, no. 2.

Ocampo, J. A. (1998) 'Beyond the Washington Consensus: An ECLAC Perspective', *Cepal Review*, no. 66.

Ocampo, J. A. (2002) 'Rethinking the Development Agenda', *Cambridge Journal of Economics*, no. 26.

OIC (Organization of Islamic Cooperation) (2012) *Pharmaceutical Industry in OIC Member Countries: Production, Consumption and Trade* (Ankara: OIC), viewed 12 January 2013. http://www.sesric.org/files/article/433.pdf

OPEC (Organization of the Petroleum Exporting Countries) (2012) *Annual Statistical Bulletin* (Vienna: OPEC)

Ottolenghi, E. (2012) 'Iran Regime Change Only Hope', *J-Wire*, 4 April, viewed 10 September 2013. http://www.jwire.com.au/featured-articles/iran-regime-change-only-hope/24234

Owen, R. (2004) *State, Power and Politics in the Making of the Modern Middle East*, 3rd ed. (Routledge: Taylor & Francis Group).

Ozcan, K. M. (2000) *Determinants of Private Savings in the Middle East and North Africa* (Ankara: Bilkent University).

Page, J. (1998) 'The State and Economic Transition in the Middle East and North Africa', in N. Shafik (ed.), *Prospects for Middle Eastern and North African Economies: From Boom to Bust?* (New York: Macmillan Press).

Palma, G. (1998) 'Three and a Half Cycles of "Mania, Panic and (Asymmetric) Crash": East Asia and Latin America Compared', *Cambridge Journal of Economics*, vol. 22, no. 6.

Parenti, M. (2003) *US Global Policy after the Overthrow of Communism*, viewed 1 November 2012. http://dimension.ucsd.edu/CEIMSA-IN-EXILE/colloques/pdf/ch-16.pdf

Parker, C., and Moore, P. W. (2007) 'The War Economy of Iraq', *Middle East Report*, no. 243.

Pasha, H. A. (2002) *Pro-Poor Policies* (UNDP: Asia-Pacific Regional Programme on the Macroeconomics of Poverty Reduction).

Pasha, H. A., and Palanivel, T. (2004) *Pro-Poor Growth and Policies: The Asian Experience* (New York: UNDP).

Pastor, M. (1987) 'The Effects of IMF Programs in the Third World: Debate and Evidence from Latin America', *World Development*, no. 15.

Patnaik, P. (1997) *Accumulation and Stability under Capitalism* (Oxford: Oxford University Press).

Patnaik, P. (2005) 'The Economics of the New Phase of Imperialism', *IDEAs Featured Articles* http://www.networkideas.org/featart/aug2005/Economics_New_Phase.pdf

Patnaik, P. (2009) 'Socialism and Welfarism', *Monthly Review*, August 30.

Patnaik, P. (2010) 'Notes on Contemporary Imperialism', *MRZine*, 20 December, viewed 3 March 2012. http://mrzine.monthlyreview.org/2010/patnaik201210.html

Patnaik, P. (2012) 'Finance and Growth under Capitalism', *IDEAs Featured Articles*, viewed 5 June 2013. http://networkideas.org/ideasact/dec11/pdf/Prabhat_Patnaik.pdf

Pempel, T. L. (1999) 'The Developmental Regime in a Changing World Economy', in M. Woo-Cumings (ed.), *The Developmental State* (New York: Cornell University Press).

Petras, J. (2008) *Fateful Triangle: The United States, Israel, and the Palestinians* (Christchurch: Clarity Press).

Petras, J. (2011) *Empire or Republic: From Joplin, Missouri to Kabul, Afghanistan*, viewed 5 March 2012. http://petras.lahaine.org/?p=1857

Petras, J., and Morley, M. (1994) *Empire or Republic: Global Power or Domestic Decay in the US* (London: Routledge).

Petras, J. F. (1976) 'State Capitalism and the Third World', *Journal of Contemporary Asia*, vol. 6, no. 4.

Pfeifer, K. (1979) 'Three Worlds or Three Worldviews?: State Capitalism and Development', *MERIP Reports*, no. 78.

Pfeiffer, K. (2000) 'Does Structural Adjustment Spell Relief from Unemployment?: A Comparison of Four IMF "Success Stories" in the Middle East and North Africa', in W. Shahin and G. Dibeh (eds), *Earnings Inequality, Unemployment, and Poverty in the Middle East and North Africa* (Westport, CT: Greenwood Press).

Picard, E. (1988) 'Arab Military in Politics: From Revolutionary Plot to Authoritarian State', in A. Dawishi and I. W. Zartman (eds), *Beyond Coercion: The Durability of the Arab State* (New York: Croom Helm).

Poulantzas, N. A. (1973) *Political Power and Social Classes*, translated from French (London: Sheed and Ward).

Poulantzas, N. A. (1975) *Classes in Contemporary Capitalism* (London: NLB).

PRS Group (various years) *International Country Risk Guide* (New York: PRS Group).

Rao, J. M. (2002) *The Possibility of Pro-Poor Development: Distribution, Growth and Policy Interactions*. (Manuscript).

Reich, W. (2013) *Sex-Pol: Essays, 1929–1934* (New York and London: Verso).

Reinert, E. S. (2005) 'Development and Social Goals: Balancing Aid and Development to Prevent "Welfare Colonialism"', High-Level United Nations Development Conference in Millennium Development Goals, United Nations, New York, 14–15 March.

Reinert, E. S. (2012) 'Neo-classical Economics: A Trail of Economic Destruction since the 1970s', *Real-World Economics Review*, no. 60.

Research Unit for Political Economy. (2003) *Behind the Invasion of Iraq* (New York: Monthly Review Press)

Rey, P. P. (1978) *Les Alliances de classes* (Paris: Maspero).

Richards, A., and Waterbury, J. (eds) (1990) *A Political Economy of the Middle East: State, Class, and Economic Development*, 1st ed. (Boulder: Westview Press).

Richards, A., and Waterbury, J. (1996) 'The Emergence of the Public Sector', in A. Richards and J. Waterbury (eds), *A Political Economy of the Middle East* (Boulder: Westview Press).

Rivlin, P. (2001) *Economic Policy and Performance in the Arab World* (Boulder: Lynne Rienner Publishers).

Romer, P. M. (1986) 'Increasing Returns and Long-Run Growth', *Journal of Political Economy*, vol. 94, no. 5.

Ross, M. L. (1999) 'The Political Economy of the Resource Curse', *World Politics*, vol. 51, no. 2.

Rosser, A. (2006) 'The Political Economy of the Resource Curse: A Literature Survey', IDS Working Paper, no. 268.

Roy, R., and Weeks, J. (2003) *Thematic Summary Report: Fiscal Policy*, UNDP Asia-Pacific Regional Programme on the Macroeconomics of Poverty Reduction.

Roy, S. (2006) 'The Economy of Gaza', *Counterpunch*. http://www.counterpunch.org/roy10042006.html

Rubin, I. I. (1972) *Essays on Marx's Theory of Value* (Detroit: Black and Red).

Saad-Filho, A. (2007) 'Life beyond the Washington Consensus: An Introduction to Pro-Poor Macroeconomic Policies', *Review of Political Economy*, vol. 19, no. 4.

Sahay, R., Cashin, P., and Mauro, P. (2001) *Macroeconomic Policies and Poverty: The State of Play and a Research Agenda*. IMF website.

Sala-i-Martin, X., and Artadi, E. V. (2002) 'Economic Growth and Investment in the Arab World', Columbia University, Department of Economics Working Paper, no. 0203-08.

SAMA (Saudi Arabian Monetary Authority) (various years) *Annual Report* (Saudi Arabia: SAMA).

Samhouri, M. (2013) 'Egypt's Hard Economic Choices', *Sada*, 30 January, viewed 4 May 2013. http://carnegieendowment.org/2013/01/31/egypt-s-hard-economic-choices/f7ib

Sawyer, M. C. (1985) *The Economics of Michal Kalecki* (London: Macmillan).

Scruton, R. (1982) *A Dictionary of Political Thought* (New York: Macmillan).

Seers, D. (1983) *The Political Economy of Nationalism* (Oxford: Oxford University Press).

Sen, A. K. (1999) *Development as Freedom* (Oxford: Oxford University Press).

Sengupta, A. (2004) 'The Human Right to Development', *Oxford Development Studies*, vol. 32, no. 2.

Shahin, W., and Dibeh, G. (2000) 'Introduction', in *Earnings Inequality, Unemployment, and Poverty in the Middle East and North Africa* (Westport, CT: Greenwood Press).

Scholch, A. (1982) *History of Palestine 1856–1922*, R. Owen (ed.) (London: Athlone Press).

Sicsú, J. (2001) 'Credible Monetary Policy: A Post Keynesian Approach', *Journal of Post Keynesian Economics*, vol. 23, no.4.

SIPRI (2009) SIPRI Military Expenditure Database (Stockholm: Stockholm International Peace Research Institute), viewed 23 August 2012. http://www.sipri.org/databases/milex

Skocpol, T. (1997) *States and Social Revolutions: A Comparative Analysis of France, Russia and China* (Cambridge: Cambridge University Press).

Solow, R. M. (1956) 'A Contribution to the Theory of Economic Growth', *Quarterly Journal of Economics*, vol. 70, no. 1.

South Africa HDR (2003) *South Africa Human Development Report: The Challenge of Sustainable Development; Unlocking People's Creativity* (UNDP: Oxford University Press).

Springborg, R. (1993) 'The Arab Bourgeoisie: A Revisionist Interpretation', *Arab Studies Quarterly*, vol. 15, no. 1.

Stewart, F. (2004) 'Development and Security', CRISE Working Paper, no. 3.

Stewart., J. (ed.) (1996) *The Hegel Myths and Legends* (Evanston, IL: Northwestern University Press), viewed 24 April 2012. http://www.marxists.org/reference/subject/philosophy/works/us/stewart.htp

Stiglitz, J. (2004) 'We Can Now Cure Dutch Disease' *Guardian*, 18 August, viewed 14 October 2012. http://www.theguardian.com/business/2004/aug/18/comment.oilandpetrol

Suleiman, N. M. (2000) *Economic Integration Tendencies in the Middle East and North Africa*, viewed 4 November 2012. http://www.al-bab.com/arab/econ/suleiman.htm

Sullivan, K. (2013) 'Saudi Arabia's Riches Conceal a Growing Problem of Poverty', *Guardian*, 1 January, viewed 30 April 2013. http://www.theguardian.com/world/2013/jan/01/saudi-arabia-riyadh-poverty-inequality

Surk, B. (2013) 'Lebanon Shiites Ousted from Gulf as Hezbollah Fans', *Associated Press*, 11 July, viewed 24 July 2013. http://bigstory.ap.org/article/lebanon-shiites-ousted-gulf-hezbollah-fans

Tabb, W. K. (2007) 'Wage Stagnation, Growing Insecurity, and the Future of the U.S. Working Class', *Monthly Review*, vol. 59, issue 02.

Takagi, S. (2012) 'Establishing Monetary Union in the Gulf Cooperation Council: What Lessons for Regional Cooperation?', ADBI Working Paper Series, no. 390.

Tarbush, M. (1982) *From the Role of the Military in Politics: A Case Study of Iraq to 1941* (London: Kegan Paul).

Targetti, F., and Kinda-Hass, B. (1982) 'Kalecki's Review of Keynes' General Theory', *Australian Economic Papers*, vol. 21.

Targetti, F., and Thirwall, A. P. (1989) *The Essential Kaldor* (London: Gerald Duckworth).

Taylor, L. (1988) *Varieties of Stabilization Experience* (Oxford: Clarendon Press).

Tilly, C. (1985) 'War Making and State Making as Organized Crime', in P. Evans, D. Rueschemeyer and T. Skocpol (eds), *Bringing the State Back In* (Cambridge: Cambridge University Press).

Tilly, C. (1991) 'War and State Power', *Middle East Report*, vol. 21.

Todaro, M., and John H. (1970) 'Migration Unemployment and Development: A Two-Sector Analysis', *American Economic Review*, no. 60.

Todaro, M. P. (1979) *Economic Development* (Englewood Cliffs, NJ: Prentice-Hall).

Transparency International (2012) *Annual Report* (Berlin: Transparency International).

Trotsky, L. ([1906] 2009). *Results and Prospects*, viewed 17 August 2013. http://www.marxists. org/archive/trotsky/1931/tpr/rp01.htm

Tschirgi, N. (2005) 'Security and Development Policies: Untangling the Relationship', European Association of Development Research and Training Institutes (EADI) Conference, September 2005, Bonn.

Tuma, E. H. (2000) 'Some Introductory Observations on Poverty and Earnings Inequality in the Arab World', in W. Shahin and G. Dibeh (eds), *Earnings Inequality, Unemployment, and Poverty in the Middle East and North Africa* (Westport, CT: Greenwood Press).

Turner, B. (1984) *Capitalism and Class in the Middle East: Theories of Social Change and Economic Development* (London: Heinemann Educational Books).

Tzannatos, Z. (2002) 'Social Protection in the Middle East and North Africa: A Review', in H. Handoussa and Z. Tzannatos (eds), *Employment Creation and Social Protection in the Middle East and North Africa* (Cairo and New York: American University in Cairo Press).

UN (United Nations) (various years) *Standard International Trade Classification*.

UN (2004) *'A More Secure World: Our Shared Responsibility': Report of the High-Level Panel on Threats, Challenges and Change.*

UN (2005a) *Geneva, 7 April 2005 - Secretary-General's Address to the Commission on Human Rights*.

UN (2005b) *Economic Survey of Europe*.

UN (2006) *Survey of the Economic and Social Developments in the ESCWA Region 2005–2006* (Beirut: United Nations).

UN (2007a) 'Unemployment EGM, Summary and Objectives of the EGM', first draft (unpublished manuscript).

UN (2007b) 'Unemployment EGM: Is a Rigid Labour Market Responsible for Unemployment?', first draft (unpublished manuscript).

UN (2007c) *The Millennium Development Goals Report*, viewed 3 February 2013. http://www. un.org/millenniumgoals/pdf/mdg2007.pdf

UN (2007d) *National Accounts Statistics: Analysis of Main Aggregates 2004–05* (New York: United Nations)

UN (2008a) 'Summary of the Survey of Economic and Social Developments in the Economic and Social Commission for Western Asia Region, 2007–2008' (New York: UN Economic and Social Council).

UN (2008b) *Survey of Economic and Social Developments in the ESCWA Region 2007–2008*, viewed 10 September 2013. http://www.arab-hdr.org/publications/other/escwa/ sum-ecosocial-dev-08e.pdf

UN (2008c) *The Demographic profile of Arab Countries' Ageing Rural Population*.

UN (2009a) Summary *Survey of the Economic and Social Developments in the ESCWA Region 2008–2009* (New York: UN Economic and Social Council).

UN (2009b) *Survey of the Economic and Social Developments in the ESCWA Region 2008–2009* (Beirut: United Nations).

UN (2012) 'UNICEF Warns on High Rates of Malnutrition among Children in Yemen', *UN News Centre*, 25 January, viewed 13 June 2012. http://www.un.org/apps/news/story.asp/html/realfile/story.asp?NewsID=41037&Cr=yemen&Cr1=#.UmSyo_mnoSU

UNCTAD (United Nations Conference on Trade and Development) (2000) *The Least Developed Countries Report* (New York: United Nations).

UNCTAD (2001) *Trade and Development Report* (Geneva: UNCTAD).

UNCTAD (2006) *The Palestinian War-Torn Economy: Aid, Development and State Formation* (New York and Geneva: United Nations).

UNCTAD (2010) *World Investment Report: Investing in a Low-Carbon Economy* (New York and Geneva: United Nations).

UNDP (United Nations Development Programme) (1994) *Human Development Report* (New York and Oxford: Oxford University Press).

UNDP (2002) *The Role of Economic Policies in Poverty Reduction* (New York: UNDP).

UNDP (2003) *The Millennium Development Goals in Arab Countries: Towards 2015; Achievements and Aspirations* (New York: UNDP).

UNDP (2005) *Macroeconomic Policies for Poverty Reduction: The Case of Yemen* (New York: UNDP).

UNDP and ILO (2012) *Rethinking Economic Growth: Toward Productive and Inclusive Arab Societies* (Beirut: ILO Regional Office for Arab States).

UNDP and LAS (2007) *The Millennium Development Goals in the Arab Region 2007: A Youth Lens* (New York: United Nations Development Program and League of Arab States).

UNDP and LAS (2008) *Growth, Inequality and Poverty in Arab Countries: Stylized Facts, Challenges and Policy Considerations for an Alternative MDG-Based Development Paradigm* (New York: United Nations Development Program and League of Arab States).

UNESCO (2012) *Education for All Regional Report 2012 for Arab States* (Global Education for All Meeting, November 21–23, Paris).

UNESCWA (UN Economic and Social Commission for Western Asia) (2001–02) *Survey of Economic and Social Developments in the ESCWA Region* (Beirut: ESCWA).

UNESCWA (2003) *Analysis of Performance and Assessment of Growth and Productivity in the ESCWA region*, issue 1 (New York: United Nations).

UNESCWA (2003–04) *Survey of Economic and Social Developments in the ESCWA Region* (Beirut: ESCWA).

UNESCWA (2004) *Analysis of Performance and Assessment of Growth and Productivity in the ESCWA Region* (Beirut: ESCWA).

UNESCWA (2004) *Analysis of Performance and Assessment of Growth and Productivity in the ESCWA Region*, issue 2 (New York: United Nations).

UNESCWA (2004) *Summary of the Survey of Economic and Social Developments in the ESCWA Region 2008–2009* (New York: United Nations).

UNESCWA (2005) *Analysis of Performance and Assessment of Growth and Productivity in the ESCWA Region*, issue 3 (New York: United Nations).

UNESCWA (2005) *Survey of Economic and Social Developments in the ESCWA Region* (Beirut: ESCWA).

UNESCWA (2005) *The Millennium Development Goals in the Arab Region* (Beirut: ESCWA).

UNESCWA (2007) *Survey of Economic and Social Developments in the ESCWA Region 2006–2007* (New York: United Nations).

UNESCWA (2007) *Population and Development Report: International Migration and Development in the Arab region; Challenges and Opportunities* (New York: United Nations).

UNESCWA (2008) *Survey of Economic and Social Developments in the ESCWA Region 2007–2008* (New York: United Nations).

UNESCWA (2009) *Summary of the Survey of Economic and Social Developments in the ESCWA Region 2008–2009* (New York: United Nations).

UNESCWA (2009) *Statistical Abstract of the ESCWA Region* (New York: United Nations).

UNHCR (United Nations High Commissioner for Refugees) (1966) *International Covenant on Economic, Social and Cultural Rights*, viewed 5 October 2012. http://www.ohchr.org/EN/ProfessionalInterest/Pages/CESCR.aspx

UNHCR (2013) *Number of Syrian Refugees Tops 1.5 Million Mark with Many More Expected*, viewed 5 September 2013. http://www.unhcr.org/519600a59.html

UNICEF (United Nations Children's Fund) (various years) 'At a Glance: Syrian Arab Republic', viewed 27 October 2012. http://www.unicef.org/infobycountry/syria_statistics.html

UNICEF (various years) *The State of the World's Children* (New York: UNICEF).

United Nations Statistics Division (various years) *Standard International Trade Classification* (New York: United Nations).

University of Texas Inequality Project (2008) 'Estimated Household Income Inequality Data Set', viewed 8 October 2012. http://utip.gov.utexas.edu/data.html

US Department of Commerce (2012) 'Annual Trade Highlights', US Census Bureau, viewed 12 December 2012. http://www.census.gov/foreign-trade/statistics/highlights/annual.html

Vandemoortele, J. (2004) *Can the MDGs Foster a New Partnership for Pro-Poor Policies?* (New York: United Nations Development Programme).

Vatikiotis, P. J. (ed.) (1972) *Revolutions in the Middle East and Other Case Studies* (London: Allen and Unwin).

Verret, M. (1999) *Le travail ouvrier* (Paris: L'Harmattan).

Vreeland, J. R. (2002) 'The Effect of IMF Programs on Labour', *World Development*, vol. 30, no. 1.

Waldner, D. (1999) *State Building and Late Development* (Ithaca, NY: Cornell University Press).

Wallerstein, I. (2000a) 'Globalization or the Age of Transition?: A Long-Term View of the Trajectory of the World System' *International Sociology*, vol. 15.

Wallerstein, I. (2000b) 'The Rise and Future Demise of the World Capitalist System', in F. J. Lechner and J. Boli (eds), *The Globalization Reader* (Oxford: Blackwell Publishers).

Warren, B. (1973) 'Imperialism and Capitalist Industrialization', *New Left Review*, vol. 1, no. 81.

Weeks, J. (1983) 'Imperialism', in T. Bottomore (ed.), *Dictionary of Marxist Thought* (Oxford: Blackwell).

Weeks, J., Huy, V. Q., Roy, R., Schmidt, R., and Thang, N. (2002) 'On the Macroeconomics of Poverty Reduction Case Study of Viet Nam: Seeking Equity within Growth', CDPR Discussion Paper, no. 2102.

Weller, C. E., and Hersh, A. (2004) 'The Long and Short of It: Global Liberalization and the Incomes of the Poor', *Journal of Post Keynesian Economics*, vol. 26, no. 3.

Wilson, R. J. A. (1995) 'Middle Eastern Trade and Financial Integration: Lessons from the European Union Experience', in H. Kheir El-Din (ed.), *Economic Cooperation in the Middle East: Prospects and Challenges* (Cairo: Dar Al-Mostaqbal Al-Arabi).

Winn, D. (2012) 'McCaskill Wants to Use Strategic Oil Reserve to Cut Price at Pump', *Connect Midmissouri*, April 4, viewed 26 October 2012. http://www.connectmidmissouri.com/news/story.aspx?id=738291#.Ui6dYManoSU

Wolff, R. (2006) 'The Fallout from Falling US Wages', *Monthly Review*, viewed 6 March 2013. http://mrzine.monthlyreview.org/2006/wolff120606.html

Woo-Cumings, M. (1999) 'Chalmers Johnson and the Politics of Nationalism and Development', in M. Woo-Cumings (ed.), *The Developmental State* (Ithaca, NY: Cornell University Press).

Wood, E. M. (1995) *Democracy against Capitalism* (Cambridge: Cambridge University Press).

Wood, E. M. (2012) *Liberty and Property: A Social History of Western Political Thought from the Renaissance to the Enlightenment* (Brooklyn: Verso).

World Bank (1995) *Claiming the Future: Choosing Prosperity in the Middle East and North Africa* (Washington, DC: World Bank).

World Bank (1997) 'Expanding the Measure of Wealth: Indicators of Environmentally Sustainable Development', *Environmentally Sustainable Development Studies and Monograph Series*, no. 17.

World Bank (2002) *Reducing Vulnerability and Increasing Opportunity Social Protection in the Middle East and North Africa*, Orientations in Development Series (Washington DC: World Bank), viewed 4 January 2013. http://www.wds.worldbank.org/servlet/WDSContentServer/WDSP/IB/2002/08/09/000094946_02073004020126/Rendered/PDF/multi0page.pdf

World Bank (2004) 'Unlocking the Employment Potential in the Middle East and North Africa: Toward a New Social Contract', *MENA Development Report* (Washington, DC: World Bank).

World Bank (2007a) *Middle East and North Africa Region Economic Developments and Prospects: Job Creation in an Era of High Growth* (Washington, DC: World Bank).

World Bank (2007b) *Better Governance for Development in the Middle East and North Africa: Enhancing Inclusiveness and Accountability: Overview* (Washington DC: World Bank), viewed 25 September 2012. http://documents.worldbank.org/curated/en/2007/09/10123610/better-governance-development-middle-east-north-africa-enhancing-inclusiveness-accountability-overview

World Bank (2009a) *World Development Indicators, WDI 2009* (Washington, DC: World Bank), viewed 17 September 2012. http://databank.worldbank.org/ddp/home.do?Step=12&id=4&CNO=2

World Bank (2009b) *World Development Report* (Washington DC: World Bank).

World Bank (2011a) *Middle East and North Africa Region, Assessment of the Local Manufacturing Potential for Concentrated Solar Power (CSP) Projects* (Washington DC: World Bank).

World Bank (2011b) 'Arab World Initiative for Financing Food Security' (Washington DC: World Bank), viewed 4 June 2013. http://www.wds.worldbank.org/external/default/WDSContentServer/WDSP/IB/2011/05/27/000001843_20110601143246/Rendered/PDF/P126506000AWIFS000PID000Concept0Stage.pdf

WESS (World Economic and Social Survey) (2008) *Overcoming Economic Insecurity* (New York: United Nations).

Wright, G. (2003) 'Wolfowitz: Iraq War Was about Oil', *Guardian*, 4 June.

Xiao, F., and Kimball, D. (2006) *Effectiveness and Effects on China's Capital Controls* (Beijing: University of International Business and Economics), viewed 12 October 2012. http://faculty.washington.edu/karyiu/confer/beijing06/papers/xiao-kimball.pdf

Yamamoto, Y. (2009) 'The Dubai Crisis', internal paper prepared for the Economic Analysis Division (Beirut: ESCWA) (unpublished).

Yang, C. (2006) 'The Downside of Cheaper Oil', *Business Week*, 9 October.

Yassiri, M. (2006) *What Is Happening in Iraq?: The ABC of the Current Situation in Iraq* (Bloomington: Xilbris Corporation).

Yates, M. D. (2013) 'Who Will Lead the U.S. Working Class?', *Monthly Review*, vol. 65, no. 1.

Zallio, F. (1992) 'Regional Integration and Economic Prospects of the Developing Countries to the South of the Mediterranean', *International Spectator*, vol. 27, no. 2.

Ziegler, J. (2011) *Destruction massive: Géopolitique de la faim* (Paris: Éditions du Seuil).

Zineldin, M. (1998) 'Globalisation and Economic Integration among Arab Countries', 4th Nordic Conference on Middle Eastern Studies, 'The Middle East in a Globalizing World', 13–16 August, Oslo, viewed 3 October 2012. http://www.hf.uib.no/simi/pao/zineldin.html

INDEX

Lightning Source UK Ltd.
Milton Keynes UK
UKOW05n0740290614

234222UK00002B/5/P